Magnolia campbellii in
Cornwall, planted 1926.
This native of the Himalayas
was first described in 1855
by Joseph Dalton Hooker.
Similar magnolias now
extinct grew in N. Europe
and Greenland 20 million
years ago. This is named
after Sir Archibald Campbell
who accompanied Hooker to
Sikkim, and was captured
there as a political hostage

Gerald Wilkinson

A history of Britain's trees

Hutchinson

LONDON   MELBOURNE   SYDNEY   AUCKLAND   JOHANNESBURG

Hutchinson & Co. (Publishers) Ltd

An imprint of the Hutchinson Publishing Group

3 Fitzroy Square, London W1P 6JD

Hutchinson Group (Australia) Pty Ltd
30–32 Cremorne Street, Richmond South, Victoria 3121
PO Box 151, Broadway, New South Wales 2007

Hutchinson Group (NZ) Ltd
32–34 View Road, PO Box 40–086, Glenfield, Auckland 10

Hutchinson Group (SA) (Pty) Ltd
PO Box 337, Bergvlei 2012, South Africa

First published 1981

© Gerald Wilkinson 1981
Designed, photographed and illustrated by the author

Set in Sabon by Input Typesetting Ltd
Colour Separations by Fotographics Ltd
Printed in Great Britain by Morrison & Gibb Ltd, London and Edinburgh
and bound by Wm Brendon & Son Ltd, Tiptree, Essex

British Library Cataloguing in Publication Data

Wilkinson, Gerald
    A history of Britain's trees.
    1. Trees – Great Britain
    I. Title
    582.160941   QK488

ISBN 0 09 146000 X

Contents

Tree families   8

1   Forests of stone   9

2   Survivors of the ice   17

3   Britain's trees 5000 years ago   23

Native shrubs   37

4   Trees and shrubs of the early Britons   41

5   Roman trees in Britain   53

6   Anglo-Saxon trees   59

7   Medieval trees   65

8   16th-century trees and the herbalist   73

Small trees for Tudor gardens   81

9   New trees from Europe and the Near East   85

10   New American trees, 1600–1700   93

11   18th-century introductions   102

12   Trees for gardeners, about 1820   122

13   The Pinetum, 1822–1861   131

14   Victorian beauties   150

Late Victorian conifers   161

Flowering cherries   164

15   New trees of the 20th century   166

Index   175

Books

AD 23–79 Pliny *Natural History* tran. Rackham and Jones, 1951

1551–1568 W. Turner *New Herball*

1597 J. Gerard *Herball*

1633 J. Gerard *Herball* ed. T. Johnson

1664 J. Evelyn *Silva*

1870 A. Mongredien *Trees and shrubs for English plantations*

1898–1919 A. C. Seward *Fossil plants*

1906–1913 H. J. Elwes and A. Henry *Trees of Great Britain and Ireland*

1921 S. Sargent *Manual of the trees of N. America*

1930 W. Fry and J. R. White *Big Trees*

1948 G. Storms *Anglo Saxon Magic*; C. Tunnard *Gardens in the Modern Landscape*

1949 H. L. Edlin *Woodland Crafts*

1955 W. G. Hoskins *Making of the English Landscape*

1956 H. L. Edlin *Trees, Woods and Man*

1957 M. Hadfield *British Trees*

1958 G. Grigson *Englishman's Flora*

1960 H. H. Swinnerton *Fossils*; H. Vedel and J. Lange, ed. Edlin *Trees and Bushes*

1964 E. J. Corner *Life of Plants*

1967 G. W. Dimbleby *Plants and Archeology*; H. Prince *Parks in England*

1969 A. M. Coats *Quest for Plants*

1970 H. C. Bold *Plant Kingdom*

1970–1980 W. J. Bean *Trees and Shrubs hardy in the British Isles*, 8th Edn.

1971 *Encyclopaedia of Garden Plants*, ed. R. Hay; R. S. R. Fitter *Finding Wild Flowers*

1972 A. F. Mitchell and A. W. Westall *Bedgebury Pinetum and Forest Plots*; A. F. Mitchell *Conifers in the British Isles*; J. H. Wilks *Trees of the British Isles in History and Legend*; B. W. Sparks and R. G. West *Ice Ages in Britain*

1973 H. Johnson *International Book of Trees*; H. C. Darby, ed. *New Historical Geography of England*; G. Wilkinson *Trees in the Wild*

1974 R. Lancaster *Trees for your Garden*; A. F. Mitchell *Field Guide to the Trees of Britain*

1975 J. D. Hunt and P. Willis *Genius of the Place*; C. A. Stace, ed. *Hybridization and the Flora of the British Isles;* Sir H. Godwin *History of the British Flora*

1976 O. Rackham *Trees and Woodland in the British Landscape*; A. Burl *Stone Circles of the British Isles*

1977 *Guide to the trees and shrubs in the University Parks, Oxford*

1978 J. Wacher, *Roman Britain*; J. Hutchinson *Families of Flowering Plants*

1979 J. Davies *Douglas of the Forests*; A. Teasdale 'Sequoiadendron gigantea' (*Arboricultural Journal*, April 1979) M. Bramwell *International Book of Wood*; F. A. O. *Poplars and Willows*

1980 F. MacRae 'Native pinewoods of Glen Affric' (*Arboricultural Journal*, April 1980); O. Rackham *Ancient Woodland*; R. Mabey *Common Ground*

1981 E. and J. Harris *Field Guide to the Trees and Shrubs of Britain*

The Burren

Killarney

Cork

Places: Arboreta and other places mentioned more than once in the text or captions

Loch Maree
○ Kishorn

○ Rothiemurchus

Mull

Glen
Dochart
Inverary
Loch
Lomond
Crarae
Inchtuthil
○ Scone
Kilmun
Benmore
○ Glasgow
○ Edinburgh
○ Dawyck

○ Tynron

R. Boyne
Glasnevin ○
○ Mountrath
Powerscourt

○ Southport

John F. Kennedy
Memorial ○ Park

○ Bodnant

Chatsworth
Cumber
Park
Sherwood
Forest

Welshpool
Cannock
Chase

○ Avoncroft
Museum

Norwich

Ely
Wicken
Fen
Wayland
Wood

Gower

Evesham
Hidcote
Batsford
Sudeley
Rousham
Ditchley
Blenheim Pk
Oxford
Woburn
Ashridge
Hatfield
Forest
Cambridge

Westonbirt
Bath
Bowood
Avebury
Kelmscott

Hatfield
Ho
Epping
Forest
Regents
Pk
Kew
Gravesend

Colchester

Longleat
Glastonbury

Silchester

Killerton
Bicton

Wakehurst
Place
Nymans ○
Mote Pk
Maidstone
Sheffield
Pk

Lostwithiel

Trengwainton
Penzance

Wistmans
Wood
Abbotsbury
Maiden
Castle
Rhinefield
Drive
New Forest
Lulworth

Kingley
Vale

Bedgebury

28 ANTHOPHYTES

ANGIOSPERMS

Dicotyledons

foxglove tree   quinine
Scrophulariaceæ *Paulownia*   Solanaceæ *Nicotiana*   Rubiaceæ *Cinchona*   Bignoniaceæ *Catalpa*

lilac   ash   olive privet   holly
Oleaceæ *Syringa Fraxinus Phillyrea Olea Ligustrum*   Aquifoliaceæ *Ilex*

sea buckthorn   vine
Eleagnaceæ *Hippophaë Eleagnus*   Vitaceæ *Vitis*   Thymeleaceæ *Daphne*

buckthorn
Rhamnaceæ *Rhamnus Colletia*

sumach   maple   horsechestnut
Anacardiaceæ *Rhus Cotinus*   Aceraceæ *Acer & Dipteronia*   Hippocastanaceæ *Aesculus*

spindle   tree of heaven   soapberry
Empetraceæ *Empetrum Euonymus*   Simarubiaceæ *Ailanthus*   Sapindaceæ *Sapindus Koelreutera*

gum trees
Myrtaceæ *Eucalyptus Myrtus*

white bryony   limes   lime
Cucurbitaceæ *Bryonia*   Tiliaceæ *Tilia*   Eucryphiaceæ *Eucryphia*

strawberry tree   heather
Ericaceæ *Arbutus Gaultheria Calluna Erica Rhododendron*   Vacciniaceæ *Vaccinium*   Tamaricaceæ *Tamarix*

sweet gale   tea
Myricaceæ *Myrica*   Theaceæ *Stuartia Camellia Thea*

elm   nettle tree   hop   mulberry   fig
Ulmaceæ *Ulmus Celtis Zelkova*   Cannabinaceæ *Humulus*   Moraceæ *Morus Maclura Ficus*

walnut   bitternut wingnut
Juglandaceæ *Juglans Carya Pterocarya*

alder   birch   beech   oak   hornbeam   hazel
[FAGALES] Betulaceæ *Alnus Betula*   Fagaceæ *Fagus Quercus Nothofagus*   Corylaceæ *Carpinus Ostrya Corylus*

sweetgum   plane   box
Hamamelidaceæ *Parrotia Hamamelis Liquidambar*   Platanaceæ *Platanus*   Buxaceæ *Buxus*

dogwood   bract tree
Cornaceæ *Swida Aucuba Cornus*   Garryaceæ *Garrya*   Nyssaceæ *Davidia*

[ARALIALES]
ivy   elder   honeysuckle   snowberry
Araliaceæ *Hedera*   Caprifoliaceæ *Sambucus Viburnum Lonicera Symphoricarpus*

willow poplar   snowbell tree   currant
Salicaceæ *Salix Populus*   Styracaceæ *Styrax*   Grossulariaceæ *Ribes*

broom   black locust   gorse
Fabaceæ incl. Papilionaceæ *Laburnum Genista Cytisus Wisteria Robinia Sophora Ulex*

[LEGUMINALES]
Judas tree   wattle
Cæsalpiniaceæ *Gleditsia Cercis Amherstia*   Mimosaceæ *Acacia*

plum, cherry bramble rose pear   apple   rowan, whitebeam hawthorn
Rosaceæ *Prunus Rubus Rosa Pyrus Malus Sorbus Cratægus Cotoneaster*

katsura   laurel
Cercidiphyllaceæ *Cercidiphyllum*   Lauraceæ *Laurus Sassafras Cinnamomum*

tulip tree
Magnoliaceæ *Magnolia Liriodendron*   Winteraceæ *Drimys*

Monocotyledons

banana   palms   butcher's broom
Musaceæ *Palmaceæ Liliacea Ruscaceæ*

---

27 GNETOPHYTES

Welwitschia and other unclassified plants

26 CONIFEROPHYTES

Pinaceæ   firs larches cedars hemlocks spruces pines

Cupressaceæ   cypresses junipers Thuja   Araucariaceæ   Taxodiaceæ   sequoia etc

Taxaceæ   yew   Cephalotaxaceæ   cowstail pines   Podocarpaceæ

25 GINGKOPHYTES

Gingko Baiera

24 CYCADOPHYTES

cycads
Cycas Dion

GYMNOSPERMS

---

23 PTEROPHYTES

tree ferns
Dicksonia

22 ARTHROPHYTES

horsetails
Calamites

21 MICROPHYTES

scale trees
Lepidodendron

SPORE PLANTS

1-20: ALGÆ FUNGI LICHENS MOSSES LIVERWORTS PSILOPHYTES

Tree families

Genera of trees and woody plants in this book arranged in botanical order according to Bold (Plant Divisions); Dallimore and Jackson, in Mitchell (conifers); Hutchinson (flowering plants)

1 · Forests of stone

Were they the bases of giant seeweeds, holdfasts in some slimy ocean floor? You can't take anything for granted in the world of two or three hundred million years ago. But no, they were roots: they fed. Hundreds of similar ones have been dug up in small pieces, and given the generic name of *Stigmaria*, because they were covered with the small scabs – stigmas – of rootlets. Then it was discovered that they could be grafted, theoretically, on to the stem genus *Lepidodendron*. The cones are *Lepidostrobus*. These were not conifers however, but spore-bearing trees. *Lepido* equals scale: they were scale trees. Here they have their roots and stand, where they lived and died, in what was the bottom of a quarry until it was planted as a rock garden in Glasgow's Victoria Park.

Spore-bearing plants in our countryside are small and low, dependent on surface moisture – for spores, unlike seeds, must swim free. In the ages represented by the Carboniferous series of rocks they were the forest giants. They grew in swamps; warm seas to the south, active volcanoes to the north – and east, for Arthur's Seat at Edinburgh is the frozen core of one of those volcanoes.

Upper Carboniferous animals were reptiles, and 15-foot amphibia, cylindrical of body, weak of leg, and toothy; many insects, some of them extremely large; a sort of scorpion, spiders, millipedes. The Glasgow fossils are internal casts of hollow *Lepidodendron* trunks from which the bark has gone without trace – this explains their unpleasant appearance. *Lepidodendron* bark was richly patterned with leaf cushions – a glorious regularity and order, great beauty of detail, long, very long, before there were men to appreciate it – long before even mammals evolved or even the remote ancestors of mammals. The bark was strong, and supported the largely pithy trunk with its narrow, central-growing core to heights of 50 or 100 feet, with a crown of branches carrying pointed leaves and spore cones. The trees were green plants in the sense that they were chlorophyllous, but in what colours this forest was painted we shall never know.

[300m bp]

bp = before the present. This is used in this book for prehistoric dates. Dates in historic time are AD

Carboniferous limestone has preserved the interiors of trunks and roots of extinct *Lepidodendron* in their native soil at Glasgow's Victoria Park. They grew about 300 million years ago

Lepidodendron bark

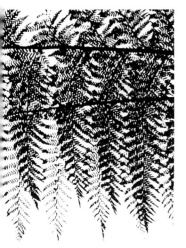

tree fern, *Dicksonia antarctica*, photographed at Penzance

A similar 'forest' in Nova Scotia was discovered with over 130 trunks rooted in fossilised clay. Such floors of clay with *Lepidodendron* and *Sigillaria* underlie nearly all coal seams. Each foot of coal represents up to 20 feet of rotting forest, and in S. Wales the coal measures are more than 8000 feet thick. This represents a very large number of generations of scale trees, seed ferns, ferns, giant horsetails (*Calamites*) and conifers: hundreds of genera, thousands of species, all extinct. How many thousands of years to produce a foot of coal? How many million years for these plants to evolve, that have now been extinct for hundreds of millions?

Cataclysmic upheavals of the earth reorientated land and sea as the ancient, nameless continents of the world merged to form one large continent, Pangea 2. The number of families of living things was reduced by more than half. Stony deserts in the northern hemisphere were leached by torrential rains and lashed by storms of sand, which sculpted the older granitic rocks. Salt lakes and land-locked seas were formed. This was the new Triassic landscape which emerged from the Carboniferous at the close of the Paleozoic era 220,000,000 years before the present. *Paleos* = ancient.

The fossil forest of Arizona dates from the Triassic and so do the first dinosaurs, so it wasn't desert everywhere. India experienced ice ages, then began to drift northwards. Plants from the southern half of the continent, Gondwanaland, spread to then equatorial parts of Siberia.

The scale trees, or giant club-mosses, did not survive, nor did the 40-foot 'horsetails', *Calamites*, but other groups of Lycopodiales and Equisetales did emerge. Even today *Equisetum* species (horsetails) colonise damp new soils, wet cinders and dune bottoms. Their ancestors grew like bamboo forests in oases of the Triassic deserts, leaving their remains in our sandstones.

The Sea of Tethys, to the east of the world land-mass, spread westwards along the collision belt which later formed the Himalaya. Eventually Gondwanaland was separated. Rift valleys opened in the infant Atlantic. In the Jurassic period Europe became largely a coral sea with islands. The climate was mild, Europe being centred on 30°N., the latitude of Cairo today.

The shallow seas at various times retreated, and several soil horizons can be traced in the limestones (deposited from the sea) of Portland. At Lulworth, high on the cliffs above the present sea, we find our second 'fossil forest'.

The Mesozoic era, of which the Jurassic is a central series of rocks, is described as the Age of Cycads. These 'bird's nest fossils' are of cycadoid plants which had short trunks and large, feathery, fern-like leaves whose broken stems covered the trunk. Flowers, probably brilliantly coloured if they resembled the cycads of today, sprang from the leaf-bases before each plant died, leaving these crowded and very tangible records of a forest of 140 million years ago. From the Yorkshire oolite came the cycad-like tree, *Williamsonia*, a feature of reconstructions of the era at South Kensington.

The Mesozoic should be called the Age of Gymnosperms. (*Gymnos* = naked: plants with seeds not enclosed in an ovary.)

Two-fifths of the world's vegetation was of cycad-like plants, and other large groups were conifers and gingkos – many and varied relations of the solitary species, *Ginkgo biloba*, which has survived. Both cycads and gingkos produce seeds, cycads in enormous cones weighing up to 30 pounds, and they have primitive motile sperm cells. These actually swim, using minute hairs, to achieve pollination. Conifers also are gymnosperms.

bird's nest fossil at
Lulworth, Dorset

Conifers resembling and probably ancestral to the Monkey Puzzle *Araucaria*, yews, *Sequoiadendron*, cypresses and *Thuja* all flourished in unimaginably large and homogeneous forests. There were also many large communities of ferns, described by palaeobotanists as an undergrowth: but where in such forests of conifers would undergrowth occur?

The detailed construction of the coniferous trees, appealing strongly to our sense of design, makes it easy to believe in their ancient origins. The fossils however are fragmentary, taxing botanical knowledge, or are solid pieces of wood turned to stone. Expert microscopic examination is required to establish the identity of a slab of stone with, say, a piece of modern Parana pine (*Araucaria* wood).

Whilst the continents had been still joined together in Pangea 2, there had grown somewhere the supposed common ancestor of the two great groups of flowering plants (Angiosperms) which now dominate the green world: dicots with 250 families or more mainly of trees – each family containing one to thirty or more genera, each genera with one to five hundred or more species – and monocots, with three or four arboreal families, mainly tropical palms. For the 50 million years of Jurassic Angiosperm evolution and for the presumed emergence of the group in the earlier Triassic, there is no fossil record at all. A poplar-like leaf, anticipating poplars by millions of years, was found at Stonesfield in Oxfordshire, a place that is the source of traditional roofing slates and epoch-marking fossils. But it isn't a missing link you need, it's a missing hundreds of thousands of years of evolution:

leaf of *Baiera*, related to *Ginkgo*, long extinct

Darwin: 'an abominable mystery'
Good*: 'One of the most perplexing things about angiosperm geography is its inherent chaos'
Darwin: 'Distribution is the key to evolution'
Corner*: 'The body of knowledge is vast, but the kingdom of plants is vaster.'

* R. Good: *Geography of the Flowering Plants*, 1953. E.J.H. Corner: *Life of Plants*, 1964.

A missing link?

'The most wonderful plant ever brought to this country and the very ugliest,' was the verdict of Sir Joseph Hooker, Director of Kew, on *Welwitschia*. It is a sort of Gymnosperm with leaves somewhat monocotyledenous and an Angiosperm-like woody stem. It has stamens recalling fossil Cycadophytes and, unlike most Gymnosperms, is pollinated by insects – various beetles attracted to nectar (as in Angiosperms, but produced on a false stigma containing an inoperative ovule). The flowers are borne on brick-red cones.

The superficially remarkable thing about *Welwitschia* is that it has only two leaves, each about 6 feet long – much longer if you include dead tissue – which continue to grow throughout its very long life. This has been carbon-14 dated at 2000 years plus. The leaves grow from the two lobes of a short trunk a few inches high, which has a root extending vertically downwards 'to unknown depths'.

Welwitschia bainesii Hook f., syn. *mirabilis*, was discovered in S. W. Africa in 1860–61 by Welwitsch and, separately, by Baines. It is a desert plant with no known relatives, fossil or otherwise. For us it may represent hundreds of families of plants, containing infinite numbers of genera and species, which have evolved, flourished and become extinct without leaving any trace.

I am indebted to Trevor Crosby of Leeds University for the opportunity to draw a young plant from life. At Leeds it grows in a 4-foot drainpipe full of pebbles. Obviously no attempt is made to simulate the desert winds which tear the leaves, but both leaves of this specimen were split into ribbons, apparently by tensions within.

The older *Welwitschia* individuals in their native habitat did not, it seems, choose to dwell in an area of nil rainfall. They have simply survived there since the climate changed.

The final Mesozoic episode, the Cretaceous, 65 million years long and, in Britain, 5000 feet thick, gets its name (*creta* = chalk) from the rocks being simply made of the dead bodies of microscopic plants and animals with shells. The seas spread and united, covering even the Sahara. A Jurassic flora of cycads, conifers and ferns remained at first on the land that was left. Such a flora is preserved in the deposits of a freshwater lake in Kent, which formed the Wealden rocks. By the end of the period the flowering plants had completely taken over in what has been described as a second Creation.

Tyrannosaurus, Triceratops, Iguanadon and other dinosaurs disappeared, and mammals roamed instead. Insects and flowering plants mutually adapted, the ovaries of the plants producing nectar instead of relying on the wind for pollination.

The flowering plants (Angiosperms) have certain advantages which have enabled them to diversify into 250,000 species, leaving the Gymnosperms in a minority of about 650. The new and varied environments of the Cretaceous, with its many coastlines and gently shifting climatic zones (actually mostly geographical shifts), over a long and comparatively settled period, provided ideal conditions for the evolution of a 'modern' flora and fauna. Probably many island habitats offered reduced local competition and limited foraging and pasturing, acting as nurseries for infant genera later to be of world importance. And those doomed dinosaurs were probably very conservative in their feeding habits, while mammals remained small and apparently insignificant.

One superiority of the Angiosperms is their ability to respond rapidly to changes both local and general. Though mammals began small, there is every reason to suppose that Angiosperms started by being big – trees, not herbs. Trees perpetuate themselves in forests which to a great extent create the habitat for more trees. But the same group of plants was able to migrate to new habitats within the forest – e.g. hanging from the branches – and outside it: pioneer trees, woody plants, herbs, and the monocot grasses which, growing from the base rather than the tip, made themselves proof against the greediest herbivores. The flowering plants have adapted even to life in the water and in some rare cases have migrated back into the sea, the domain of their remote ancestors, the seaweeds.

Not only is the group superbly adaptable to virtually every habitat available in the world, but species themselves split into, often, many subspecies and varieties according to terrain, and frequently hybridise, gaining new territory. Many Angiosperms reproduce vegetatively as well as sexually and, it is said, can even evolve vegetatively, adopting and rejecting natural mutations of the body tissues. All the older groups of plants except perhaps the oldest, the minuter algae and moulds, are much more cumbersome both in reproduction and in evolution.

The late Cretaceous forests of Greenland, to which, then subtropical, continent the unsubmerged part of Britain was then attached, contained Gymnosperms such as ginkgos, *Araucaria*, *Sequoia* and cypress-like conifers, and the *Sciadopitys* genus now known by the Japanese umbrella pine (page 148). There were also trees resembling *Athrotaxus*, now native of Tasmania. Among Angiosperms were the archetypal magnolias, the most primitive flowering plants we know. There were trees resembling the tropical breadfruit, *Artocarpus*, and *Cinnamomum*, *Ocotea*, *Dalbergia* – none of these four genera are represented elsewhere in this book, for they will not grow in the temperate zones. There were also walnuts, figs and willows now extinct, in America and Europe.

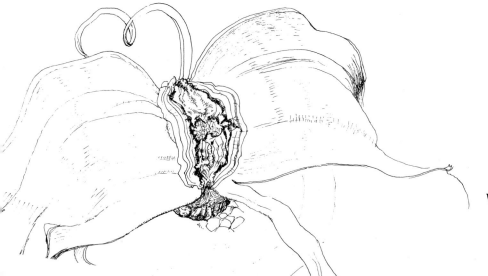

Welwitschia at Leeds

13

flower buds of *Magnolia*

The present distribution of the Magnoliaceae in southern N. America and E. Asia is described as discontinuous. It is only to be explained if we are aware of the ancient nativity of the magnolias in Greenland, whence they spread west and east along a band of country varying from warm temperate plains to tropical highlands. Tulip trees (*Liriodendron*, page 95), members of the Magnolia family, are now known from two species, one E. American, one central Chinese. The missing parent species, or its near relatives, grew in Britain and Europe and may have originated there or further north. It is difficult to imagine a tulip tree 'emerging' but it must have happened somewhere – or it was created – and the sub-tropical Scottish highlands are as good as anywhere, I feel.

The image of the Cretaceous is one of a great calm sea and a land surface heavy with green, all undisturbed by extremes like volcanic eruptions. There must have been enormous changes in 65 million years, but at least one author, Swinnerton (1960), suggests that evolution, as illustrated in the unparalleled richness of Cretaceous fossil sea animals, continued as if driven by its own power. 'On that vast sea floor, with its uniform and stable conditions, its inexhaustible store of food and apparent absence of competition, the precise influences which stimulated these serial changes [in the test of *Micraster*, a sea urchin] must have largely internal and genetic.'

'Uplifting' of the land and a retreat of the seas at the end of the Cretaceous saw the British land surface as continuous chalkland, soon to be defined, in Tertiary times, by the formation of the North Sea. The Tertiary, some 60 million years, is the last period before the Quaternary in which we live. The various departments of the Tertiary and Quaternary which together make up that part of the Cenozoic Era which has elapsed, are based on the proportions of living molluscan species identified in the rocks. There were 15 per cent at the start and 35 to 50 per cent in the more recent. Similar proportions apply to recognisable genera of plants, though not of living species. The earth was cooling, or the equator was moving southwards, or the land was moving north, or all three.

MESOZOIC ERA	CAINOZOIC ERA						
Cretaceous	Tertiary				Quaternary		
	Eocene 58m 'dawn of recent'	Oligocene 38m 'somewhat recent'	Miocene 28m 'less recent'	Pliocene 12m 'more recent'	Pleistocene 1m 'most recent'	10,000 yrs 'modern or recent'	present

In a last shuddering twist of the now largely separate continental plates, the Alps and the Himalaya had yet to be squeezed up from the bottom of the Tethys sea, while a 'stupendous vulcanism' was to accompany the equivalent tearing apart of the crust in the North Atlantic rift – Iceland is still affected.

Tertiary trees

seed of a tropical palm, a *Nypa* species, from the London Clay

As, in the Cretaceous, the flowering plants gradually achieved dominance over the older Gymnosperms and ferns, so in the Tertiary at least in the European zone, the 'modern' deciduous forest gradually displaced a tropical and sub-tropical flora of palms and large-leaved evergreens. Trees, as always before, far outnumbered herbs. This is typical of tropical forest but it also agrees with evolutionary theory.

That paragraph is of course a vast simplification, and conifers still reigned supreme in cooler and mountainous areas, as indeed they still do. The deciduous conifer *Glyptostrobus*, rediscovered in 1945 as the dawn redwood, *Metasequoia glyptostroboides*, in China (being known as a fossil, it had to take over the lumpish fossil name) ranged over the whole northern hemisphere. The swamp cypress, *Taxodium*, also deciduous, was now common, as were *Sequoia* species closely resembling the Californian redwood, *Sequoia sempervirens*, and the Big Tree, *Sequoiadendron*. There were *Thujas* and *Libocedrus* – incense cedars, now natives of the Far East and the Far West and Chile. *Cryptomaria*, the Japanese cedar, grew in N. Ireland, and there were many pines. Ginkgos and cycads still flourished in the early tertiary forests. But the discovery of tropical palm seeds fossilised in the London Clay gave a more vivid idea of what the land was like. The seed was of a species of *Nypa*, one of the oldest known monocots and now native as *Nypa fruticans* in Malayan swamps. There were other palms in south England: *Sabal* and *Phoenix*. Among dicots were *Platanus, Liquidambar, Catalpa* and, still most important, *Magnolia*.

By Miocene times, about the middle of the Tertiary, the tropical element of the flora had migrated and the Magnoliaceae were the dominant plants, making up more than half the total. They are represented in the decreasing E. Asian and N. American elements of the diagram. But while families and genera are recognisable, species are all extinct: evolution continues. It comes as something of a shock after all these more or less familiar generic names to realise that not until the middle Pliocene, in rocks perhaps only 6 million years old, is a living European species of plant found in the fossil record.

several-million-year-old leaf print of *Cercidiphyllum* from Ardtun, Mull. The tree is now native to Japan. Below, 'Outer European' fossil floras of the Tertiary (after Godwin)

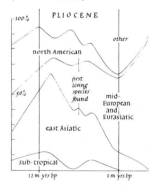

spruce forests, presumed to be *Picea abies*, grew in Cheshire 60,800 years ago. This is Loch Long

By the end of the Pliocene, European trees resembled those of today, but in a richer 'spectrum'. The last hickories and magnolias disappeared into America and China. Lower temperatures preceding the great Ice Age of the Pleistocene ('most recent') removed a last group of trees which have now a refuge in the region of the Caucasus: wingnut, horsechestnut, walnut, some limes, maples and elms; while only one pine (the Scots), one spruce (Norway) and one fir (European silver fir) remained in northern Europe. Of these, only the Scots pine has continued in Britain, to form with yew and juniper a very small remnant of the former Age of Gymnosperms.

Homo erectus already lived, not on fruit alone, in Africa, as the ice ages began in the north.

Pterocarya fraxinifolia, Caucasian wingnut, extinct in Europe since the Ice Ages; photographed at Kew

right: chart of an interglacial, after West. Note the late spread of hornbeam. The interglacial maple was *Acer monspessulanum*, now native to S. Europe

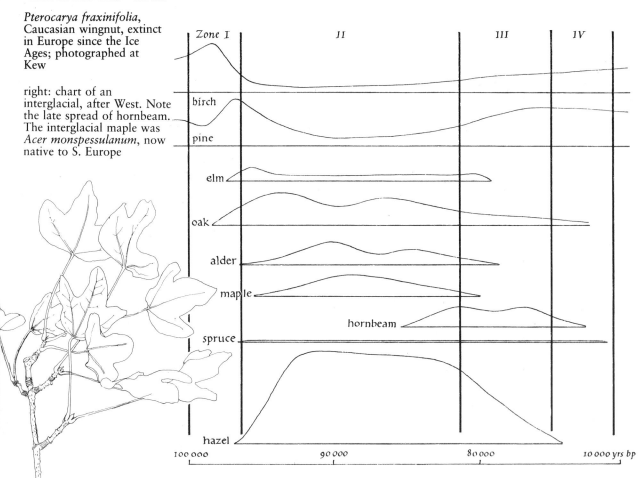

2 · Survivors of the ice

juniper, Tynron, Dumfries

Juniperus communis is the widest-ranging tree species of the north. Variable from a 12-foot spire to a plump bush, and on high ground prostrate as subspecies *nana*, it grows on chalk downs, Welsh clifftops and Scottish mountain sides. In the last ice age it increased enormously as soon as temperatures began to rise. Godwin says, 'the evidence is strong for indigeneity from the middle Pleistocene', which takes it back well beyond 200,000 years.

Our one remaining pure juniper wood looks tame and tidy in the sun, like a cemetery. Once among the trees with your legs trapped in slimy deadwood, you fear it may be yours. The grotesque fingers of the older trees look ominous as the sky darkens.

The timber is strong. It carves well into 'dirk handles' (Edlin) and, with cedar-like fragrance, 'spits and spoons imparting a grateful relish' (Evelyn). The wood turns very well – it contains a resin once used for varnish – and the smoke inhibits pestilence or cures hams, giving them a ginny flavour. For gin, to which juniper gave its name, the Scots exported the berries to Holland, and they wove baskets from the roots, not having many willow trees.

The berries made a brown dye and a whole range of medicines – oil of juniper is still a carminative, BP. The Swedes made a healthy juniper beer, and certain Bohemians, known for wonderful good health, drank nothing else but juniper-water. North American juniper woods harboured illicit stills.

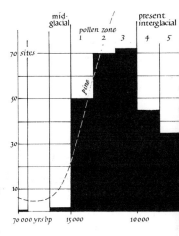

juniper pollen chart

Sea buckthorn

sea buckthorn

Hippophaë rhamnoides, sea buckthorn, sallow thorn, is of the oleaster family, not the buckthorn. It is only by adaption a seaside plant, being also native to landlocked Switzerland, where up to 6000 feet it clothes the sides of Alpine streams – as it must have the streams of Britain's melting glaciers. It is scaly, silvery all over, with prominent warts, and spines. It spread very suddenly after the ice, then was as suddenly eclipsed by more familiar native trees. It needs the fullest light and cannot have been any sort of undershrub. On the Lancashire coast, planted or escaped, it shares the dunes with the equally silvery creeping willow. It can grow up to 20 feet or more; a hairy Chinese variety native to Szechuan up to 60 feet. Sea buckthorn forest is not out of the question for late glacial Britain. Those small green flowers (males on separate trees) surely cannot produce the pollen mass of pine, oak or hazel, so it could be under-represented in the pollen record. The berries, a strange, attractive reddish yellow, are very acid – they are disliked by birds and stay on the silvery twigs until February. They are a good source of vitamin C and are used, it is said, as part of a fish sauce on the Baltic coast and to make a delicate jelly in Tartary. I tried the jelly, but there was a peculiar, putrid aroma from the cooking berries, and the clear golden jelly, pleasantly tart, still had some of the smell.

Dwarf birch

dwarf birch

Salix reticulata

Betula nana now grows practically everywhere north of Ben Nevis and Riga, according to the distribution maps. On the ground you must look for it among the heather of certain high moors. It grew widely, and probably much more thickly, in the tundra of mid- and late-glacial Britain, including Upper Teesdale, where, strangely, it has survived a hundred centuries of assorted threats. Elsewhere, the forest has come and mostly gone away again, leaving no place for this attractive miniature tree in the lowlands. In Sweden it grows with and hybridises with the silver birch.

Never taller than 4 feet, it is ignored by writers of tree books, except Bean, who recommends it by garden streams and notes its leaves, 'prettily net-veined beneath'; and Edlin, who forgets nothing. It took me a week of walking the hills to find it, and then not without the help of knowledgeable Highlanders, who kindly led me to a hummocky moor west of the Spey. Red deer observed us from a distance: the plants bore the marks of their teeth.

Herbaceous willows

In similar places grow several herbaceous and dwarf willows, including *Salix herbacea*, only 3 inches high; *myrsinites*, disguised as a billberry; *lanata*, woolly and *lapponum*, Lapland or downy; and the very attractive *reticulata*, the net-veined willow. All are more or less round-leaved, native sub-arctics with a much more southerly range in the ice ages. The silky, silvery and very vigorous creeping willow, *S. repens*, has narrower leaves and a scattered, less montane distribution on poor, wet soil and sand – it also is a native of very long standing.

All this tundra or sub-forest grew against the background of advancing tree birches and Scots pine, *Pinus sylvestris* a survivor of at least three ice ages. Pine was at first confined to river valleys and lowland heaths, but soon spread all over Britain, up to 3000 feet and from shore to shore – and further, into the Dogger Bank and what is now the sea of Cardigan Bay. Bog trees, deep in the peats of Scotland, Ireland and East Anglia are part of this forest: some have been dated by carbon-14 to 7000 years old. Though often preceded by birchwood and containing juniper, it was virtually a blanket of a single species. The hairy mammoths retreated, to freeze in Siberia.

[10 000 bp]

Corylus avellana:
hazel tree, self-coppicing in the mild, damp climate of the W. Highlands

Hazel

Very high frequencies of hazel pollen, sometimes mixed with sweetgale, from which, formerly, it could not be distinguished, are shown in the fossil record of the early part of the present interglacial. Though hazel produces much pollen, no doubt carried far on the winter winds and pushed into the soil by February rains, the early presence of large hazel woods in Ireland and N.

England is a fact. Botanists observed hazel as an undershrub in modern oakwoods. They forgot that this pattern might be the result of many centuries of cultivation and management. The very high 'Corylus maxima' were regarded as aberrations and hazel was not included in the totals of tree pollen. Shortly after 9000 bp hazel pollen rises to four or even seventeen times the total of all other trees.

In a wet, luxurious ashwood preserved on a limestone platform near Kishorn, W. Ross – a few acres which we surely must accept as once typical of thousands now grazed to semi-desert by sheep and deer – are many hazels, old and gnarled but indubitably trees and not shrubs. The trunks are split and collapsed with age, but from these trunks stout coppice poles continue their upward growth – these are natural coppice trees. The climate, untypical of Britain as a whole, may yet be close enough to that of the early post-glacial.

The British forest

To return to the late Ice Age: oaks with 90-feet clear trunks have been found in E. Anglian bogs, and pieces of oak from S. W. England have been dated as 9000 years old, along with hazel about three centuries older. These eastern and south-western areas were also early strongholds of pine, with a more important concentration in Hampshire. The pattern of pinewoods and hazel woods occasionally invaded by oak (pollen frequencies of oak are low) is an unfamiliar one. Elm was also present. Alder, *Alnus glutinosa*, also has an early record and one that extends back to previous interglacials, with a good correlation between macro remains and pollen percentages. It is a waterside tree and an important element of fen carrs, but certainly not limited to fenland. Every river in Britain has alders beside it at some point, and while the water meadows of England cannot be typical of early post-glacial habitats, the vigorous conditions of the Scottish sites illustrated here surely can.

tenacious alder (right) in a N. Scottish river bed and by Loch Lomond

Silver birch

Whilst early interglacial hazel woods are only grudgingly admitted to the history of our vegetation, the high pollen frequencies of *Betula* show that 'we must presume dominant birch forests throughout the British Isles' – in pollen zone IV (Godwin). Birch, among a very few native trees, behaves now as it must always have done in its long history here. Common everywhere, it will colonise grassland of almost every type, wet or dry, and quickly forms thickets and small woods – even on soil as poor as that of colliery slag heaps. In far northern Scotland and Scandinavia, and in Greenland and northern Russia, it is the only or the dominant tree. It is more tolerant of cold than any other tree above shrub height, with *B. pubescens* (hairy) slightly more hardy than *B. pendula* (or *verrucosa*), 'warty' but not always pendulous. Edlin (1956) remarks that exceptionally fine individuals are sometimes met with in Scotland, suggesting a once-common superior strain. Constant use of the better trees, over the centuries, has encouraged a poorer type of 'Lady of the Woods' – a ragged, ubiquitous urchin, none the less elegant. Loudon, in the 1820s still in better touch with tradition than we can be, describes some of the uses of birch, which may well go back to the Stone Age:

> The Highlanders of Scotland make everything of it. They build their houses, make their beds, chairs, table, dishes and spoons; construct their mills; make their carts, ploughs, harrows, gates, and fences, and even manufacture ropes of it. The branches are employed as fuel in the distillation of whisky; the spray is used for smoking hams and herrings, for which last purpose it is preferred to every other kind of wood. The bark is used for tanning leather, and sometimes, when dried and twisted into a rope, instead of candles. The spray is used for thatching houses: and, dried in summer, with the leaves on, makes a good bed, where heath is scarce.

We might add that there was a flourishing iron industry in the Highlands. A beer or wine can be brewed from the spring sap, but perhaps there was enough whisky in Scotland. A fungus parasite, *Fomes fomentarius*, surgeon's agaric, used for tinder and, perhaps later, for dressing wounds, was collected by Mesolithic people. Another tinder fungus, *Piptoporus betalinus*, razor-strop fungus, is now more common in Scotland – hard as a stone, in conical brackets, its appearance signifies the death of quite young trees.

Often preceding the forest, birch also quickly fills deforested areas. It is light-demanding and relatively short-lived, so forest takes over again: oak, holly and beech can invade a birchwood, as can pine in Scotland. So our birchwoods are all secondary woodland of inferior strains. Purer woodlands probably existed at Birkenhead, Birkdale, Bricket wood and Betws (from *bedw*, the Welsh name of the tree).

The frequently observed hybridisation of the two species is now said to be impossible genetically. They were formerly lumped, sensibly, as *B. alba*. The witches' brooms, twiggy bundles in the branches, are cluster galls: harmless.

The pinewoods

As with birch, the natural pinewoods of the Highlands have been said to consist of unwanted crooked or short-stemmed trees and their offspring.

shade-intolerant shrubs of the British tundra as their pollen rises and declines in the first 2000 years of the postglacial

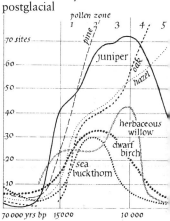

However, the great pinewoods are impressive, and they are the only remaining large areas of native British forest. They can be seen at Rothiemurchus (Cairngorms), Loch Maree, Loch Rannoch. The pine forest of Glen Affric, said to have been preserved only through its remoteness, has been taken over by the Forestry Commission which undertook a large and timely conservation and regeneration programme. Combining judicious planting from local seed and natural regeneration, the Commission's officers, after initial failures, found it necessary to exclude the red and roe deer entirely from their plots. Black grouse and capercailzie also damage seedlings, but this was tolerable. Rowan, birch and willow were allowed to grow up as well as pine.

An air of drama enters the report in the spring 1980 *Arboricultural Journal*: 'The Rangers were now instructed to shoot all deer on sight, irrespective of species, sex, age or season.' An increase in the price of venison in 1967 (which I must admit I never noticed) gave extra point to the enterprise. The Commission deserves our gratitude for this considerable and well-controlled action to let nature regain her balance. The successful part of the operation so far concerns Loch Benevian, West and Central, a total of nearly 4000 acres. Visitors will judge whether the work has retained the natural character of the forest. Plans will be reassessed in 1990.

The alternative, slower method is to cull and fence out all deer and rely entirely on natural regeneration, scattered though this might be.

Scots pine has a wide natural range, east to Okhotsk, and is the most common conifer in Europe. It is also our second most important softwood tree after Sitka spruce – we had 623,000 acres in 1965. It is imported as red deal, Baltic redwood, Norway fir, Archangel fir and, formerly, as Riga fir, Danzig fir. It is a *fyr* in most other languages. Var. *rigensis* is a tall form used for ships' masts. A silver-leafed variety originates in the Caucasus – the metallic or blue lustres evolved, presumably towards the warmer limits of the tree's range, to reflect heat away from the leaves.

Specimens in England are often of mixed European parentage. Scottish timber, from slow-grown northern strains, is superior.

pine, birch and juniper:
a native forest,
Rothiemurchus

small-leaved lime trunk.
Below, dominant trees in
Britain 5000 years ago
(after Rackham, 1976)

3 · Britain's trees 5000 years ago

Between 7000 and 5000 before the present the British forest reached a climax of luxuriance, enjoying a climate both warmer and wetter than ever since. Melting ice continued to feed the ocean and the sea level rose to flood the Rhine delta in the southern North Sea and break the landbridge with Europe. About 5000 bp elm and lime, which had spread and increased over much of the lowlands, were suddenly reduced, perhaps largely by human action. Elm never recovered, while weeds such as the ribwort plaintain increased, as did the ash, the tree of farm tools.

From this time on, plants which increase enough to appear in the pollen record cannot truly be called indigenous. Birds may carry berries across the Channel, of course, but successive landings by farming peoples cannot be ignored. They surely brought, with their skills, their favourite plants, as inadvertently they brought their weeds. (Some that we call weeds – such as corn spurrey and black bindweed – were part of the diet of prehistoric people, as has been found from the stomachs of bog corpses in Sweden.)

The more that is known about Neolithic people, the less simple they appear. So the notion that plants are native if they were here before the Romans has ceased to be useful. The Romans were, on the whole, unreliable and biassed reporters on plant-life. The famous woad of the Ancient Britons turns out to be itself a Roman introduction, while Julius Caesar, marching over the chalk hills, claimed that we had no beeches. Our guide must be the records of fossils and subfossils.

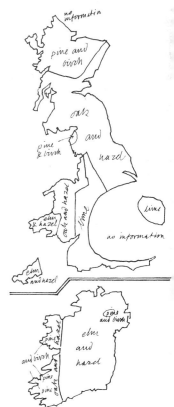

The durmast oak

durmast oak with solar halo

Of the two species of British oak – both of which are European and even Asian oaks as well – the durmast or sessile oak, *Quercus petraea*, formerly *sessiliflora*, is the more northerly and westerly in distribution. Taking all those names in order, we may explain something of its nature. *Mast* = food, but durmast seems an unlikely combination of Latin and Old English. The mast of the sessile oak, if not hard, is certainly fixed close to the twig, being sessile or stalkless, following its flower. This oak is not the better one for pig food, so it may have been dȳr mast. *Petraea*, stony; for which read acid or sandy, but certainly of stony places. The names do not tell that the leaves are not eared, are stalked and have down on their undersides in the form of microscopic star-patterns.

Older names were white oak and maiden oak, while Evelyn called it 'quercus urbana, which grows more upright, and being clean and lighter is fittest for timber'. But these were not the crooked forest oaks, planted wide apart, that the navy was so much in need of.

Q. petraea is the only native oak in Ireland and was very likely the first to establish itself in England – later, perhaps, neglected in favour of its brother. Pollen and macro remains are indistinguishable from *Q. robur* (page 34).

Yew

The present stronghold of the yew is a wild wood at Kingley Vale, near Lavant in W. Sussex. This is a Nature Conservancy site, with very necessary fences and a lot of unnecessary notices. The stone memorial to Professor Tansley at the top of the Vale is not out of place, however.

Other coombes in the S. Downs indicate a possible succession from scrub, with juniper, to yew. There are wild trees on the Marlborough Downs, the Chilterns (Watlington Common) and on limestone in S. England generally: not the S.W., then more again in the Welsh borders, Derbyshire and Cumbria. A wood at Mucross, Killarney may be of wild origin.

There are obviously no fossil records from the chalk, but the distribution otherwise, and the apparent quantities, of yew about 5000 bp appear to have been as now, with the addition of some East Anglian and Lincolnshire sites. But there's nothing to prove that the southern chalk hills were not covered with yew woods as some people would like to believe. By the Bronze Age yew is found at nearly a quarter of all sites excavated: a high proportion considering its preference for sheltered, calcareous positions.

yews on Watlington Common

The oldest wooden artefact in the world (about 13,000 years) is a spear of yew found at Clacton. Some yew bows from the present interglacial in Somerset are dated about 4600 bp.

'Since the use of bows is laid aside amongst us, the propagation of the yew-tree is likewise quite forborn,' wrote Evelyn in 1664. Yews planted about this time, in spite of him, are now 12 or 13 feet in girth. Many churchyards in the South and West have yews of 30 to 40 feet in girth. The oldest tree in Britain, the Fortingall yew, Perthshire, was about 52 feet in 1769, and is now 1500 years old at a very conservative estimate. The Celtic *iw* is our oldest tree name.

It is hard to escape the connection of this tree with religion, Christian or pagan, though speculation about the Druids is baseless. The shapes of wild trees are clearly such as to have given shelter to our earliest ancestors. The interior gloom and the poisonous foliage and seed add to its portentous atmosphere.

The timber is valuable – sometimes ruinous to band-saws because of deeply embedded stones and nails. It is now sliced for richly figured veneers – English yews are knotty. Wood for Agincourt-style long-bows was imported, by decree, with barrels of wine. The best explanation for the churchyard

ancient yew at Kingley Vale

yews is that they were believed to 'absorb the vapours of putrefaction'.

The yew, *Taxus baccata*, a Gymnosperm of the family *Taxaceae*, is distributed over most of Europe, south and central, with extensions into Asia. *Bacca* means a fleshy berry. The Sussex name, snotty-gogs, refers to the soft, non-poisonous aril, not quite enclosing the seed; and ruddier than any cherry.

The wych elm

Elm entered the British woodlands a little before oak, both quite late in our post-glacial period. *Ulmus glabra* is the only native of the genus in Ireland and, probably, in Scotland. Flowering later (March/April) than other elms it sets fertile seed. We may visualise its progress across England as a bushy tree of riversides – as we see it now in Scottish glens, with sallows, holly and alder – sometimes forming small woods, sometimes growing into a large, rounded, somewhat pendulous tree, in either case heavy with early fruit, and then most noticeable – as it is in autumn, by the gold of its leaves.

The Elm Decline, where pollen totals drop to half or less about 5000 bp, has been repeated in our own time. The wych elm, mostly dead in England, will survive in remote glens. Clearance for arable crops remains the best explanation for the prehistoric Decline.

leaves of wych elm, Dumfries

Glabra, smooth, refers to the shoots and can be applied to the branches and the trunk, to a degree. Older names are *U. montana*, self-explanatory, and *U. scabra*, the opposite of smooth, for the texture of the large, beautiful leaves. *Wych* is quick or pliant, as in switch, from the Saxon *wice*: the timber for bows and cart-shafts and a tough, handsome brown wood for furniture. It was witch hasell in Gerard's day. The inner bark can be, and was, eaten; and beaten into coarse fibre – seemingly irreconcilable uses. The leaves were a fodder crop: important for woodland farmers.

Willows

The native willows are small trees which flower before the leaves come out. The dwarf, round-leaved group of the previous chapter are arctic, or nearly so, now restricted to northern mountains. *Salix viminalis*, the common osier, with leaves not round but narrow and longest of all, up to 10 inches, has a reputation of having survived the last ice age, along with creeping willow, in County Louth. These two willows hybridise elsewhere as the rosemary-leaved willow. But the osier belongs to freshwater margins. Its more recent history, in lowland Britain, is of wide exploitation as a coppice tree, cut annually for basket making. Baskets, and particularly fish 'kettles' or kiddles, creels for ponies, riddles and storage baskets have been essential for survival in their time, and the craft, and perhaps the cultivation of osier beds, goes back to the Stone Age. The industry is now centred on the Somerset levels.

Many varieties of osier are known for different qualities, but they can be referred to three or four botanical species and their hybrids. Purple osiers are from *S. purpurea*, a European cousin: black osiers from *S. triandra* ('three-anther'), the almond-leaved willow: brown and yellow from *viminalis*, the narrow- and downy-leaved native. A triple hybrid of the last with a *purpurea* cross produces simply Fine Basket Osier. There are odd old names like Glib Skins, Whining Gelster, Dark Dicks: 'skins' are skeins, produced by splitting certain varieties. Strong baskets are made from shoots cut in winter and, for the best buff material, boiled in their bark, which contains a natural dye.

Osiers are withies (Anglo-Saxon *wipig*), in Scotland and N.E. England 'saughs,' giving rise to or deriving from *saleach* or sallow. Sallow or goat willow, *S. caprea*, is the hedge willow, a weed to foresters – it grows in woodland as well as by streams and ponds. It is cut for Palm Sunday or, more likely now, for a hint of spring in the parlour, the catkins of the male tree being pussy willow: when finally yellow, 'goose chicks'. In Ireland, where it is undoubtedly native, 'sally' is lucky on journeys, and a twig binds and protects the creamery churn, or used to. Gypsies used to cut it for clothes pegs, first bound in tin cut from old cans, nailed, and then split. It was familiar enough for the first Australian settlers to name some of their eucalyptus trees sallees.

Other sallows are *S. aurita*, round-eared, and grey willow, *S. cinerea* ('ashen' as in Cinderella). This is also eared, but with longer, harder leaves. All are small, rounded trees, lovely in a quiet way. The round-eared willow, so called from the conspicuous stipules persisting on the shoots, belongs to acid wetlands of the N. and W.

All withies and sallies interbreed, and the textbooks are clearer about the situation than I am from my limited observations. While the forester weeds them out, Hillier's seed catalogue lists them all lovingly. In fact, you can strike them easily from ripe shoots. The osier leaf reproduced here was gathered at a first-floor window of my house. The tree was a stick in the ground four years ago, by the kitchen drain.

All three willows have a long and continuous history in the British Isles, says Godwin. I have seen incredible hulks of old sallows, broken in the mire, yet with strong, vertical branches – another natural coppice tree. A fallen trunk may give rise to a natural line of trees – and to archaeological speculations. The marshier habitats are now rare in England, but sallows are

ancient sallow in a S.W. Irish swamp. Above, osier leaf, actual size happy to survive in odd corners, margins of plantations, stream sides, hedges, heaths, and by ponds full of old prams. The female trees, with catkins like caterpillars, later very woolly, are ignored by the palm pickers. Pollination is by early bees and late March winds.

Holly and ivy

ivy in snow

With its precious cruciform flowers, blood-red berries, and thorns, holly has a well-known religious meaning. In folklore it is the male to the female ivy, and the pair are re-united in ecology by their intolerance of persistent frost. Like yew, whose range it nearly follows, holly has flourished in earlier interglacials, and in the Atlantic stage of our own it increased rapidly, with yew and ash, in response to Neolithic clearances.

It is a ruggedly adaptable and variable tree, thorny only at animal height, fertile to the edge of its range. It is at its vigorous best in frost-free, wet Killarney oakwoods, where it extends out into pure holly wood. The stems are shining white with mossy patches and exuberant, often fantastic anatomy.

Ilex aquifolium (needle- or constellation?-leaved) is *holegn* or holm (hulver in East Anglia) perhaps from the Gaelic *cuillean* (killin in Cornwall). The leaves were a tonic and some sort of cure (Paraguay tea or maté is an *Ilex*). The berries are strongly emetic, but not to the birds which spread the seeds: 'thristilcok and popingay' in a poem quoted by Grigson: ivy has 'no fowles but the sory howlet that singeth "How how"'.

The wood is pure white, good for inlays and chessmen: stained black it resembles ebony. It is a wonderful fuel – but (also from Grigson): 'who so ever against holly do sing/ He may wepe and handes wring'. And this applies to any abuse of the tree.

Ivy also varies its leaves: it dispenses with lobes on fertile shoots. We may wonder which is the ancestral form. Other members of the family, Araliaceae, have five-lobed leaves and at least one, *Echinopanax horridus*, of Asia and America (?originating in Europe) has fierce prickles.

Ivy will revert to a tree form if a cutting of the flowering shoot, with its oval pointed leaves, is planted. Otherwise it creeps – horizontally and in all directions until a vertical surface presents itself. Climbing stems put out tiny root-like fingers into the crevices of bark or stone. It will not flower until it reaches the light, but it can spread on woodland floors too dark for grass.

The flowers are five-petalled, yellowy green, autumnal; unpleasantly scented – but not to bees, wasps and flies. The shoots have hairs in the form of pointed stars. The dull black berries are five-ribbed and contain two to five seeds.

Hedera is Latin for ivy, *helix* Greek for a screw, or the snail which creeps as harmlessly as the plant. The wood was used for cups to turn cow's milk into cough medicine, but holly would do as well. With holly, it was brought indoors at Christmas; and hung outside taverns whose wine needed a bush.

In the last but one interglacial it was abundant and fed upon by hippopotami at Clacton. It is distributed over most of Europe and Asia Minor, avoiding the deep frosts of Continental Europe and Russia. There is a Caucasian ivy, very large leaved, a Himalayan one with yellow berries and a Japanese ivy with leaves slightly three-lobed.

holly trunk, Kerry

Native limes

The small-leaved lime and the large-leaved lime are *Tilia cordata* (cordate = heart-shaped) and *T. platyphyllos* (Greek *platy*, broad, *phyllos*, leaf). They were lindens up to about 1600, then lines, then limes. The Welsh is, literally, 'elm-lime', *llwyf teil*, apt because the two go together in many ways, or are complementary. German *Lind* is bast (American limes are basswoods), and bast is fibre. Bast trees are important in primitive communities, especially where such plants as *Cannabis*, hemp, are not grown.

T. cordata, the more important of our two native limes, leapt to prominence in prehistoric studies when it was stated by the Danish botanist Iverson, in 1969, that '*Tilia*, not *Quercus*, was the dominating tree in the climax forest of the post-glacial warmth period'. At least one lime-dominated area of woodland had been discovered in this country – in alluvium dated 7500 to 2500 bp, near Birmingham. Pollen deposits of 20 per cent or more are common for most of England, and the pollen of lime, not scattered carelessly but reserved for the bees, under-represents the tree in fossil records. Lime suffered a decline, like elm, but has been much reduced over the historical period by the gradually worsening climate and because the seedlings are nutritious and taken by animals, children and pigeons. To explain the original decline, barking trees and consuming seedlings is a more effective way of wiping out trees than clear felling – especially in the case of lime and elm which coppice easily.

leaves of large-leaved lime; below, small-leaved lime

Rackham (1976) discovered four or five lime woods within 10 miles of Sudbury in Suffolk: 'These and similar groups of woods in Essex, Norfolk, Lincs, Derbyshire etc. are almost certainly the fragmented remains of parts of the wildwood that were particularly rich in *Tilia*,' he says. But ancient coppice stools and modern coppices point to traditional use and management, as with elm, and with oak/hazel and ash/hazel in northern, western and midland countries. (We have little evidence from the non-peaty areas of the country at 5000 bp or before.)

Ash

It would be naïve to assume that any ashwood or complex of ash, oak and hazel is of natural origin. But ash undoubtedly colonises open shrub, and hedges, which are a sort of secondary scrub in strips.

As elm declined, ash increased – phenomenally. It was already present in small quantities. Light-loving, it would have a hard time in the climax forest, where it arrived somewhat late, having travelled from some Ice Age refuge in Europe. Everything points to its active cultivation, or at least encouragement, by the early farmers who used the method of temporary clearance – of elmwood perhaps – but who had some permanent bases.

Ash wood is known for its great strength and is virtually the only wood in Britain for tool handles, especially axes – the American hickory is slightly superior. It is sometimes supposed that Yggdrasil, the old Scandinavian Tree of Life, was an ash tree. In the folk-healers' magic – the sickly child passed through a cleft tree to absorb its strength – its quality passes into the supernatural. Ash trees may have been sacred in the Neolithic period.

Notable ashwoods remaining on limestone platforms have probably done

so because farmers had no other use for those sheep-destructive clints and grikes: planting is not ruled out. Ash is also known as a component of woodland following calcareous fen carr: you have to look a long way for this now. Gilbert White complained that practically every ash tree in the hedges was pollarded. This offended his eye, but it shows how eagerly the wood was used. There is no doubt in my mind that most patches of ashwood in the west and north of Britain were put there on purpose. They have not been regularly cropped like the midland coppices: pieces of various shapes were needed, not just poles.

In the coppices, ash trees are often seen as standards. The later, more sophisticated craft of the tool-maker required trees at least 30 years old. The wood was invariably cleft (using the froe or side knife) to ensure that the grain followed the length of the piece. Shafts could be bent to the shapes required by soaking in water (try making a shepherd's crook from any other timber). This flexibility – later achieved by steaming – is almost as important a quality of ash wood as its strength and resistance to shock. Britain actually exported ash to Russia for Red Army sledge runners in the Second World War; but now we have to import straight-grown ash for the implements of sports, trades and crafts which we have taught to the world.

pollard ash, Oxfordshire

When our industrial strength finally collapses, shall we have the hardwoods to sustain our traditional crafts? You might ask: shall we have the craftsmen? There are signs that we shall. Plastics have great qualities, properly used, but I think there is no future for pressings and mouldings of whatever material that are never quite up to the job.

Edlin (1949) describes an interesting example of what craftsmanship can mean in woodland terms. Walking sticks were once fashionable – 'ashplants', they were called. These were ingeniously grown in the shape required. Young saplings were transplanted, set sideways with the leading shoot removed. When a vertical pole had grown up, almost at right-angles, it was cut, with the original shoot as the handle. Finished with the bark on, it went perfectly with tweed plus-fours.

You may have used a broom made of birch twigs. The handle may not have been of ash – hazel or sallow would do – but the twigs may have been bound on with light-coloured bands of wood. This was certainly ash, soaked in a stream for months, then beaten into strands.

opposite:
ash tree in Devon, self sown in a hedge now cleared for pasture. Below: native beech, cut down last year as unproductive of timber

Ash was the supreme coach-builders' timber for framing, equally strong in straights or curves, and persisting in railway carriages, cars and aircraft, until sometimes superseded by laminated spruce, then by metal. The frame of the *curragh* built on 5th-century lines for Tim Severin's *Brendan Voyage* was of native Irish ash, mountain grown. The masts and oars were of wood 'hand-picked from the tough, north-facing sides of the ash trees'. *Fraxinus excelsior*.

Beech

The beech, *Fagus sylvatica*, has a similar story. The beechwoods are a result of industrial use and management. It is a native tree and was certainly here before 5000 bp. But no beechwood can be called natural: the wood has been so useful. Even the leaves were good for bug-free mattresses. The hangers on the downs are windbreaks, cover for game, living timber yards, but not

31

beech in old boundary
hedge, Herts

survivors of some vast beech forest. Of course the beeches have spread, and
many have grown up into the tree cathedrals discovered by Victorian
nature-lovers. These high beechwoods may, for all we know, resemble the
original cover of the downs and chalk hills.

The early distribution of beech in Britain is surprising. It appeared in the
warm Boreal climatic period (before the Atlantic, or oceanic warm and wet
period of optimum growth conditions) equivalent to pollen zone VI. It was
found in the Hampshire basin, where we might expect it as a European
invader, and in the Somerset levels. Then suddenly, there is beech on Bodmin
Moor, in East Anglia, at the centre of England, at the Derbyshire Peak, in
W. Stafford, at Bootle, Kendal, Grasmere, Carlisle, Corbridge and 35 miles
up the Dee from Aberdeen. None of these places is much like High Wycombe
and I would not be surprised to be told that the beeches moved in with
human settlers. Not perhaps a magic tree, the beech is a worthy companion
with nutritious mast which might have acquired magical properties as an
ancestral food.

There was a great period of planting beeches in modern times, in the late
18th century and the early 19th, perhaps by the new owners of great estates
– certainly so in Lancashire and the Scottish lowlands. It is time that enthusiasm was revived, for many of these plantations are now old.

Near the High Wycombe centre of the furniture industry the beeches were
cut at between 20 and 30 years old, sawn up and split and turned into chair
sticks by bodgers who lived in the woods for half the year. The stick-back
chair was one of our more distinguished contributions to furniture design –
and look at its American echoes. Now we import beech from Hungary and
go to admire the beechwoods on Sundays and Bank Holidays. Wendover
Forest has had its beeches cleared, and softwood planted instead by the
Forestry Commission, but they also maintain tall beechwoods at Queen's
Wood near by. Burnham Beeches is a wood of old pollards, used to supply
domestic charcoal to London – it is near the Thames for transport. There
are disused pollards in Epping Forest, and along many a lane and common
land boundary in the home counties – and in the New Forest, well
documented.

The native poplar

The history of *Populus tremula*, the aspen, asp, aps or quaking ash, is simple.
Our only native poplar, it seeds itself in damp hollows and spreads by
suckers. If is of no particular use, growing neither fast nor large, the timber
soft and perishable. It is used in Sweden for matches and matchboxes, and
it *was* used for arrows.

The aspen is, however, beautiful, from its clear-patterned folk-weave bark
to its early, purple catkins and *pointilliste* round leaves which chatter in
summer breezes and go yellow, attractively spotted, in autumn. It has survived, quite commonly in Scotland, perhaps because ignored: but Grigson
says it was cursed and avoided. Local names refer monotonously to 'old
wives' tongues'. The leaves were described as palsied.

Now drowned out by lustier hybrid poplars, the aspen's leafy speaking in
the mostly silent Ireland of the 8th century was of distant battle. In J. C.
O'Keefe's translation:

Aspen a-trembling
At times when I hear
Its leaves rustling
I think it is the foray.

[5000 bp]

I will not quote the arsenal of assonances that Hopkins uses to evoke the aspens in a 'Sweet especial rural scene'. I prefer Thomas, whose aspens seem at first to be talking about the weather; then, perhaps not: '. . . men may hear/But need not listen . . .'

rowan in Glen Dochart

Rowan and bird cherry

The rowan, small northern tree, is our only important native *Sorbus*, in spite of the claims of numerous whitebeams and the wild service. *S. aucuparia* ('bird-catcher') is a rowntree, rune tree, a magic tree; quicken or wichen, quickbeam, witchwood; or stodgy 'mountain ash'. There was even a Rowan Tree Day, 2 May in Yorkshire, according to Grigson, who gives a catalogue of the rowan's powers in old beliefs.

Rowan grows all over Europe and extends into Siberia. It can be found at 2000 or even 3000 feet in the Highlands, silvery barked. The same species in a London park will be pewter, in the Cotswold greeny-brown. The flowers are cream-white on woolly stalks, the berries a healthy, evil-repelling vermillion. They can be made into a vitamin-C-rich jelly if you can get them before the birds. There is a variety with orange-yellow berries, another with pink bark, otherwise see various Chinese rowans for garden specimens. The genus *Sorbus*, clear enough to Linnaeus in 1753, was included in *Pyrus* (pears) for a hundred years or so.

Our only native *Prunus* is the bird cherry, *P. padus*; virtually a N. Irish and Scottish tree, in prehistory as now, and little known. Out of flower (and the birds soon take the small black cherries) it is neutral-looking, though elegant on closer acquaintance: light green and fine-boned.

bird cherry

33

Padus is obscure – some sort of Roman shrub. Northern names are hackberry, hack merry, hawkberry, heckberry, eckberry, hegberry, hagberry, all Grigson tells us, from Old Scandinavian. The bird cherry also grows in the north as far as Kamchatka and south to the Alps and Caucasus.

Bird cherry has been reported from the ancient Wayland's Wood in Norfolk, presumably native. The tree is planted in gardens, and there is a variety with 'double' flowers.

Hawthorn

Still with Rosaceae we can, not surprisingly, claim the hawthorn as a native. It does not seem to have been common, however, until the Roman period, and is now very common because it has been popular as the quick-thorn hedge since the earliest enclosures of the Saxons. The two species cannot be separated as fossil pollen or wood.

Crataegus oxyacantha ('thorny') or *laevigata* (polished) is a woodland tree. *C. monogyna* (one-pistil) is equally thorny but with acute, deeply lobed leaves. Haw is invariably the popular name for the fruit (as against hips for the rose) – Old English *hagg*. In districts where the May festival – by the old calendar it would be now about the middle of May – coincided with the blossom, it is the May tree. It is highly charged with fertility symbolism in England, and is an untouchable fairy tree in Ireland. Though a 'quick' tree it seems not to have a very long tradition of being a witch tree. May was only one of the 'Maying' plants, listed by Grigson as hawthorn, oak, ivy, cinquefoil, buttercup and maple, and represented in the carved capitals of the chapter house at Southwell. But the heavy scent of the blossom with its hint of decay, and its undeniable beauty, are the essence of early summer to the English townsman, out for a walk or the first picnic of the year.

After the legend of the founding of Glastonbury Abbey by Joseph of Arimathea took hold (his staff broke into bloom on Christmas Day, originating Christianity in England *and* the cultivar 'Biflora' of *C. monogyna)*, the May symbolism became ritualised and obscure. The Green Man, Jack in the Green, or May King had been already absorbed, physically, into the church in carvings such as the roof boss illustrated on page 63, from Norwich Cathedral. But it is still unlucky to bring hawthorn into the house. Christ was crowned with thorns of the very tree which provides the blossoms of May.

Many thorns grew to a great age as landmarks or boundary trees, as at Hethel, near Norwich. The tree, measured in the 18th century at 9 feet girth, still stands, reduced to a bush. It was called the Witch of Hethel, possibly only because of its curiously contorted branches.

English? oak

Āc in Old English gave us *acer*, a field: they had oaks in their fields. This is the truth underlying the Domesday Book estimates of woodland on the number of swine they would feed (midland woods were measured by length and breadth). The pedunculate oak was the tree of the pig-pasturing Saxons, great builders in wood, and it persisted at the heart of our tree-based economy, until ships of oak became our wooden walls (Evelyn, 1664) and 'heart

hawthorn at Glastonbury

the Hethel thorn

of oak were our men' (David Garrick, 1770s). The trees were open-grown to get the spreading crooked shapes for 'cruck' houses and ships 'knees'. Then, very quickly in the 1830s and 40s, ships began to be made of iron and the picturesque trees were left to stand in the Royal forests, bearing a heavy aura of ancientness. Of course, oaks were venerated, preserved on village greens and at cross-ways, preached under, hidden in by fugitive kings. They are still our most admired trees, tolerant of 284 insect species, ecological king-pins and sentimental symbols of Olde England. Wilks (1972) mentions 135 named or famous old oaks. The Marton Oak in Cheshire has a girth of 42 feet, not counting splits.

Quercus robur, with leaves eared and almost stalkless, is distributed all over Europe, except Spain and N. Scandinavia, and is found in Asia Minor. There is no proof that it is native to Britain, but we will give it the benefit of the doubt, in the circumstances.

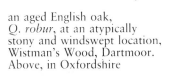

an aged English oak,
Q. robur, at an atypically stony and windswept location, Wistman's Wood, Dartmoor. Above, in Oxfordshire

English elms

By 5000 bp elm pollen is found at 90 per cent of all sites. It is assumed to represent several English species besides the wych elm, native to Ireland and Scotland, but there is no way of proving that these other English elms are natives. Research into the distribution of particular clones, and estimates of their likely movements by suckering over the centuries points towards the Roman period 'or earlier'. This merely suggests local cultivation in Roman Britain, which we would expect. Coppices were managed to fuel foundries and heating systems. Coppicing types of elm are usually hybrids, with one parent the wych elm. Were the other parents found as natives or introduced?

The best arguments for the native elms are based on their present geographical variations – present, that is, before the elm disease epidemic of the 1970s. For instance, Melville (1948) found a spectrum of leaf forms of the Coritanian elm related 'harmonically' to their geographical sources in such a way as to suggest a natural distribution – and this is an area of central England where human interference was likely to have produced the opposite effect.

The unusually wide range of elm species (or subspecies according to some authorities) endemic to lowland England suggests a long history of nativeness. *U. carpinifolia* has a European range, and *U. angustifolia*, the Cornish elm, has some slight distribution in northern France. The others are unknown as native trees anywhere else. There is at least one other English species still to be accounted for. The small-leaved elm, *U. diversifolia*, was found to be a hybrid by Melville; but one of its parent species remains unidentified. It may be extinct, lost under the North Sea.

Seed capsules of a Chiltern box tree. Box, *Buxus sempervirens*, is firmly included as a native by many botanists though it has no fossil record to prove that it is indigenous

British trees in 5000 bp

alder	*Alnus glutinosa*
ash	*Fraxinus excelsior*
beech	*Fagus sylvatica*
birch	*Betula pubescens, B. verrucosa*
box	*Buxus sempervirens*
cherry	*Prunus padus*
elm	*Ulmus glabra, U. procera*
	U. carpinifolia ⎫
	angustilfolia ⎬ *U. nitens*
	plotii ⎪
	coritana ⎭
hawthorn	*Crataegus monogyna, C. laevigata (oxyacantha)*
hazel	*Corylus avellana*
holly	*Ilex aquifolium*
ivy	*Hedera helix*
lime	*Tilia cordata, T. platyphyllos*
oak	*Quercus petraea, Q. robur (pedunculata)*
pine	*Pinus sylvestris*
poplar	*Populus tremula*
rowan	*Sorbus aucuparia*
willow	*Salix caprea, S. cinerea, S. aurita*
yew	*Taxus baccata*

oak apple

alder buckthorn carr,
Wicken Fen,
Cambridgeshire

Native shrubs

Of the warmth-loving shrubs which invaded Britain before it was separated
from the continent, **alder buckthorn** has the strongest claim to nativeness. It
is not now very well known, and it hides behind the names of other shrubs
and trees – black alder, black dogwood – but it has straggled across four
interglacials and it probably covered large areas of marshy land. It forms a
shapeless, thin sort of woodland or carr in wet, acid soil, over a loose
basketwork of dead wood – or it will grow in the open, with willows. It is
not thorny, though it has fiercely armed relatives like *Colletia* (page 154),
Wild Irishman in New Zealand, and jujube in India. The bark is poisonous
when fresh, which probably kept away the interglacial rhinos: more delicate
grazers would avoid the tangle of stems.

dogwood on the Chiltern
escarpment

When dried the bark is a gentle purgative, preferred to the purging buckthorn, and the American *Rhammus*, 'cascara sagrada'.

Rhammus frangula or *Frangula alnus*, alder buckthorn, has white flowers
followed by berries which turn from green through red to deep purple. Dyes
were obtained from the bark and the berries, and a fine charcoal for gunpowder from the wood. For this, black gunpowder, used in fuses, it was
cultivated in Kent and Sussex until 1946.

Bean describes it as 'rather handsome . . . cheerful green' – I hadn't thought
of it like that. But sure enough, you can buy plants for your garden from
Hilliers, even choose a willow-leaved variety. A large-leaved form grows in
the Caucasus, that last home of northern Tertiary plants.

Dogwood, *Cornus sanguinea*, spreads easily over abandoned pasture and
nature reserves in the chalkland and it crops up as a hedge and scrub plant,
never a tree, in S. England – and, I read, in E. Wales. It is generally recognised
as *Cornus* but now confusingly named *Swida* or *Thelycrania* – the specific
sanguinea is constant, and so are the red twigs. Dogwood, perhaps dag wood

37

but also cat wood and gatter (goat) wood, are rude names for a low bush with useless berries. But it was also a skiver tree, useful to gypsies who made skewers to sell – at least more attractive then twisted metal ones.

As a scrub plant it is soon shaded out by trees. But it spread over England to Wales and Ireland with, or just before, the Boreal deciduous forest.

Comparing it with garden *Cornus* species, Bean is right to call it undistinguished. However, it flushes to a most impressive red-ink colour in autumn and it is an ornament to our countryside. Grigson calls it splendid, and so it appears here.

For a native shrub, **Guelder rose** is the least appropriate of a whole string of native names which describe *Viburnum opulus*, with its five-lobed leaves, magnificent white flowers and shiny red berries. Marsh elder, water elder, dwarf plane tree, white elder, rose elder; best of all is Gerard's Ople tree, opal or opulent as you please. It is another of those skewer trees, and had its share of dog and goat names, from folk with no eye for its beauty. From Guelder Land came a cultivated variety, the sterile snowball tree which country wives planted in cottage gardens. The name was transferred to the wild tree. The snowballs were used for picturesque games of tisty-tosty among Devonshire yokels.

The fossil record goes back two interglacials before our own. It is a surprise to find that there are records from Skye, the Cairngorms, Galloway; and apparently Guelder rose still has a Scottish range. Seeds are found in archaeological sites from the Mesolithic on. 'It must not be thought that the fruits were collected for food, for they are made most unpalatable by the valerianic acid they contain,' warns Godwin. But two authorities mention their use to flavour a honey and flour paste, in Norway and Sweden – they are fermented for a drink too. The same species, apparently, in Canada, is used for a substitute cranberry sauce; ideal for the venison-weary Stone Ager. As with sea buckthorn, my experiment in jelly-making produced a powerful smell, not very pleasant. But the jelly seems innocuous. I am, as I write, about to try it on my editor with some roast mutton.*

To the herbalists, Guelder rose berries are known as an anti-scorbutic. The bark, which also contains valerian, had some currency as 'cramp-bark'. It had been used for centuries by people who live, like the tree, in marshy country and by the damp edges of woods, and suffer from stiffness of the joints. It's also good for lockjaw.

The earliest records of buckthorn are from excavations of prehistoric habitations in Cambridgeshire, then from Westmorland – these just establish it as native. The tree is found in Cambridgeshire fens today, but is best known as a shrub of the chalk, particularly common on the Chiltern escarpment, where it forms, in the hedges, thick, ragged trees about 20 feet tall, with cherry-like bark. The thorns are terminal to the shoots; lower down, the green flowers spring from leaf axils, clustered but neither loose, as with the alder buckthorn, nor terminal as with dogwood.

buckthorn

The black berries of **buckthorn**, *Rhammus cathartica*, were well known as a purgative in medieval times, and, while it is difficult to imagine Stone Age people suffering from constipation, the fact remains that nearly all fossil records are linked to habitations. A range of dyes also can be got from the bark and the fruit. Berries were collected in the Chilterns near Aylesbury up

*Innocuous – Ed.

38

to the late 19th century. They were pressed and the diluted liquid sold to drug firms. So the plant would be protected: it was worth something. The medicine was eventually removed from the BP list as too violent.

The painter's pigment sap green was obtained from the juice of the berries, with alum. It was not a very permanent colour and it is now produced chemically. Dyes for cloth were a grey-blue from the berries and strong browns from the bark; yellowish with alum, dark with copperas.

Buckthorn has no long list of popular names, only waythorn, and from Gerard, Laxative Ram.

Also present in Britain before 5000 bp was **mistletoe**, *Viscum album*, with a range rather wider than at present. We do not know which trees the mistletoe grew on – the Druid's oaks were mostly an 18th-century fantasy, based on a classical reference, though at least one Anglo-Saxon spell refers to mistletoe of the oak. It is not now common upon oak, though not unknown: it now prefers hybrid lime, hybrid black poplar and apple.

Mistletoe's powerful magic came from its unearthliness. It was a fertility charm – in extreme cases of credulity it opened locks, but this is a sort of symbolic play upon virginity – now reduced to a mere kissing game at Christmas.

Traveller's joy, old man's beard; bullbine, bedwine, withywine, climbers, Devil's guts, hag-rope; hedge feathers, honesty, maiden's hair, tuzz-wuzzy; *Clematis vitalba*. (What would I do without Grigson?) Many of the names describe the persistent silky fruit, so common in southern hedges. But in overgrown coppices – as, surely in the native woodland – it may reach 40 feet or more, with thick stems and lianas of tropical appearance. Then the middle group of names is appropriate.

The ropes were used for basketwork. There is only one record, of wood, carbon dated 6300 bp. That is enough, considering its range in non-peaty soil where fossils are unlikely.

Honeysuckle, *Lonicera*, also grew in the British forest.

Clematis vitalba

39

[5000 bp]

sweetgale

Native shrubs

(Chapter 2)

Dwarf birch	*Betula nana*	
juniper	*Juniperus communis*	
sea buckthorn	*Hippophaë rhamnoides*	
sweetgale	*Myrica gale*	
willows	*Salix herbacea*	least
	lapponum	Lappland or downy
	lanata	woolly
	myrsinites	whortle leaved
	phylicifolia	tea-leaved
	polaris	
	repens	creeping willow
	reticulata	net-veined
	viminalis	osier

Guelder rose in an
Oxfordshire hedge

(Chapter 3)

alder buckthorn	*Frangula alnus*
buckthorn	*Rhammus cathartica*
dogwood	*Cornus (Thelycrania) sanguinea*
Guelder rose	*Viburnum opulus*
honeysuckle	*Lonicera periclymenum*
mistletoe	*Viscum album*
traveller's joy	*Clematis vitalba*

not mentioned in the text

cranberry	*Vaccinium oxycoccus*
cowberry	*Vaccinium vitis-idæa*
crowberry	*Empetrum nigrum*

crab apple in Cheshire

4 · Trees and shrubs of the early Britons

Britain was certainly an island by 5000 bp (3000 BC): the date of the formation of the English Channel is sometimes given as 6000 bp. The North Channel, between Ireland and Galloway, is deep, and Ireland was cut off early with a correspondingly limited native flora – and a few species, difficult to explain, shared with Portugal.

The decline of elm and lime about 5000 bp is associated with small forest clearances and burning by immigrant farmers of Neolithic culture. Their ancestors, Neolithic but then without pottery, had built, or at least settled within the massive walls of Jericho while half Britain was still sheathed in ice. The English branches of this culture arose both from the Danube and from coastal West Mediterranean stock, progressing northwards. No record has been found of the boats they used to reach our shores. I like to imagine the eastern group crossing the Rhine delta, now the Dogger Bank – perhaps driven from there by ever-higher tides. They might have brought with them the smooth-leaved elms, one of which, *U. carpinifolia*, has a European range extending along the Elbe. The western group might follow a curving shore line from N. France to Sussex with only a mile or two of sea to cross, while the cliffs of Dover were still under downland extending to Artois, clothed with beech and yew. But such speculations are unscientific.

Native and not so native

The absence of a plant from the fossil record does not prove its absence from the flora. At the same time, we cannot say that a plant is native because we think it ought to be. A list of arboreal plants anyway cannot tell the whole story, though trees are more likely than herbs to leave solid records. We must stick to our trees, and stick to the facts available.

ancient hornbeam,
Carpinus betulus

Even making allowances for the likely absence of calcicoles from the 600 or so English sites from which pollen has been analysed, none of the tree species in this chapter are indigenous. That said, there are some borderline cases: whitebeam (see page 46) is one, hornbeam is another. Hornbeam, regarded as an important indicator of temperature (or of absence of spring frosts), established itself as a considerable forest tree at very late stages of previous interglacials and appears to repeat the pattern in the present one. There are very low levels of pollen and a distribution rather like that of beech in the period about our deadline. Hornbeam prefers clays and gravels, and its present range is to the S.E. of the country. It should be regarded as a native, but it rises to importance only in the Bronze Age. Since it has been much coppiced for fairly specialised mechanical uses and as an excellent fuel, perhaps ever since the Bronze Age, we are left to form our own conclusions. Its continental range extends to Greece and S. Sweden. See pages 16 and 72. The pollard hornbeams of Epping Forest are famous, and have been fought for by the commoners and by William Morris in a diatribe against the Experts of Essex (1895), who had plans to tidy the place up. Epping Forest belongs to the Greater London Council.

Crab apple

The ancestry of the wild apple, *Malus sylvestris*, is lost. The fruit is the food of pigs and birds, and of men. The crab may be described as a wild native apple without anyone contradicting: but is it either wild or native? It was certainly used by prehistoric people, and is said to have been cultivated in the European Neolithic. The first British records are mainly of charcoal and of impressions of pips on pottery found at the Neolithic causewayed camp on Windmill Hill, just above Avebury, Wiltshire.

'Crab' comes from the Norse word which also gave us scrub – the tree is a scrab in the North. It has a bushy, wide, rounded crown on a single trunk. Crabs need a full light and cannot be expected in dense woodland, though they are sometimes to be found there, perhaps marking an early settlement site. The seeds are sown in the hedges by birds.

A species *M. pumila* ('dwarfish') has downy leaves and is identified by some authorities as a descendant of cultivated forms – while the smooth-leaved crab is an ancestor. Gerard distinguished four types of crab: the red, the white, the smaller and the 'choking leane crab-tree: the difference is known to all'. How do you eat crab apples without sugar? Perhaps they were roasted, with pigs, or fermented, with honey. Richard Mabey (1972) reports that they can be buried and dug up in the spring with some of their bitterness removed. Storage pits are typical of Iron Age villages at least.

Small plums

All fossil records of *Prunus* are sparse and occur late in the prehistoric period. The blackthorn, *P. spinosa*, has a minor history in the two previous interglacials. Finds of *Prunus* type pollen from the last glaciation are referred to *P. spinosa*. Charcoal from archaeological sites in S. England comes later and is taken to indicate blackthorn firewood – not necessarily on domestic hearths, for this fiercely burning brushwood could have been used for ovens and kilns (clamps is a better word for the Iron Age versions). Then, strangely, we hear of a wheelbarrow full of sloe stones dug up at the Glastonbury Lake village – and there are very many Iron Age villages on dry land whose details are lost to us. What use are sloes, apart from flavouring gin? They *may* have been used for dye.

But we have only to consider our present-day fruit diet, the great variety of which includes almost nothing that was available to our early British counterpart, whether hunter or vegetarian or a bit of both. Most of the fruits which we consider far too sour to eat can be improved by boiling or slow cooking, and can be made acceptable or even delicious by the addition of honey. Add to this the medicinal virtues of wild fruit. Even sloes are a standard remedy according to Culpeper: 'A conserve is of very much use and most familiarly taken' – or a decoction of the berries, fresh or dried – for a range of ills familiar in old herbals 'lask of the belly, bloody flux, bleeding at the nose and mouth or any other place, pains in the bowels and guts that come by over-feeding . . .' the traditional remedies are mostly forgotten now, but when did the traditions begin? Certainly long before they were written down. By far the greatest number of plants recorded as used by American Indians were for making medicinal brews and beverages. The human lot is to suffer, at least occasionally, and the human reaction is to take something for it.

cherry plum

The nearly related bullace (*P. insititia* – it means 'grafted') is still popular with old country people for wine and jellies: and sloes are 'bullens' in some places. A house I once rented for a while, in Essex, had a variety of fuit trees, one of which was a heavily cropping bullace. An aged neighbour informed me that she had always had the 'bullets', and she stripped the tree very thoroughly. But she never offered me any of the produce. The cherry plum, *P. cerasifera*, often confused with the blackthorn (it flowers even earlier in the hedges) has a long history of cultivation, but no fossil history in Britain. Supposed to be a parent, with *P. spinosa*, of the modern domestic plum, it is of Asian origin and probably reached here in the Middle Ages as a *mirabelle* – it is known as the myrobalan plum to some authors: *P. domestica* var. *myrobalan* to Linnaeus.

However they came, various small plums were eaten from the Iron Age onwards. The damson, distinct enough to the palate but botanically the same as the bullace, turns up in Roman British towns.

Wild service

The wild service, *Sorbus torminalis*, has been identified from Late Iron Age charcoal at Maiden Castle. It has no other prehistoric record in Britain, except for several seeds from a late interglacial.

It is the only *Sorbus* with plane-like leaves, and has brown berries (*serves*, deviously from the Latin) like its tame counterpart, *Sorbus domestica*, which has leaves like a rowan. Gerard, who did not recognise the rowan as a *Sorbus* (it was a Quick-beam or Wild-ash) clearly identifies *Sorbus torminalis*, so named in Pliny. He called it the common service tree: it grew abundantly near Southfleet and Gravesend, also at Islington. *Torminalis* refers to colic, *tormina*; it was a medicine for tummy ache. The berries, called chequers in

wild service tree in
Ditchley Wood,
Oxfordshire

Kent and Sussex, are mentioned by a Victorian author as sold in the markets – mainly to children: a sad tale.

The wild service is a very distinctive tree, its leaves smoother and its bark rougher than other *Sorbus* species. It is popular with botanists: said to be the origin of all those pubs called The Chequers (as if their signs were not the hatchments of local gentry). Here a drink made from the berries was sold to keep away the plague. The trees, and some of the pubs, can be found in oakwoods in S.E. England. The natural, or naturalised, range extends to Oxfordshire (and to Worcester and Yorkshire in the textbooks). Its European range is wide and it is also found in N. Africa and Asia Minor.

large cherry trees in
Ditchley Wood: the wood
is now coniferised

Wild cherry

All records of the wild cherry, *Prunus avium,* come from archaeological sites
of the New Stone Age, Bronze Age, and later periods. There are no pollen
records – all are wood or fruit stones. Pollen of *Prunus* is generally sparse in
the post-glacial period, and all or most of it is blackthorn.

Wild cherries are sometimes bitter and certainly mostly stones, but not to
be despised if one had never seen the cultivated sort. Those the birds miss
turn to blackish red. The English cherry, gean or mazzard, gaskin or
merry-tree (at least two of the names are French) is widely distributed in

Europe, and as far as western Asia. It is most common on rich soil and clay over chalk or limestone. It is a hedgerow tree in the Wychwood forest area. Large trees, up to 100 feet, are found in beechwoods on the Chiltern tops. The cherry is the only deciduous tree that can compete with beech. It may well have been encouraged, for the timber is valuable and the trees grow very straight in the woods. Some Chiltern villages are well known for cherry orchards, and the wild cherry is used as a rootstock.

Now, there are many fine specimens going to waste. But the foresters do their calculations in hectares, not single trees – which may be valuable but are too much trouble to extract.

Whitebeams and French hales

The basic European *Sorbus* is the whitebeam, *S. aria*, with brilliant white undersides to the leaves. It is said to have been identified from Neolithic remains in Ireland and Dorset. The Latin *aria* is obscure, and the English probably is not as old as it sounds. Anglo-Saxon charters mention a 'hoar withy' which is supposed to be this tree – why, I can't imagine, since there are at least two willows which can be described as hoar.

To Gerard it was a sort of hawthorn, the *Aria* of Theophrastus. 'It grows in shadowy woods of Cumberland and Westmorland, with leaves like the pear tree or alder, but white beneath, and fruit like the berries of the hawthorne, in taste like the Neapolitan medlar.' His editor Johnson adds, perhaps drily, that it grows on Hampstead Heath. It was in many places of the West of England, and some 'refer it to *sorbus*, and that not unfitly: in some places of this kingdome they call it a white Beame tree'.

It was probably called a beam to link it to and differentiate it from the most common *Sorbus*, the rowan or quick beam, and the hornbeam, whose similarly cream-white (and harder) wood has similar uses – for mill cogs and tool handles. In the chalk hornbeam may be found on the dip slopes where whitebeam grows on the escarpments.

Were there ever woods of whitebeam? The search took me, guided by Fitter (1971), to a wood quaintly called a barn on the Beds/Herts border. I came face to face with a tawny owl, found a tramp's residence, was very throughly stung and scratched, and found a few whitebeams, rather straggly amongst beech, oak and cherry. Out of the valleys, whitebeam is common in the scrub and very white in spring against its neighbour yews.

A *Sorbus* of the Western Isles is *rupicola* ('rock inhabiting'), and this has a pollen record early enough to make it native. Other species or subspecies are local to the west of England, notably the Mendips, and the Avon and Cheddar Gorges: *S. anglica* and others. One quite common in the S.W. is *S. devoniensis*: the fruits, French hales, were sold in the markets, perhaps for mixing with apples in pies or to make one of those jellies that were an important part of our winter diet long ago. French hales = French *alisia*.

Many local forms, as with the elm, argue for nativeness.

Ramblers

The wild rose, a native in previous interglacials, appears doubtfully in the present one before it is identified in the Iron Age (in Cambridgeshire). There-

whitebeam

French hales

after it was obviously collected for food; as it was by thousands of school children for the Ministry of Food in the Second World War, for vitamin-rich rose hip syrup. This is another tree with a dog name: *Rosa canina*. Burnet rose appears in the sands of Clacton, something over 100,000 years ago, then disappears as far as I can see until the sixteenth century: the Pimpinelle Rose in Gerard.

The raspberry, *Rubus idaeus* ('of Mt Ida' says Gerard) and blackberries, a whole tribe of species and subspecies lumped under *R. fruticosa* ('shrubby' not fruity), have records from previous interglacials but appear late in our own and almost entirely associated with habitations. The cloudberry, *R. chamaemorus* ('false mulberry'), with amber-coloured fruit, a plant of bogs and high moorland, has a 'permanently native status' (Godwin) with a strong record in the late glacial. It would have been included as a 'survivor of the ice', except that there happens to be no record from the last interglacial.

[after 5000 bp]

bramble leaves mined by the larvae of a micro moth, *Nepticula aurella*

Elder

Elderberry, *Sambucus nigra*, ought to be a native, it is so familiar. This or another *Sambucus* lived here in previous interglacials. But the only post-glacial record for our 'native period' comes from the Dogger Bank. It then appears at two sites in the Mesolithic; three Neolithic, six Bronze Age, six Iron Age, eight Roman – all at habitations.

Since elders characteristically flourish alongside human (nitrogen-rich) refuse (and badger setts) we might be forgiven for classifying the elder as a tree-weed. But it is much more than that. The fruits are not only abundant but easily fermented into good wine, and even the flowers are edible – though not to *my* taste. They were used for a skin lotion until quite recently. The berries made a black dye, said to be used by the Romans. The medicinal uses of the berries, green or ripe, were manifold. Aubrey refers to vast quantities of them sold in London at 'not inconsiderable profit'.

The timber is extremely hard, away from the pithy twig and the soft, unpleasant bark. Elder has strong associations with witches, as the hawthorn has with fairies – both are trees respected for different reasons by the Celtic people: with hazel as the archetypal magic tree, perhaps of an earlier race.

elder hedge mechanically slashed

47

maple in the hedge,
Chilterns

Field maple

The supposed native maple is *Acer campestre* – 'of the fields' – it lives in the hedges and is rarely allowed to grow tall. But a specimen at Mote Park, Maidstone, is about 72 feet. There is no record of the species before the Neolithic; the wood is found at many later archaeological sites.

The timber is hard and lends itself to fine carving and turnery. Saxon harps were made of it, and it was used for ceremonial bowls in old Wales, and fine tables in antiquity, particularly the intricately grained burs of trees which had been lopped. It was 'far superior to beech for all the uses of the turner' according to Evelyn – it could be worked so thin it was almost transparent.

After Roman times *mapuldor* was clearly encouraged and gave its name to many places in southern England. It was a dog-oak and a cat-oak in Yorkshire and elsewhere, the fruits kitty-keys in Yorkshire and boots-and-shoes in Somerset. The native range extends over Europe to the Balkans.

New habitat

Three thousand years, between the isolation of Britain by the sea and the Roman occupation in 43AD, is a long period. It witnessed the addition to our flora of only a small number of trees. But some very important plants were introduced, the cultivated cereals.

Most of the trees are small and bear berries. The exception, maple, included in this chapter, may well have flourished on the chalk and limestone, unrecorded before 5000 bp. We are left with a collection of 'fruit' trees: crab, sloe, cherry, wild service, whitebeam, rose, elder, bramble. Their records are closely associated with sites of human occupation – but this only indicates that they were collected.

All these berries could have reached our islands with the help of birds. Few birds are moving north in the autumn, but waxwings sometimes visit S. England in thousands when berries are short in France, and some finches wander in flocks in the winter looking for feeding sites. Summer migrants might bring last year's seeds over long distances.

Even if the berry-bearing trees had reached northern France or the low countries in the post-glacial warm period it seems rather a coincidence that they should all have been ferried here by the birds. The explanation is that even small clearances of the high forest produced new habitats where light-demanding shrubs could grow, and overspill populations of waxwings could be accommodated – probably making do with hawthorn at first.

Wild service and wild cherry are mainly seen as incidental woodland trees, but the others need open woodland or a full light to produce fruit. At the forest margins in the Atlantic period were either newly formed bogs or grasslands, reduced and under heavy pressure from such grazing animals as survived the almost total afforestation.

Whether introduced by birds or man, and whether we call them native or not, these berried small trees occupy a man-made habitat, and men clearly had uses for them. Clearances also favoured hazel and ash, as is shown in many pollen charts. We have to admit that clearings may have been made deliberately to encourage useful trees, even if we cannot believe that the trees were planted.

Britain's first farmers belonged to Neolithic cultures: that is, they are identified by axes of polished stone. They were probably herdsmen. They cleared, or at least killed, elm and lime for grazing space and used the leaves for fodder, the bark for food and fibres. They burnt over the brushwood and planted (it is not certain that they sowed) semi-wild wheat which they perhaps used only for cattle feed. When the soil on their patch was exhausted, they moved on, leaving the land to return to scrub. The climate was now becoming drier and cooler, and not all the scrub returned to woodland.

Neolithic farmers had pottery. They needed fast-burning wood for the firing, such as hawthorn, blackthorn, holly or juniper. If their diet was mainly meat they would need drinks or preserves made from the wild fruits to supply essential vitamins and trace-elements. Both cookery and storage are implied in the use of pottery. Some of the pots, in shape and decoration, seem to imitate baskets.

Speculations about the uses they made of wood for building are mostly based on holes in the ground long since filled up, and shoring and shuttering long since rotted or even burnt away. The massive stone tombs which were built in the Neolithic Age are not representations in stone of wooden houses for the living. The settled people were capable of similar feats of organisation, however, in building giant causewayed camps, long barrows, dead straight ditches miles long, and, later, great circular and oval henges with banks and ditches, with multiple poles or standing stones. A fully furnished Neolithic village at Skara Brae in the Orkneys has stone beds and cupboards that must be copies of those made of wood elsewhere. There was trade in the polished axes which were manufactured at sites in N. Wales and the Lake District. The galleried flint mines of Grimes Graves in Norfolk are late Neolithic.

The only large surviving examples of the Neolithic use of wood are the trackways of the Somerset levels, then marshland. The oldest of these, says Rackham (1976) is the most sophisticated. It is contemporary with the Elm Decline with a date of 5173 bp. 'It involves wood of oak, ash, lime, hazel, alder and holly, of different sizes and selected for particular functions in the structure. The sizes and shapes of the assemblage of poles are remarkably like those produced by a medieval coppice on a rather long rotation.' Other writers mention alder poles and bundles of hazel and birch, and birchwood pegs in tens of thousands. Some of the tracks were miles long. In some the poles are laid along the direction of the track, in others across it.

Wheeled vehicles were in use in Europe from about 5000 bp. Unlike the Ancient Egyptian wheels, rather later, which employed imported elm, some two-wheeled carts dug up in Holland have solid wheels of oak. Elsewhere in Europe alder was used – light, shock-absorbing and wet-resistant, like Lancashire clogs. This use, with the discovery of fifteen dug-out canoes of alder in Denmark, suggests a timber stature for alder trees – certainly *Alnus glutinosa* – that we rarely see now. Dug-out canoes, usually later than Neolithic, were made of almost any wood, oak predominating, but also of elm, poplar and pine. A canoe of solid yew was discovered in Sussex in the last century; it had overturned with a load of brambles, gorse, thorn and hazel.

The oak-wheeled carts of Holland are 3000 years old. This takes us into the Bronze Age. Large forest clearances – in Shropshire – first occur around 3000 years ago, but the many micro-cultures of the copper, tin and gold seekers, users and hoarders are of little importance in telling the story of the

alder of timber quality, Blenheim Park

trees. Much barley was grown, almost to the exclusion of the semi-wild wheats of the earliest forest farmers. It has been suggested that the barley was used only for brewing ale, and this sorts well with a general impression of warrior chieftains, buried in all their finery – their women had nothing but hand mirrors. A class structure seems to enter our pre-history (if it had not done so before, with the beaker people) and many must have found themselves in a dilemma – whether to use their limited supply of bronze tools to improve their lot, or keep them to improve their status. The flint and wood technology of earlier times continues.

Stone circles

The Wessex culture of the Bronze Age was responsible for Stonehenge in the late form which has partly survived. The movement and erection of very large stones must have depended on a good supply of very consistent coppice poles or forest-grown trunks, for rollers and lifting scaffolds or platforms.

Besides Stonehenge there are 900 stone circles known in the British islands. They were built between 4600 and 3750 years ago by many tribes known not by their bronze but by their pottery – there are many classified styles of beaker as well as other jars and urns. The relatively small Rollright Stones circle, which I can see from my windows, is supposed to have served, to what purpose is not known, an area of twenty square miles of inhabited, probably wooded country – several hundred people, plus one or two hundreds of upland pastoralists. This estimate (Burl, 1976) takes into account the territory of some nearby henges. At Avebury, one of the two largest monuments, the bank and ditch alone are estimated to have taken 1,500,000 man-hours to build, and a population of 1500 within about 50 square miles is suggested. The area would be 90 square miles if the people were, as is believed, animal farmers shifting from lowland to upland pastures in summer. Some parts of the forest were certainly reduced, and this not only in Wessex, for there are important concentrations of stone circles in N. Wales, the Peak, Cumbria, central, N.E. and S.W. Scotland, N. Ireland, Cork and Kerry, and of smaller circles in S.W. England. The cultural centre of Britain seems to have been on the Boyne, north of Dublin.

It may seem ironic to use stone circles as indicators of woodland or its removal. But the circles themselves may have derived from 'wood henges' (Burl, 1976) and the timber circles could well have been representations of woodland sanctuaries, built in the (recently cleared?) upland sites which are typical. Natural circles occur in undisturbed woodland, particularly around great elms and limes, which send up surprisingly perfect circles of suckers from their roots. This vastly increases the protectiveness of a large tree: inside, undergrowth is quite shaded out. The old tree may die, leaving behind a magical-seeming circle to mature. Limes layer their lower branches in a similar, remarkably regular pattern. Yews in relatively open ground form perfect circles beneath the conic crown, the ground beneath quite dry and bare. Often there is a rich growth of scrub and grass round the edge, almost forming a protective bank.

If monumental circles originated in this way it would suggest a primary protective purpose. Early Neolithic families in the forest may well have felt insecurity as a major emotional drive. The circle's function was presumably

Rollright Stones,
Oxfordshire

adapted over the centuries to the more outgoing magic of fertility rituals or the reciting of sagas. Neolithic clearings, in a context of almost complete forestation, must have made startling changes to the landscape. The extraordinary habit of burying charcoal and rubbish in pits and foundations of stone circles was almost certainly an attempt to perpetuate woodland spirits in places that were no longer forest homes: deposits of powerful earth, Burl calls them. Archaeologists of the distant future may come to similar conclusions about our town parks and gardens.

Other circles that the Neolithic builders may have seen, besides their own pottery, were, probably extremely common in their damp woods, large rings of fungi, still called fairy rings. They could see circles in the sky of course, and according to Professor Thom saw a great deal more. The sun was a god, and appears in carvings of the Boyne, where close spirals and concentric circles are major motifs. But here, having drawn a few patterns ourselves, we must depart.

Says Godwin, reassuringly and sweepingly: 'by and large the forest did not shew signs of permanent or widespread modification until the opening of the Iron Age'. By and large ... but the pattern was changing. There seems to have been so much Neolithic and early Bronze Age activity that one might suspect the population to have been reduced in the second millenium before Christ, and much of the forest replaced as secondary woodland and scrub.

Gorse and broom

There remain two familiar plants to be incorporated in this very superficial account of our prehistory. *Ulex europaeus*, gorse, or in Ireland furze (both are Anglo Saxon words), whin, a Norse word, in Scotland, is a shrub of western uplands, its native range restricted to N.W. Europe. *Ulex* species (there are two lesser ones as well) left some trace in Brittany before the Neolithic, and were perhaps present in Cornwall, but there are no British records before 5000 bp. To us, gorse is pretty and scented throughout the summer, and prickly, but to western farmers (and Sussex ones in the Bronze Age) it has been very useful. Even if its nitrogen-fixing properties were not understood, it was a prime fuel for bread ovens and therefore for primitive smelting. With blackthorn and hawthorn it forms a group of stock-proof small trees that, however uncomfortably, can be gathered into faggots for a sure-fire source of sudden heat. Gorse was certainly planted near habitations for this purpose in Devonshire, and in Ireland and Wales. Dried, and beaten with flat mallets, it has been an important fodder plant – it is virtually evergreen – and was even a substitute for straw within memory. The flowers were used to make wine.

broom

It looks as if gorse, unlike most of our invaders, may have come in from the south and west, perhaps from Ireland to England – it is such a feature of Co. Kerry now. It will not grow at all in the shade of trees, so, like other shrubs in this chapter, had to wait for suitable habitat before it could expand. I do not doubt that it was assisted by man.

Broom, *Cytisus* or *Sarothamnus scoparius* (*scopae* = a broom), has one record of wood establishing it as native. Is one record enough? It appears again in the seventeenth century, used as its name suggests, and planted as a medicine for sheep to help themselves to. It will tolerate the poorest soils and survive destructive frosts by means of hard seeds which can germinate after years in the ground. Like gorse, it adds nitrogen, to the soil – it is sometimes planted on motorway verges for this reason.

Spindle tree

spindle berries

A small tree with one positive record in the early British period is the spindle tree, *Euonymus europaeus*. The luminously coloured berries (or popcorns, hot-cross buns, pincushions) are useless except for de-lousing, dried and powdered: they have the name of louse berries in the Avon area according to Grigson. It was named around 1560 by Turner, who knew what a spindle was: it could also be called the square tree, because of the four-sided twigs. It was a skewer tree and had a variety of cat and dog names, being never large. It is a calcicole, which may explain its lack of fossil records. It is lovely and elegant, and, *fusain* in French, good for fine drawing charcoal. It may not be native, but it is a lot more native than the rabbits which nibble its green bark.

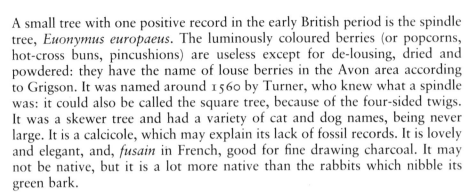

Iron, and its smelting, forging and tempering was introduced to Britain about a thousand years before the Roman occupation. Patterns of post-holes, storage(?) pits and Celtic fields (though it seems that Celts came late in the period) have been used to reconstruct the homes and farms of the Iron Age, and the daily lives of the people are familiar to millions from television documentaries. Very impressive 'hill forts' or raised towns can be seen and touched, the best known being Maiden Castle (Mai Dun) near Dorchester. Arable farming, including bread wheat instead of the Bronze Age barley, reached the stage where a surplus could be exported, which probably impressed the Romans, entrenched in Gaul. All of which suggests a sophisticated approach to woodland management: but little is known. We think of all this prosperous activity on the southern hills of England and a clearer light seems to dawn. But it may be illusory. In Scotland, the people hid themselves from history in brochs and round houses of stone, and remained untouched, even by the Romans.

Arbutus graveyard, Killarney woods. The strawberry tree, *Arbutus unedo*, may be native to W. Kerry but has no ancient fossil record

damson, part of a hedge
near Evesham

5 · Roman trees in Britain

UT IOVI AESCULUS, APOLLINI LAURUS, MINERVAE OLEA, VENERI MYRTUS,
HERCULI POPULUS. To Jove the chestnut-oak, to Apollo the bay, to Minerva
the olive, to Venus the myrtle, to Hercules the poplar (are dedicated). So
appear, at a time when probably no Briton could write his own name, the
names of some of our familiar trees. The quotation is from Gaius Plinius
Secundus, *Naturalis historiae*, written about half a century after the birth of
Christ. Doubt enters the record immediately, in that AESCULUS, a Roman
acorn-bearing tree not certainly identified, had its name stolen for the
horsechestnut, discovered to science in 1557.

The Roman genius for communication is evident from the brevity and
clarity of even this small fragment of a textbook, compared with the fussiness
of the simplest English equivalent. The 5000 miles of Roman main roads of
Britain, straighter than any for centuries after, are well-known. Along such
roads over the whole Empire ordinary people thought little of sending jars
of olives or warm underwear to their soldier relatives. The traffic in wine
and in dried fruit (as well as, apparently, a strong fish sauce) was considerable, as is shown by the discovery of amphorae and casks in various places,
including a shipwreck in the Thames. The importing of fruit certainly con-
fuses the record of fruit trees in Britain. Various timbers can be identified

53

from charcoal, which survives longer than wood, but the original timber might have been imported as furniture or tools.

The damson (PRUNUS IN DAMASCO MONTE NATA) is described, with a dozen other sorts of plum, by Pliny: it had been grown in Italy for a long time, had a large stone in relation to the flesh, did not wrinkle in drying. Some types of plum could be stored in jars. It is reasonable to suppose that the relatively hardy damson was introduced to Britain and grown here by the Romans – perhaps unintentionally – and has remained ever since.

The tree in the picture is part of a hedge near Evesham – half a mile of a single species. A few minutes' picking provided my family with the material for several jars of good jam, but the fruit was obviously ignored by the local people. Orchard-grown damsons are larger, and can be round or somewhat pear-shaped ('prunes'), but in flavor they are quite distinct from other plums – *P. domestica* – said to derive from hybrids of the blackthorn and the cherry plum. Damsons are *P. insititia* (as the bullace) or *P. damascena*. Stones of larger plums have been found at Silchester, near Reading, the most completely preserved Roman town in Britain.

A Roman pine

After the obviously useful and therefore important vine and olive, Pliny places the pine which produces the largest fruit of any tree. This seems a curious way of looking at a pine cone, until we consider it as a possible meal. The cone of *Pinus pinea* is certainly large: at four inches wide it is exceeded only by two Californian pines, *P. jeffreyi* and *P. coulteri*. The seeds are found in Roman wells in Britain – why in wells?

The kernels, inside the hard shells, can be eaten raw. They have a rather oily taste, but can be roasted and salted like peanuts. They have a place in traditional Italian cooking. But Pliny describes only medicinal uses: slightly crushed and boiled down with water for colic and 'contrary humours' of the stomach; eaten whole for coughs and kidney trouble, as well as for that persistent disease in all herbals, spitting of blood.

We cannot pretend that the Romans grew stone pines here, or even that some of their kernels germinated. The tree is difficult to grow here – but perhaps not as difficult as is believed, for the specimen illustrated was in a field near Calne, the great open cones rotting amongst cow pats.

Pinus cembra, the Arolla pine of Switzerland, also has edible nuts. But the stone pine is closely associated with Italy and Rome: familiar in Turner's paintings of Italy – he had some models in Twickenham, near his villa.

Sweet chestnut

Chestnuts were known to the ancient Romans in four or five eating varieties, and a common black 'cooking' chestnut – others were fed to pigs. Flour was made from chestnuts for making a sort of bread 'for young women fasting'. Chestnuts, in Pliny, were eaten to cure diarrhoea and 'promote the growth of flesh'. The nuts *are* very nourishing, so the young Roman women had a curious way of fasting – but it is said they were addicted to vomiting.

Chestnuts and cherries grew only reluctantly near Rome, and Pliny mentions that there were no cherries in Italy before 74 BC: in 120 years the

stone pine in a field near Calne, Wiltshire

young cone of stone pine × 1/3

cherry had even reached Britain, TRANS OCEANUM – it is the only time he mentions Britain in connection with trees. This at least proves that the Romans were conscious of transplanting trees to the provinces.

Chestnut timber was ranked with larch, oak and walnuts as 'slow to age' – cypress, cedar, ebony, nettle tree (*Celtis*), box, yew, juniper and olive were ageless. On this showing the Romans would hardly bother to plant chestnuts for timber in a country rich in oakwoods. Oak is as good a fuel – much better – and it can be coppiced as easily. The present-day, healthy chestnut coppices of the Sussex Weald, where the Roman iron industry was centred, tempt one to believe in a Roman introduction, and there is evidence for Roman chestnut woods in S. Essex. I think the Romans would be contemptuous of the fruit which ripens here. Chestnut charcoal has been identified from sites in Sussex, London, Hertfordshire, Wiltshire and Dorset.

The main use of our English coppice chestnut is for palings and hop-poles. The wood is naturally durable.

sweet chestnut, a roadside tree in W. Scotland

Juglans regia

It is generally agreed that the Romans introduced the walnut to the Netherlands, and whilst there is only one British record, at Rotherley, Wiltshire, Godwin accepts that the same may have happened here. The walnut seems a Roman tree, with its resounding name (construed as 'Jove's acorns'). The shell being made in two parts, it was 'consecrated to weddings'. It may have been thought essential for British-Roman marriage ceremonies. Walnut trees remained a status symbol for bridegrooms in Germany until Evelyn's time.

Roman walnuts had many domestic uses. They were put in wine which was boiled down to make it keep – an interesting explanation, perhaps, of the colonial Romans' habit of diluting their wine with water: it was a concentrate. From the nuts themselves a wine, CARYNIUM, was made, and dyes came from the unripe shells, hair stain from the nuts. The oil was used to treat ear troubles, headaches, baldness. The timber, with beech, was preferred for work underground, and was also used for roofbeams: if about to break, it would give warning creaks. The wood was stained chemically to look like ebony. The tree was grown from seed – it should be planted between the 1st and the 15th of March.

But the nuts, it seems, were not especially valued as food. They were thought to cause headaches as well as cure them. They may have got a bad reputation from the Greek herbalist Dioscorides. Translated by Goodyer, the assistant editor of Gerard's *Herbal*, the Greek text says:

> Nuces regia, which some call Persica, being eaten are hard of digestion, they hurt ye stomach, engender choler, breed headach, are naught for such as have ye Cough, but good to make one vomit if they be eaten by one fasting. They are Antidots against Poysons, being eaten before, or after, with figgs & Rue: being eaten in a great quantitie they expell ye broade wormes.

This surely cannot be the innocuous walnut.

The timber, it seems, was not valued by the Romans for its more recent supremacy in coachwork and cabinet-working. The shade of the tree, wrote Pliny, is undoubtedly poisonous to other plants.

Roman tree-lore

acorn of Turkey oak:
'bitter and rude'

Of all trees, mast-bearing species, GLANDIFERI, always had the highest place in the esteem of the Romans. This included the chestnut and beech as well as oaks. Julius Caesar noted that the superior warships of the Veneti had hulls made entirely of oak, and would stand up to any amount of rough handling. The cross timbers were beams a foot thick, fastened with iron bolts as thick as a man's thumb. These are exactly the dimensions used in the woodwork of some of the northern British forts built by the Roman army.

Civic wreaths of honour – for services to the Empire – were of oak leaves: first of the evergreen oak, later of the AESCULUM sacred to Jove, and sometimes of the common oak – but only if it bore acorns. Acorns were still, in outlying provinces like Spain, treated as food. Pliny's oaks were ROBUR, QUERCUS, AESCULUS, CERRIS, ILEX, SUBER. The best acorns were of QUERCUS, next best AESCULUS; those of ROBUR were small and those of the turkey oak, CERRIS, bitter and rude in a prickly cup. The best tree was the broad-leaved oak, but its acorns were variable.

The ROBUR is usually taken to be the Valonia oak, *Quercus macrolepis* or *aegilops*, with semi-evergreen leaves and impressive acorn cups; the common oak, *Q. robur*, AESCULUS may be the Kermes or the Macedonian oak, for their evergreen leaves, suitable for wreaths, or if the tree dedicated to Jove ought to be big, perhaps the Hungarian oak, also native of Italy. The translator identifies AESCULUS as the chestnut-leaved oak, but unfortunately that is a Caucasian tree. The rest are easily identified, SUBER being the cork oak. But Pliny introduces also HEMERAS, a bushy tree with large acorns, and AEGILOPS, the tallest, INCULTIS AMICA – wild-country-loving. These may have been sub-species, as it were, to his main group.

The romans in Britain built fortresses of wood, often, it is said, using prefabricated units. Oak would be preferred, but we may imagine that the native pinewoods offered suitable timber in Europe and North Britain. All of Pliny's six 'resinous' trees were useful for timber except his PICEA, fit only for roof shingles. This is likely to have been a spruce, as its name would now indicate, or a cypress.

Wacher estimates that 37,000 cubic metres of timber were felled and sawn by the Roman forces to build the 80 or so forts of Northern Britain – about 11,250 acres of woodland. This would be one-fortieth of the acreage of woodland lost in the 1914–18 war. It would hardly dent forested Britannia, but the clearings, as we have seen, introduce new elements into the ecology. The Roman army engineers built in a massive carpentry of posts, beams and lattices, covered with carefully prepared mud, and finished in plaster. Wattle and daub doesn't quite describe this: rather the walls were of unbaked clay or dried mud on timber armatures locked deep into the soil. The walls were thick and carried rainwater away from the foundations into wooden surface gutters. Some of the military camps in England had walls of turf. Forts had timber gateways, the several posts, commonly 12 inches square, held together by assorted nails, up to 10 inches long. The gateways, and the walls at intervals, were surmounted by defensive towers with, according to the carvings on Trajan's column, diagonal bracing. Only the post-holes remain, deep, square and tidy, surrounded by heaps of bent nails – for the timber-work was dismantled when the troops left. Trees were nowhere scarce, but squared

Roman building

timbers represented many hours of skilled work. At Inchtuthil, the most northerly fort and where the timbers are believed to have been salvaged, 12 tons of unused nails were found. Perhaps they were left accidentally on purpose by the sappers, already struggling with 12-foot beams.

Rackham insists that the Romans maintained coppices to fuel baths, kilns, furnaces, salt pans, and this is only reasonable, since it would be necessary, over four centuries, to limit the distances fuel had to be carried.

Ploughs with iron coulters are of Roman date or earlier and a great deal of land must have been cleared for agriculture. Oats entered the cereal list in Iron Age time, and rye in Roman. The population of Britain at the height of the Roman occupation is estimated at between half a million and one and a half million. This is only the number of people living in one of our prov—incial cities now.

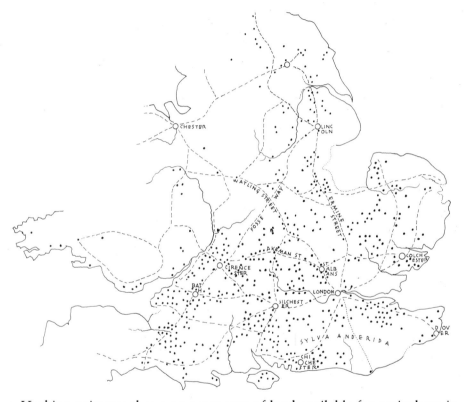

Roman villas in Britain

Hoskins estimates that 2 or 3 per cent of land available for agriculture in the early twenties was in use in Roman times. Vast forests occupied most of Britain. The only one to have a Roman name was SYLVA ANDERIDA, later Andredesweald, the Weald of Kent, Sussex and Hampshire. In 892 it was still 30 miles wide and 120 miles long.

The Roman soldier had a shield of laminated limewood and a spear of ash. Ash was 'better than hazel for spears, lighter than CORNUS, more pliant than SORBUS': Gallic ash, especially, had the suppleness and light weight required for chariot building – how true! Elm would have been suitable, says Pliny, if it were not so heavy. It was used for door frames and hinges, but care had to be taken to set it upside down – reversing the direction of the growth. I wonder if there is any sense in that? Pine and alder were hollowed to make pipes for running water. Since Roman manufacturing industries tended to be centralised we can expect that there were large coppices of all these trees, except pine, which will not coppice.

Returning to the archaeological record, there are a few more trees to be considered for Roman Britain. There are single records from Silchester of charcoal of silver fir, and seeds of medlar, mulberry and fig at three other Roman sites as well. At four sites, again including Silchester, the grape vine has been identified.

This rather thin evidence needs interpreting. The odd man out is of course the fir, and this is confidently assumed to have arrived in the form of wine casks – it was a Roman use of fir wood. Silchester, undisturbed by later building and fully excavated, may be regarded as typical rather than unique among Roman-British towns, often excavated without much attention to botanical remains. All the fruit seeds found there, nevertheless, could be from imported fruit. Did they grow the trees? Probably we shall never know.

There was a law against provincial vineyards until the 3rd century, and by that time the climate was worsening. It did not improve again until the early medieval period, when grape-vines were certainly cultivated.

Mulberries have never been regarded as essentially more valuable than blackberries – often called dwarf mulberries – until the possibility of home-produced silk was envisaged early in the 17th century. Figs are difficult. Ripened in Britain they can be delicious, and the Romans had a fashion for eating them fresh with cheese. But English figs can never compete as dried fruit with the produce of Mediterranean countries. The Romans dried and boxed their figs, too, the best coming from Ibiza and the east coast of Italy.

Medlars however are hardy, and are (rarely) found growing wild in Britain. MESPILUS was the generic name for thorn trees in Ancient Rome, the Gallic MESPILUS being the hawthorn, SETANIA the medlar. We may assume, I believe, that this tree was introduced to Britain by the Romans. Figs, mulberries and vines they may have cultivated, but it is unlikely that any of these have been in continuous cultivation ever since, and they are in no way naturalised. The Romans also introduced lentils, peas, radishes, celery, buckwheat, and the herbs, fennel, coriander and dill. They grew cannabis, for the fibre, and opium poppy, belladonna, henbane and vervain, some or all of these for use as anaesthetics in surgery. They introduced dozens of weeds.

medlar, *Mespilus germanicus*

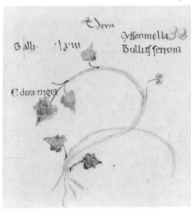

ivy as two separate species: a Saxon version of the classical *Herbarium* of Apuleius Platonicus

6 · Anglo-Saxon trees

Two centuries of silence follow the withdrawal of the Roman army in the 4th century, until the spread of organised Christianity to England about 600 AD. Under this silence Saxons, Angles, Jutes, Frisians and Swabians settled the land, and, with some exceptions, the Celts and Britons withdrew to the west. Many old Celtic homelands on the downs of southern England were deserted, never to be occupied again. They had lost their woodland. After centuries of stock-raising and, probably, dairy farming for the nearby concentrations of Roman habitation, the chalklands and limestone upland had become untenable sheepwalks.

Now the pattern of our rural landscape began to be marked out, based on the essentially lowland arable cultivation methods of the Saxons, with their nucleated villages – communities arising out of that loyalty to a leader which was the first rule of Anglo-Saxon behaviour.

They came in wooden boats, well made, with tall prows and many subtly shaped ribs to which the planks were fixed with nails (as against the Celtic *curragh* of tensioned wood, lashed with thongs and covered with oiled skins). Such people would certainly be capable of efficient woodland management, though we cannot suspect them of transplanting their native trees such as spruce, fir or maple. It is possible however that our stock of native willows was increased at this time, and that some additions were made to the complex genealogy of our elms. The white willow and some types of 'Dutch' elm (hybrids with *Ulmus glabra*) have a strongly eastern distribution and yet are clearly old-established.

Anglo-Saxon records of trees come from magic spells and from land charters, our knowledge of their woodland from place names and by inference from the eleventh-century Domesday Book. Some hint of their use of wood in building is to be got from the rare Saxon stonework, in a style that emerged from the traditional use of timber construction.

Our language is half Anglo-Saxon, and so are more than half our tree names: there are few Celtic ones and relatively few from the Norman French. The language of Anglo-Saxon literature is rich in words for actions and feelings, life and death, sea and land; and almost empty of detail and description. There are many names for death, for burning, for brightness and glory; many names for the sea (including *brim, flotweǵ, ǵelagu, holm, lagu, lagustrēam, mere, mereflōd, sǣ, sund* and *hwaelweǵ*, whale-path), and for the tools of war. One name for spear is *aesc*, ash; one name for ash is *axe*. One name for shield is *lind*, the same as linden, the lime. (It is odd that the Romans should have used limewood shields too.) A Saxon spell confirms it; part of a cure for rheumatism – against elf-spears:

I stood under linden wood, under the light shield,
where mighty women showed their power
and screaming sent forth their spears

In Beowulf too '... hand grasped shield, yellow limewood' (*geolwe linde*). Many other tree names are Anglo-Saxon, including treo, treow, apparently the same for truth, tree and cross.

alder	*alor*	hazel	*hæsel*	pear	*pirige*
aspen	*æsp*	hawthorn	*hæþorn*	sallow	*sealh*
birch	*birce*	holly	*holen*	sloe	*slahþorn*
bramble	*bremel,*	ivy	*ifig*	sweetgale	*gagel*
	brembel	maple tree	*mapuldor*	willow	*welig, wiþig* (withy)
elder	*ellen*	mistletoe	*mistel-tan*	woodbine	*wudubine*
elm	*elm*	oak	*æc āc*		(honeysuckle)
wych elm	*wice*				

Wudu was any kind of timber, whether growing in the ground, held in the hand or floating as a ship.

Surprisingly, there are words for myrtle (*wyr*), and olive (*elebaum*) – plants used in spells, as is the butcher's broom, not much of a tree perhaps: *cneow-holen* (knee-holly). The vine makes its presence felt in later decorative patterns, perhaps derived from Latin sources. But the climate is supposed to have improved at around the 7th century. There were vineyards at Berkhamsted in Domesday times – about 2 acres, against nearly 1000 acres of meadow land, and woodland forage for 1000 hogs, in that delightful vale of the Bulbourne.

Little useful can be learnt about Anglo-Saxon trees from the land charters, though these have been studied for this purpose. Rarity, unusual size or shape, distinctive character, are surely the qualifications for boundary marks. Yet oaks are mentioned nearly as often as thorns, which tend to be conspicuous, isolated in pasture or left alone for superstitious reasons. Large old oaks may well have been singled out by old tradition as sacred trees and then remained as landmarks – as indeed hundreds of them still do.

Apples, willows, pears, elder and lime come in for fairly frequently mentions, in a selection of 150 charters given in Rackham (1976). Birch, ash, maple, aspen and service tree are mentioned: no yews, poplars or pines, distinctive though these would be in the landscape; and no elms, even in Worcestershire, where elms became the 'Worcestershire weed'. Perhaps they were too common to be used as marks, or too much lopped.

Magic trees

In the magic spells of the Anglo-Saxon herbalist witch-doctors oak is frequently used, thorn never. Oak, ash and hazel have special properties. Even aspen is specified, as are bramble, elder and sallow, often for qualities inherent in the character of the tree – strength, vigour, suppleness – even wartyness. Buckthorn (*þefeþorn*) has peculiar virtues apart from the purgative berries. Some of the spells put in practically everything, even repeating some species to make sure. Omissions are notable, as in this long, but, I think diverting example:

Against the disease called shingles. Take the bark of the trembling poplar and of aspen, and apple-tree, maple-tree, elder, willow, sallow, myrtle, wych elm, oak, blackthorn, birch, olive tree, goat willow; of ash there must be most, and part of every tree that one can get, except hawthorn and alder; of all these trees most that are mentioned here. And also gale and butcher's broom; houseleek, elecampane, radish, dwarf elder, the great nettle, wormwood, lesser centaury.

Boil strongly, removing the barks and putting in fresh three times, then strain and add a measure of butter; stir. Let it stand for two or three days, then take the butter out. Take catkins of gale and a cluster of ivy berries, tansy and betony, elecampane, radish, bonewort, basil: pound them together, boil in the butter, then remove the butter as far as possible. Take barley meal and burnt salt, prepare it in the butter, stir strongly away from the fire, add pepper. Then first eat the preparation after one night's fast.

Thereafter drink the potion and no other liquid for ten nights or for 30 if possible. Then take mistletoe of oak, pound it small and dry it, and rub it to a mealy powder, then weigh it against a penny. Put that in the best wine. Drink this for nine days and do not eat new cheese or fresh goose, nor fresh eel, nor fresh pork, nor anything that comes from mulberry wine, nor fish without shells, nor web-footed fowls. If he eats any of this let it be salted and let him drink no beer and be moderate in the way of wine and ale. If a man follow this prescription then he will be well.

By contrast, another tree formula is simple and easy:

Against deafness. Take a green stick of ash, lay it over a fire, then take the juice which comes out, put it in wool, wring it in the ear and stop up the ear with the same wool.

Oak and hazel sticks are the mediums for the symbolic extraction of poison:

Against the bite of a spider. Cut five incisions, one on the bite and four round about it. Throw the bloodied stick in silence across a cart road.

Clearly the cuts are to be made with the stick. Iron would be undesirable. Another spell says 'Let the blood run on a green hazel stick, then throw it across a road'. Another, against 'flying venom. Cut four incisions on the four sides with an oaken stick'.

The four sides are related to the magic circle, but were easily adapted to the Christian symbol when this became important. The magic number was three, with its multiples – and this long before the Holy Trinity became a force to be reckoned with.

If a man's stomach has become sour or swollen take two handfuls of leaves of holly, cut very small, and boil in various kinds of milk until tender. Select bit by bit. Eat six slices, three in the morning and three in the evening, after food, for nine days or longer.

The holly leaves are clearly believed to contain a healing substance, and in fact they have been used in herbal medicine until recent times; particularly for jaundice. But Culpeper used the leaves and bark as a poultice for broken bones. This seems not to have proved effective and holly was edited out of later editions of his herbal.

Trees are of course only part of this magic. For balance I include some spells using animal materials.

Against the bite of a spider. Take a hen's egg, cut it up raw into ale and fresh sheep dung, so that he does not know: give him to drink a good bowlful.

Against synovia (water on the joints): Dwarf elder, burn and pound a dog's head and a baked apple. Mix all this together and lay on.

If a man intends to fight with an enemy, let him stew sand-martins in wine and eat them.

The last one seems quite painless. Ears were treated gently too:

Heat juice of celandine and mother's milk in an oyster shell and drip into the ear.

Many spells take note of the power of silence. And there are special instructions that bark should be removed from the east side of a tree. Storm (1948) from whom most of these spells are taken (he got them from Cockayne, 1864), believes that this was because the east side had absorbed the power of the rising sun. But it is worth remembering that green algae form on the opposite side.

Against dysentry. Take half a poor cheese, not greasy, add four slices of English honey, boil in a pan until brown. Then take a handful of bark of young oak and bring it home in silence and never into the house of the patient. Scrape off the green outside. Boil the juicy chips in cow milk, sweeten the drink with three slices of honey, then take it with cheese. After the drink you must abstain from ale for seven days and you must drink milk that has not turned sour.

From a bone-salve recipe: many herbs with hazel, pounded with ivy berries:

And take the bark of ash tree and twigs of willow and bark of oak and bark of myrtle and bark of crab-tree and bark of sallow and leaves of woodbine. All these should be taken near the ground and of the east side of the trees . . .

Hazel, notable for its straight, supple shoots is not a surprising choice for repairing bones. Ivy berries add ingredient x, then other strong or resilient trees are added to complete the cure, with a final reinforcement, of weaving and binding plants.

The mother of all herbs, however, was no tree but the great plaintain, a humble weed, a native survivor of ice ages, now adapted to roadside habitats – waybread. It comes second, after mugwort, in the Charm of Nine Herbs.

And thou, Waybread, wort-mother
easterly opened, innerly mighty:
chariot crushed thee, queen rode over thee,
over thee, women wept, bulls breathed.
You withstood all – and rebounded:
so you withstand poisons and plagues
and loathsomeness roving the land.

fly now, poison hater, against greater poison; you the lesser
Are mightier than lesser poisons: until he be cured of both.

This two-part approach is typical. Often the tree barks are placed in the second, healing and strengthening part.

Dig up waybread without iron before sunrise

Iron: 'the grey enemy of the forest,' is part of black magic, not of healing.

What should we infer from the mention of mulberry, myrtle, and olive in the spells: that these trees survived in old Roman-British orchards? That the names are mistranslations or had survived from Latin originals? Latin and Irish are both used for bits of abracadabra, but the spells are surely rooted in the heathen faith of Odin, Thor, Freyr and of the world-tree Yggdrasil, 'stretching its branches afar, green both in winter and summer. No one knows what kind of tree it is'.

We need not underestimate the resources of the spell-givers, but we cannot assume that olives, myrtles and mulberries were common in Anglo-Saxon England, the last in quantities sufficient to make wine.

Elebaum and *oleastrum* are translated variously as olive tree, wild olive and sea buckthorn. Since the coasts of Suffolk and Norfolk are now the only native home of the sea buckthorn in England I think we can safely leave out the olive and the oleaster. Mulberry is a local name for *Rubus* species in Suffolk (Grigson 1958) and there are extant many recipes for blackberry wine. The language is diverse and might well have mulberry for the wine and bramble for the twigs, though it must be admitted that a single blackberry is called a *brembelaeppel*.

Myrtle and gale are mentioned together in the spell on page 61. Bog myrtle is a modern name for sweetgale, Dutch myrtle a folk name. Gale, so called all over eastern England, was once very common in the Fens, and popular for its fragrance – not because it pleased the senses but because it was supposed to keep away fleas. It was used in beer before hops came into favour.

A spell which can mention goat willow, willow and sallow all in one breath can, I feel, use two names for gale. It certainly seems unlikely that *Myrtus communis* was grown in Saxon England, but – it is a Mediterranean plant – it might have been grown in sheltered plots by the herbalists.

Perhaps the spell books were sometimes extravagant, like some cookery books. One last quotation; and you may hear the voice, from twelve centuries ago, of the authentic English sceptic.

Against the bite of an adder. If he obtains and eats bark which comes from Paradise, no poison can hurt him. Then he that copied this book wrote that this would be hard to get.

green man, Norwich, early 14th century

7 · Medieval trees

How much was the native forest modified during the eleven centuries between the Iron Age and the Norman invasion? The answer is: quite completely in parts of southern and eastern England, but for the rest of Britain only patchily.

There were in Roman Britain as many as 1000 villas (more than 500 are actually known) each of which farmed about 1000 acres. There were also at least as many native settlements – 'Celtic' farming has been underestimated. Many sweeping statements are made, and I felt the need of some rough calculations. In a 10 km square of Oxfordshire the effect of three Roman villas and the native farms, here side by side in a relatively heavily settled area, would be to fill roughly a quarter of the square with cultivated land. This hardly agrees with Hoskins's estimate of 2 or 3 per cent, but our 10 km square may well have been at the maximum. The other three-quarters of the square must have been largely dense forest – it was Wychwood – but there would be large marshes and some open grazing on high land. Where there are ancient boundary ditches (usually called Grimm's Dyke on the map) we can assume that forest was absent. Breaks in such boundaries are taken to mean impenetrable woodland, not necessarily, of course, primeval, or other natural hazards. All these features are present in my 10 km sample. The three Roman villas are only one or two miles apart. A modern farm near one of them (Ditchley) is called Assart Farm, and *assart* was a Norman name for a new clearing of the forest. Of course, the forest may have crept back after the Roman period.

Modern researches tend to show that there was more Roman occupation, even of heavy clay soils, than was formerly suspected. Cultivation of Roman farmlands seems often to have continued through the Dark Age, with the Saxon settlers frequently taking over existing Roman and native farms rather than pioneering. The later Vikings, though they threated isolated settlements, particularly monasteries near the coast, made hundreds of new villages (ending in *by*, *thorpe* or *thwaite* in the N.E. and N.W.), and Saxon villages certainly multiplied in the 'Magna and Parva' style. Even so, the population at the time of *Domesday* is given as 1¼ millions, the same figure for England (without the four northern counties) as the more generous of the estimates for Roman Britain.

Some authors are at pains to show that the wild woods were already gone when the Romans withdrew. Historical writers generally, however, are happy to visualise Norman Britain as, at least, heavily wooded:

From Blacon Point to Hillbree
A squirrel may jump from tree to tree

sings the author of a volume in *The Pelican History of England*. The trouble is, I don't know where these two places were. Cheshire?

A population only one-fortieth of today's! But this is no guide to the

opposite:
pollard willows in
Kelmscott village

settlement and use of the land. In eastern areas the number of people to the square mile was as many as 35: in most of the country between 5 and 10. Nowadays there are an average 350 to the square mile. But most of *us* live in towns, most of *them* lived in villages, hamlets and isolated tribal homes. The rural population of, say, Norfolk or Lincolnshire was therefore much as it is today, and it was using between four and ten times as much land per head to feed itself, so much has the yield per acre increased.

Such areas had certainly lost their native woodland, and the trees they did have were managed so as to produce their maximum of pasture, building materials, fencing and fuel. Surveys of woodland, Domesday or modern, take no account of the incidental trees and small patches of wood that are now largely decorative (though very important for with animals and birds). Then they were used to the full, being cut at intervals by pollarding or shredding. Domesday seems not too clear, either, about coppices. 'Underwood' was only spasmodically recorded, yet every village must have had enough for its needs, unless it drew upon a large waste or forest.

The intensive use of trees tends to perpetuate ancient woods, and it favours certain species at the expense of others, some native, some hybrids. It can lead to the extinction of species which do not regenerate easily. This seems to have happened to the Breckland pinewoods in the Neolithic, and the black poplar in the Middle Ages.

In E. Anglia today we find a sharp difference between hedgerow and incidental trees on the one hand and woodland on the other. While the ancient woods investigated so thoroughly by Oliver Rackham reveal species dating back to prehistory, the landscape as a whole has a very different character, with willows and poplars the ground bass to a disorderly concerto of native and alien trees from which such members as maple, hornbeam, small-leaved lime, aspen, are absent. Elms (but of different inheritance) are common to both woodland and farmland. Ash, oak, beech and alder vary according to local conditions.

In the rest of England there is a closer correspondence between woodland and incidental trees, because the pressures which altered the indigenous forest have been gentler. Enclosures, using native trees as hedges, are often very much older. With the exception of the limes, all replaced by the hybrid apart from some rare woods, the native species often dominate the open landscape

very old pollard elms –
'dodders' – in Knapwell,
Cambridgeshire, mark the
lines of former boundaries

as they do the older woodlands. It is not difficult at times to imagine the
fields as carved out of the forest. Changes in elevation are frequently signalled
by changes from ash to oak, oak to elm, elm to willow. Dropped blindfold
anywhere in England you could soon say where you were by sampling the
major trees. But a varied and intricate web of usage and law has shaped the
countryside.

Forest and commons

A hundred years after the Norman invasion almost one-third of the country
was under Forest Law. This only meant that the King got the deer, just as
the Queen today gets the swans on the Thames. It wasn't all trees, but it is
some indication that there were patches of waste, some of it wooded, around
which, in 140 separate areas, the laws of the Royal Forest operated to protect
red deer. King William, who laid waste practically every village in Yorkshire,
is said by the Anglo-Saxon Chronicle to have loved the deer as if he were
their father. It was probably he who started the English fashion of being
kinder to animals than to people. Poachers ran the risk of being blinded. But
these were brutish times: by the Saxon laws of Wessex you could be killed
outright if you wandered into a strange wood and forgot to halloo or blow
a horn.

The Forest system tended to slow down development at least, while the
King's demesne forests accumulated large timber trees. Undergrowth and
new growth were removed by the combined effect of protected deer and the
people's exercise of various rights of common.

Elsewhere, the trees of the waste belonged to the lords of the manors,
while the villagers took deadwood and underwood, and had some rights to
timber for repairs. Rights of turbary (turf removal) and the use of woodlands
as pasture prevented the growth of new wood, but pollarding the trees, to
allow usable wood to grow above the reach of the beasts, very much prolongs
the life of the tree.

Coppices, where the trees are cut systematically to ground level, were the
almost universal system of woodland management by the middle of the 13th
century. Coppices formed parts of forests as well as interpenetrating with
wood pastures, parts of which were fenced for long enough to establish the
new growth.

hawthorn, once part of a
hedge, in Epping Forest

Almost all the native trees, and many aliens, can be coppiced. In midland and eastern England hazel, with some lime and elm, is the main coppice tree – and the system favours hazel, for it can set new seed only two or three years after cutting. Ash and oak have often been left to grow up as standard timber trees in the coppices. Alder coppice is not unknown and may have been much more common before all the land was drained.

Industries, whether salt pans, glassworks, iron mines or foundries, had to have a measurable amount of coppice, on a given rotation, to keep them going. Even in Domesday time Droitwich used 500 cartloads a year. Such resources had to be renewable. Towns and cities also required a supply of wood or charcoal, and this could not be taken at random.

Old laws for Tiptree Heath, summarised in 1523 and quoted by Rackham (1980), give an insight into some of the complexities of commoning. Tiptree was a very large common shared by seventeen parishes: 'like a Forest but without deer'. Part of it was compartmented into woods – that is, parts of the woods were protected against grazing by hedges or banks and ditches. Part was heathland with scattered trees, usually pollarded.

The woods belonged to the lords of the manors, but these lords could not fell trees if the commoners wanted to keep them for lopping. The commoners could take cartbote, ploughbote, and hedgebote, by lopping or shredding. If they couldn't find enough by these methods they were allowed to cut trees to the ground – not, of course, uprooting them. The people could cut broom, gorse and thorns at will, for firewood. During February they could coppice 'bircheses, willoughes, salloughes and alders'. If the supply of these ran out they could lop and crop maples and beeches, and if they were still short of firewood they could lop such oaks as were already pollarded, or 'shredde such as hath not been before lopped'.

Willows

Willows have been grown along the banks of rivers and by ponds at least since the 13th century. We can take it that grown means planted, at least initially, for few lowland river banks are the permanent etchings into the soil that they seem. Cattle and water traffic rapidly erode the banks, but a few stakes of willow, needing very little protection because the stems are bitter, can soon strengthen the soil, and will provide a constant supply of fencing material. The trees survive flooding. (Regular 'floating' of water meadows was established in the 16th century.) Pollarding keeps the shade to reasonable proportions – and still has to be done today, when there is little demand for hurdles. The Thames Water men burn the cuttings of millions of willows, while the coal trains trundle southwards to Didcot Power Station. Of course, there's no comparison, but experiments *have* started in Scandinavia with willow beds as a source of energy. . . .

The crack willow, snap willow, *Salix fragilis*, open bark willow, wrong willow, is the less tidy and useful of the two willows which can form tall trees (70 feet or more) and which flower in summer, with the leaves, The white, or Huntingdon willow, *S. alba*, has downy, usually smaller leaves, darker green but white beneath. It has pendulous shoots and forms a more compact and regular shape than the crack willow. It is often pollarded, like its sister. Which you think the more common may depend on whether you

white willow, R. Nene

travel L.N.E. or L.N.W. (railways tend to follow watercourses).

A cross results in the Bedford willow, which used to be valued highly for its timber, used for artificial limbs. The very popular weeping willow, and the proud, elegant cricket bat willow, are varieties of *S. alba*.

Both *fragilis* and *alba* are taken to be native trees; though there are only tentative identifications of Iron Age and Roman charcoal, all from southern England. Edlin very reasonably supposes that both were indigenous to the undrained, once very extensive East Anglian fens; and this would place them easily within their European range, north to Denmark. Since their spread throughout England and Wales is largely the work of man and a function of husbandry I have included them as medieval trees: certainly they are features of any medieval landscape, and long may they remain a feature of ours.

Populus nigra var. *betulifolia*

Poplars: black, white and grey

The black poplar, *Populus nigra*, is a European tree with a vigorous and distinct strain (*betulifolia*) native to N.W. Europe and Britain. 'Popeler' is taken by Rackham to refer to this massive tree of riverside meadows, never found in woods. It was one of the commonest trees in Suffolk and Essex in the Middle Ages, and was also found all over the midlands. It seems to have been cut to extinction in some areas, being a source of cruck beams for early buildings – and not so much valued and possessed by lords and kings as were the oaks of the forest. It should have been planted like the elms in the Enclosure Act hedges, but was forgotten. Now we have only a thousand trees left, and most are too scattered to pollinate each other. If there is a case for planting landscape trees, this very English poplar ought to be high on the list, though we cannot say that the timber is so straight or produced so rapidly as with the many hybrid poplars in use today. Black poplars of European origin are sometimes planted as screens in industrial areas.

The white poplar, *P. alba*, had a distinctly 17th- and 18th-century image until it was discovered that its, supposedly Dutch, name, *abele*, featured as that of a large tree *abel* in 13th- and 14th-century documents. This, says Rackham, implies that it is native or of ancient introduction. Well, it could have been introduced in the 12th century, not exactly ancient in my book.

The abele is very white, and has prominent diamond markings on the light-coloured bark at least down to about 6 feet above the ground. Below this, the bark of old trees is immensely coarse and black. Sucker leaves and leaves of young shoots are five-lobed, and all are intensely white beneath, the stalks and the shoots being hairy. It is rarely a very large tree and has usually a ragged outline – elegant in a coarse, swashbuckling way. This is a favourite tree of farmers' wives and property developers, and is often to be seen near ring roads. In the right place it can be superb.

The grey poplar, *P. canescens*, is a hybrid or intermediate form between the native aspen and the white poplar. It is more impressive than either as a large landscape tree, almost elm-like under the weight of summer foliage, and statuesque in the field hedges or on the roadside – though it looks nothing like an elm in winter. It is naturalised in some woodlands.

The leaves are never so white or so deeply lobed as those of the white poplar, more like a coarse version of the aspen, usually light grey and hairy

black poplar, Oxfordshire

white poplar bark

grey poplar,
Gloucestershire

beneath. But leaves of the suckers which spring from the roots near the tree are often very similar to the white poplar's. The bark is grey and regularly fissured on most of the trunk, usually only the branches of large trees showing the distinctive light colour and diamond patterns of one parent, modified by the horizontal streaks of the other, *P. tremula*. Female trees are less common than male, because people tend not to plant female poplars, disliking the fluffy seeds. The grey poplar will stand up to strong winds and is tolerant of some shade.

The white and grey poplars are supposed to be impossible to lop without injury – unlike the black poplars, which will stand any amount of cutting. Elwes and Henry (1913) had never seen a pollarded white poplar, and

Turner, the painter, made a note in a sketchbook of the early 1800s, 'Polled arbele', as if to remark on a rarity in the landscape. The timber of both trees tends to be lumped as abele in the timber trade. It is useful, has possibilities of pulping – it has been described as a non-coniferous softwood – and is light, strong and not easily split by nailing. It has been used in coach-building. It is said to be non-inflammable.

Late medieval wood and timber

If coppicing favours the spread of hazel, the use of small timber and particularly wattles creates a demand for it. Hurdles and wattles-and-daub building can of course use almost any young growth of wood – oak and willow are both used – but hazel grows fast and straight, and is tough and pliable.

History books tell us that the half-timbered style of building was a response to a general shortage of wood. But buildings entirely of wood are draughty without very careful tongue-and-groove construction of well-seasoned timber, all of which has to be sawn and planed. Even the beautifully made Saxon ships had seaweed stuffed between the planks. The native tradition was of turf supported on small timber, and it is not difficult to see this evolving into wattle-and-daub or cob for walls, and thatch for roofs.

Saxon houses tended to a long shape, a main roof beam supported by vertical posts. The roof often sloped right to the ground. Ground sills were of timber, later replaced by stone, which would not rot. By the 11th century the centre posts had disappeared, but the long shape seems to have been retained, and the roof was supported by a series of pointed arches or A frames, which preferably had convex sides to give more headroom. Such houses are cruck houses. A single large tree was split into two or four to make perfectly symmetrical crucks. Splitting a large tree trunk is a considerable undertaking. I imagine it to have been attended by some ceremony as the tree, gently penetrated by the cumulative force of wedges, yielded its protective soul to the family roof.

The smallest wood from the coppice was used for firing ovens, and firewood was gathered from every possible source close to the village. The medieval landscape apart from the forests must have been very neat and tidy, the horizon only rarely broken by the silhouettes of large trees. The open field system of the midlands did not perhaps lend itself to many incidental trees. But there were boundaries upon which trees could grow, and there were soon permanent pastures with hedges, where certain trees would always be allowed to grow up. Other fences were of moveable wattles, the product of the coppices, and these were even more in demand as sheep farming increased. Elms were encouraged near habitations for the heavy timbers essential to animal husbandry. Oaks in the coppices were allowed to grow up as standards: the hazel/oak pattern came to be recognised as the typical woodland of lowland England.

Large timber trees for important buildings were often supplied from the royal forests – the gift of the king to the Church. Windmills, first recorded in 1191, became common in the 13th century. Posts for mills were the most massive timbers ever handled by the village craftsman – 40 feet by 2 feet square is mentioned for Gamlingay mill by Rackham (1980) – there was also a bill for repairing a cart which broke under the weight. Large timbers appear

poplar frame of cruck barn, early 17th century. The split oak infilling dates from 1974 when the barn was rebuilt at the Avoncroft Museum of Building, Bromsgrove, Worcestershire

coppiced hornbeam in
Hatfield Forest

to have been carried half across the kingdom for various reasons, not always a local shortage – which gives some idea of their value. Transport was by water wherever possible. Oak was actually imported as sawn planks in the 13th century, but this does not imply a dearth of oak, only European competitiveness. 600 years later, we found it cheaper to import American elm wheelhubs than to make our own from the plentiful and superior elms of the countryside, and 700 years later it was economic to import elm from Canada, with, in this case, disastrous consequences.

The idea that later medieval and Tudor industries, glass and iron in particular, finally destroyed the native woodlands is now discounted: they had been destroyed long before, and present-day woodlands grown up from old coppices actually mark the sites of old industries. This can be only partly true and is not true at all of Northern England and Scotland. The 16th-century expansion of industries into new areas, whose woods were only loosely managed, must have been destructive. One iron master in 1550 to 1580 is said to have reduced Cannock Chase to something less than its present tree cover. New blast furnaces in Derbyshire and Yorkshire were using woodlands with no history of careful management and no future except as poor grazing for sheep. Pinewoods in Scotland were cut indiscriminately then as later: pine regenerates only by seed, and then only if rigorously protected from grazing.

Many areas of Forest, at least partly woodland, were disafforested bit by bit in the Middle Ages, the land often converted to arable. Monasteries were disbanded and their timber sold. New landlords needed quick returns, from produce or rent. It was cash, not grey iron, that was the enemy of the forest.

The Black Death occurred in 1348–50. Before that, the English had already outgrown the, then, resources of their country: people were weakened by malnutrition and many were starving after a string of bad harvests. The plagues decimated or more than decimated the population, but only a few villages were actually emptied of people. There was some reshuffling of roles and territory, and much of the less productive land was left to revert to pasture or scrub.

Prosperity returned, but the population continued to fall, except in some provincial towns and cities where it increased. The map of deserted medieval villages is heavily pock-marked through the south midlands and in Norfolk, Lincolnshire, Yorkshire and Northumberland. By various means, legal and not, much more land was devoted to sheep in the 15th century.

Derelict buildings were a common sight in the countryside. There must have been considerable regrowth of incidental woodland and generally less determination to pollard every tree. A Great Rebuilding at the end of the 16th century may have used a good deal of the timber which had grown up. Very many oaks and elms must have been felled – and black poplars if there were any left. In itself, of course, the use of timber does not reduce woodland; it merely stimulates new growth. But the process of conversion to grazing still continued, and a population rising again put more pressure on the land for food production. Fens were drained and wastes enclosed.

In another hundred years, people were to talk seriously of a national timber shortage, and of planting more trees.

hop poles, Kent

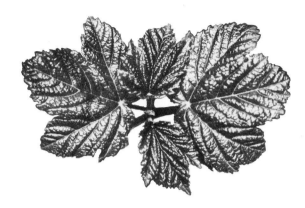

8 · 16th-century trees and the herbalist

Printing came to London in the late 15th century. Our knowledge of introduced trees in the following century comes from herbals printed in English, notably those by William Turner and John Gerard. The herbalists, who supplied the 'poticaries', had to know a lot of botany and a great deal about classical authors. Occasional nuggets of personal experience are found amongst their heaps of sad erudition, and these help us to date the introductions of new trees.

Sycamore or great maple

Acer pseudoplatanus, the sycamore, is called a plane in Scotland, where, unlike any other south European tree, it is naturalised to the point of ubiquity – as it is everywhere in Britain. It is often the most westerly tree of the mainland, where the Atlantic winds merely shape the crown. Summer gales burn the leaves, but the trees produce more. The sycamore colonises, without quite threatening, native woodland everywhere. It is planted to shelter houses and farms on the moors, and forms considerable woods in W. Yorkshire and Lancashire, seeming to like the acid soils of cloughs and valley sides, and spreading over the sour banks of mills and factories. In Lancashire it is characteristically green with algae on one side and black with soot on the other. It has been planted extensively in mill country as a source of white timber for large rollers.

Sycamore is first recorded in England in 1578 (H. Lyte, *A niewe herball*), but it may have been planted in Scotland before that. It is supposed to be recognisable in the carvings of St Frideswide's shrine in Christchurch, Oxford, dated 1282. The young figure of Frideswide, sadly noseless, lies beneath a range of beautifully carved stone foliage, whcih varies from clearly represented pedunculate oak to grape vines – without, I fear, quite hitting on sycamore.

'The Great Maple, not rightly called the Sycamore tree', was Gerard's heading for a woodcut obviously of the field maple – perhaps a printer's error. The *sycomorus* of the Bible is usually identified as a fig species native to Palestine: common in the lowlands in Solomon's time according to the

sycamore trunk

Jerusalem Bible. Seeds of *Acer pseudoplatanus* may well have been brought from Europe by Crusader knights.

In the *Herball* of 1597 it was still 'a stranger in England, only it groweth in the walkes and places of pleasure of noble men, where it especially is planted for the shadow sake'. But Evelyn (1664) would have none of it: 'for the honey-dew leaves, which fall early, like the ash, turn to mucilage and noxious insects, and putrifie with the first moisture of the season; so as they contaminate and mar our walks; and are therefore by my consent, to be banish'd from all curious gardens and avenues'. Sycamores continued to be planted, and were quite well known to poets, but by 1690 the tree was not, according to the botanist Ray, to be found wild: it was planted in churchyards.

In Scotland it has often been a 'dool tree', weeping maple-syrup tears. A 'plague tree' at Mapperton, a tiny village near Beaminster in Dorset, is a sycamore, called the Posy Tree, where parishioners gathered, with herbs and flowers, to watch the coffins carried to a mass grave, well away from the church. The tree, though hollow, does not look old enough but it may be a replacement. Perhaps even sadder is the Martyrs' Tree at Tolpuddle, a great sycamore on the tiny village green. It is now a monument of the Trade Union movement, propped, filled with vermiculite, banded with iron, yet vigorous.

Older trees can be 30 feet in girth, this mostly in the north and in Ireland. An old sycamore near Mountrath, in central Ireland, miraculously leans to contain the water of St Finton's Well. Its trunk is completely metalled over with Irish pennies beaten into the bark.

Seedlings of sycamore, with distinctive pointed, opposite, seed-leaves, spring up on bits of bare soil and moss every year. Grass will shade them out. Saplings are said to be deer-proof. The alien sycamore is now an inseparable part of our flora, with, it is said, 183 different epiphytes and parasites.

The timber is traditionally used to make the bodies of violins, violas and 'cellos – and, no doubt, double basses, see page 86.

plague tree at Mapperton

sycamore surrounded by its own offspring

Mulberry, black and white

The black mulberry, *Morus nigra*, has appeared twice in this story already. It was a Roman tree, and it may have flavoured Saxon mead, but nobody can be sure that it grew here before the 14th century. Gerard, at the end of the 16th, refers to it as a common tree of the orchard; certainly no stranger. It grows slowly and lives long, so that many old trees in Oxford colleges and by old houses will date from a Royal enthusiasm for home-grown silk worms, about 1604. Since Gerard's trees are 'high and full of boughs: the body thereof many times great, the bark rugged', we can assume that *his* generation of mulberries goes back at least to the 14th century.

It is a singular fact that the berries on all the dozen or so mulberry trees that I know are left on the tree to rot or feed the birds. And why are there so many trees in Oxford?

The white mulberry, already known to Gerard in 1597, is a native of China, long cultivated in Europe because it is the preferred food of silkworms. *M. alba* is a variable tree, both in leaf and habit, while *nigra*, despite its even longer history of cultivation, has no known varieties. Even the fruit of the white mulberry is variable, ripening white, pink or purple – though I have only seen pink. They taste the same as black mulberries, which are red.

Mulberry timber is yellow, turning brown, and said to resemble that of *Robinia*. It has been used for cabinet work and 'takes a good polish' – Elwes.

mulberry at Sudeley Castle

Holm oak

Quercus ilex was a stranger in Gerard's England, 'notwithstanding there is heere and there a tree thereof, that hath beene procured from beyonde the seas; one groweth in hir Maiesties garden of White Hal, neer to the gate that leadeth into the street'. The 1633 edition, added 'Privy' to 'garden'.

The holm oak is perhaps the first foreign tree to have been introduced to Britain for its own sake, and not for its use or associations (imaginary in the case of the sycamore). It has, however, classical associations. A tree in Pliny's Rome was said to have survived from Etruscan time, when it had been a sacred tree. *Q. ilex* is, as Bean says, 'in many respects the finest of all evergreen trees, apart from conifers, cultivated in the British Isles. Its foliage is most abundant, and the branches form heavy dark masses on the tree.'

It has usually a well-shaped, spreading crown, 70 feet high or more. The bark is regularly and distinctively patterned, sometimes black, sometimes a warm brown. The leaves open silvery, then turn through yellow-green to shiny dark green, khaki below, and remain on the tree for several years. Old leaves are often shed in the summer and are offensive to tidy gardeners. But Bean has a remedy for this: grow ivy under the tree.

Holm oaks are common enough not to be remarkable, but they rarely seem to get the space they need to be properly appreciated. They are sometimes planted as windbreaks and as avenues, and can be seen as healthy bushes on southern sea fronts. There are half a dozen cultivated varieties of which 'Fordii', with glossy, narrow, curling leaves, is the most common. The timber of holm oak is harder than ordinary oak, but as durable and more flexible. Evelyn recommended it for stocks of tools, mallet heads, axle trees, wedges, beetles and pins.

holm oak

Oriental plane

The plane, *Platanus orientalis*, also has classical associations. It was planted by the ancients as a shade tree, and cared for lovingly, even fed with wine instead of water, by keen Roman garden owners. Xerxes is supposed to have fallen in love with a plane tree and stopped his mighty army on the march while he stripped his concubines of their jewellery to decorate the tree.

William Turner, who published the relevant part of his *Herball* in 1562, had seen two planes, in Northumberland and at Cambridge. He included the tree in his *Names of Herbes*, 1548: their leaves 'in all poyntes were lyke unto the Italian playn tre. And it is doubtles that these two trees were either brought out of Italy or of some far countre beyond Italy, where unto the freres, monks and chanones went a pilgrimage'. The woodcut in the *Herball* is nearer to a plane than a sycamore, and Turner would have seen both on his travels.

The 'largest tree in the world' in 1831 was a plane by the Bosphorus with a trunk measuring 140 feet in circumference – but this certainly included several subsidiary trunks, one of which was hollowed out to make a cabin for the keeper. Planes easily layer their lower branches.

Oriental planes in this country are to be found in the gardens of grand houses, usually low-branching with massive gnarled trunks. The bark peels in the same way as with the familiar London plane, of which this tree is one parent. The leaves of *P. orientalis* can be very large, but on average are taken to be smaller and more deeply lobed than those of the hybrid.

Gerard's trees

John Gerard's *Herball* is a fine summary of our botanical knowledge in the Tudor period. The author has been criticised often, and not least by the editor of his second edition (1633), Thomas Johnson, for unoriginality and inaccuracy. Most of his (excellent) woodcut illustrations are said to have been taken over from a Frankfurt herbal of 1588, and his text from an English translation of Dodoen's Latin herbal of 1583. Even so, we like him (and since when did you have to be original to be a bestseller?). He is sensible, encyclopaedic, not too short-sighted to include relevant curiosities and not afraid to admit ignorance. Plagiarist though he may be (not unusually so for his time) he still gives us much information from his own experience – often of plants in his own garden. And he writes, throughout his 1392 pages, with bounce and clarity. Like many authors after him, he needed his editor. Johnson's additions are invaluable, but he might have spared us his frequent remarks about 'our author'.

The 'Third Booke of the Historie of Plants' contains the 'Trees, Bushes, Fruit bearing plants, Rosins, Gums, Roses, Heath, Mosses': some Indian plants, etc – and some plants omitted earlier 'for want of perfect instruction, and also being hindered by the slacknesse of the Cutters or Gravers'.

He begins with the rose, which deserves the first place for its beauty, 'vertues' (it has a surprisingly long list of medicinal uses), and its smell; and because it is an English symbol. The roses are: white, red, damask, and one without prickles: musk; with yellow, double yellow and cinnamon: wild roses, which grow in most parts of England. Of the last, the Pimpinell is

Gerard

2 *Rosa rubra.*
The red Rose.

from Gerard's *Herball*

plane tree at Pusey House, Oxfordshire

plentiful at Graies in Essex and in a pasture near a village called Knightsbridge – and in many other places.

Gerard's Oke Tree with his Acornes and Mosse, and his Common Oke with his Apple or Greene Gall are the leaders of a confused tribe, and his conifers are difficult to sort out, after the Great Cedar tree of Libanus, which is clear enough. The cedar does not at this time grow in England, nor does the *Picea* or Pitch Tree. His pines, which all look the same, do not help us much. Only one, *Pinus sativa*, the tame or manured Pine tree, seems to be growing in England. It has sweet kernels: I take this to be an argument for the Roman introduction of *Pinus pinea*, or its later re-introduction. The Firre he has seen growing in Cheshire, Staffordshire and Lancashire. This is interesting, but it's *all* we know. The cypress, obviously *sempervirens*, from Italy, grows in gardens around London. Compact and accented, it was clearly a favourite tree in the formal gardens of Europe.

Then Gerard springs a surprise. He has a specimen of the *Arborvitae*, the American tree of life, growing in his garden. This is *Thuja occidentalis*, the white cedar, from Newfoundland. It had been introduced to France earlier in the century, the first of the many American conifers brought to Europe. Gerard describes the scent of the crushed foliage as an 'aromatick, spicie or gummie savor, very pleasant and comfortable'. Mitchell (1974) says it smells of apples, and Gerard's description suggests the richer aroma of *Thuja plicata*. Gerard's small tree is, he says, easily multiplied by cuttings.

The juniper grew in Kent 'to the stature and bignesse of a faire great tree'.

Arbor Vitæ.
The Tree of Life.

Hedges and bushes

The tamarisk was a Tudor introduction from Germany. It is often regarded as a native, even to the point of splitting *Tamarix anglica* from *T. gallica*; but it is only naturalised on the Sussex and Suffolk coasts. It grew in Gerard's garden: it was an important medicinal plant for disordered livers, or hard spleen.

Tamarisk now is a notable hedging tree of Cornish coastal pastures (and caravan sites). The fresh-coloured feathery foliage is supposedly evergreen, but the trees are sometimes stripped naked in hard winters. The sometimes old, gnarled trunks, supply pieces of very hard wood, and the shoots have been used for weaving lobster pots. The small flowers, in spikes in summer, are of a dull pink, like persicaria.

tamarisk denuded of leaves after a hard winter, Cornwall

Privet, or Prim Print, *Ligustrum*, grows, says Gerard, 'naturally in every wood', and in the hedgerows of London gardens – but Turner had already noticed it in the hedges of Cambridgeshire and 'almost every garden in London'. Privet leaves were of some importance in herbal medicine. Gerard used them to cure 'swellings, apostumations and ulcers of the mouth or throat, being gargarised with the juice or decotion thereof'. London and other town hedges are in our time of the Japanese *L. ovalifolium*; vigorous, but soft-leaved and dull. The native privet, *L. vulgare*, has only a doubtful record from fossil pollen, the only certain identification being from Lincolnshire and after 5000 bp.

Gerard had a mock-privet, or *Phillyrea* in his garden 'found by our industrious Pena in the mountaines neere Narbonne and Montpelier'. It was only a hedge bush. The tree is hardy, certainly in the south, but is still described as infrequent in gardens, in spite of its attractive character. The white and blue Pipe Privet turns out to be *Syringa*, the lilac, growing in his garden in very great plenty.

There follow several obscure bushes, including Mezereum and Spurge Laurel; the first he got from Poland, the second was abundant in the woods in most parts of England – I think he exaggerated here. The Bay or Laurell he 'defended from cold', at the beginning of March especially. 'It cureth them that are black and blew' . . . and the leaves could be eaten, the morning after, by common drunkards. He lists *Laurus Tinus*, and the native box – on sundry waste and barren hills in England. Myrtle he has in no less than six sorts, the last two of these being nourished in the garden of Mistresse Tuggy in Westminster. One of these ought to be butcher's broom by the description. Then there is Sweet Willow, Gaule, or Dutch Myrtle, which grows plentifully in the Isle of Ely – enough for it to be used in faggots for the oven – also by Colebrooke and in sundry other places. I can't find Colebrooke near London, unless it be a tributary of the river Roding at Loughton.

Passing by several lesser shrubs, we find Gerard lists four sorts of Elder, including the cut-leaved variety, which grows in ms garden. The Marsh or Water Elder, which follows, is our Guelder Rose, but this name, Gelders Rose, Gerard gives to the Rose Elder, our snowball tree: 'in my garden there groweth not any fruit upon this tree, nor in any other place, for ought that I can understand' (it is an infertile double-bloomed variety).

snowball tree

From the Near East

Gerard knows the Judas tree well, and it is in his garden, though it must be a recent introduction: its temperature and vertues are unknown. 'The floures come forth in the Spring, before the leaves: the fruit or cods be ripe in Sommer.' It was a hedge plant which 'groweth up into a tree of reasonable bignesse'.

He is confusing about Laburnum – *Anagyris* or stinking Beane Trefoile – but the description is unmistakable, and Master Tradescant has it in his garden. We are rather surprised to learn that the smell of the leaves and flowers annoys passers-by.

There are more exotics which we pass over except for the Bladder Wort, *Pistacium germanicum*, which seems to be grown widely in S. England in Gerard's time. It has no old name, unless it be *Staphylodendron plinii*. It is still called the bladder nut today, and is *Staphylea pinnata* Linnaeus, which I read is naturalised in some parts. It may be found in old gardens as a small tree.

The Hasell, of which he has the Filberd and the wild hedge nut, is of course native, but Gerard also includes the Filberd Nut of Constantinople or small Turkey Nut. This is *Corylus colurna*, which is generally said to have been introduced in the 16th century.

'The Wallnut groweth in fields neere common highwayes, in a fat and fruitfull ground, and in orchards . . . it loveth not to grow in waterie places.' The chestnut grows on mountains and shadowy places, and valleys: it loves a soft black soil. There are sundry woods of chestnuts in England, as a mile and a half from Feversham in Kent. The Horse Chestnut is now growing with Mr Tradescant at South Lambeth – this is Johnson's addition, in 1633.

Turkish hazel nut from Gerard's *Herball*

Fruit trees

Gerard is a useful guide to the Elizabethan orchard. Almonds are in London gardens and orchards, in great plenty. They were perhaps cultivated since Roman times. Of peaches, Gerard has four sorts: white, red, yellow and d'avant. But Johnson adds the names of several choice varieties, which are to be had of his friend Mr Millen in Old Street. The names are poetry, but we must hurry on, mentioning only the Melocotone, the Romane, the Peach du Troy; and Nectarins – Roman red, the bastard red, the little Dainty Green, the yellow, the white and the russet, which is not so good as the rest. There are Great and Lesser Aprecockes, and Johnson's friend can also supply these.

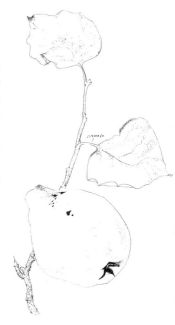

Here is even included the Pomegranat (and the wilde Pomegranat). Gerard has 'recovered' several trees from the seeds: they are three or four cubits high, and he is attending God's leisure for flowers and fruit. He is patient, for there are at least eleven distinct medicinal 'Vertues'.

The quince, *Cydonia*, he knows as *Malus cotonea*, in gardens and orchards, and often planted in hedges – not wild. Miller's *Cydonia oblonga* was based on the variety *pyriformis*, introduced from Portugal by Tradescant in 1611, and it is a much larger fruit than the older form Gerard describes, which however still grows in our orchards as *maliformis*.

quince 'Pyriformis'

As with every plant, Gerard lists foreign names, and one of the Spanish names for quince is *marmellos*. He remarks that marmalade, or 'Cotiniate,' is good for strengthening the stomach, and he gives recipes. In both, the fruit is strained after being softened by boiling, so that the result would be a jelly. Quince jam is better, I think, perhaps too sweet, but aromatic. Gerards adds rose water and a few grains of muske (from the petals of the musk rose?). He recommends the seeds, soaked in water, to make a mucilage or jelly, to take away roughness of the tongue in fevers. It is also a mild laxative, according to the modern herbalist Hans Flück, but separate out the seeds; they contain prussic acid.

The medlar, another fruit rather neglected today, Gerard has in four forms, two of which are recognisable as the orchard medlars of today – particularly the second, a larger fruit with narrow leaves. The woodcut for the 1633 edition exactly corresponds with a neighbour's garden 'Dutch medlar'.

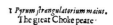

1 Pyrum strangulatorium maius.
The great Choke peare

Johnson dealt savagely with Gerard's pears, pruning the diagrams (which look splendid in a hand-coloured copy at the Bodleian Library) to save a couple of pages. But he kept the original names: Katharine, Jenneting, St James, Royal, Burgomot, Quince pear, Bishop's and Winter pear. John Millen in Old Street could supply them. The wild pears are interesting, very various. The wood Gerard praised for its use in 'many sorts of pretty toies'. The fruits varied from 'austere' in taste to so choking that they were not to be eaten by wild beasts, much less men. Wild pears are now the rarest of our native trees, so that Rackham says there are only five single specimens living in Eastern England. Yet Gerard could identify six types: 1, the great Choke peare tree, 2, the small Choke peare, 3, the wilde hedge Peare, 4, the wilde Crab peare tree, 5, the Lowsie wild peare, 6, and the Crow peare: 'all growing of themselves without manuring, in most places as woods, or in the borders of fields, and neere to high waies ... Their nourishment is little and bad.' Perhaps pears do not coppice well and have all been used up to make 'pretty toies'?

Crabs were of four sorts, which I have mentioned on page 42. Gerard also knew a garden crab tree, *Chamaemalus*, dwarfe apple or Paradise apple, in London gardens. The cultivated apple had already multiplied into so many types that he 'had heard of one that intendeth to write a peculiar volume of apples'. Johnson cut out some pictures, but kept those of the Pome Water and the Bakers Ditch Apple. The fruits of both are curiously shaped, like a pear in reverse. Two others have a familiar name, Pearemaine. A recipe:

> The pulpe of the rosted apples, in number foure or fiue, according to the greatnesse of the Apples, especially of the Pome-water, mixed in a wine quart of faire water, laboured together vntill it come to be as apples and Ale, which wee call Lambes Wooll, and the whole quart drunke last at night, within the space of an houre, doth in one night cure those that pisse by droppes with great anguish and dolour; the strangurie, and all other diseases proceeding of the difficultie of making water; but in twise taking it, it neuer faileth in any: oftentimes there happeneth with the foresaid diseases the Gonorrhæa, or running of the Raines, which it likewise healeth in those persons, but not generally in all; which my selfe haue often proued, and gained thereby both crownes and credit.

Or, as we say, an apple a day keeps the doctor away.

The plums are unsurprising, except that the myrobalan is a 'great tree'. There is an 'almond plum', long, with a cleft down the middle, of a brown red colour and pleasant taste – it sounds familiar. In the cherries he includes a double-flowered variety, bearing fruit, and another 'exceeding double' like a white marigold smelling of hawthorn, with seldom or never any fruit. The Bird's cherry is plentiful in Westmorland and in almost every hedge in Lancashire: a harsh and unpleasant taste. It seems to have gone from Lancashire, these days.

There are several varieties of cherry in London gardens: one, jet black and of a most pleasant taste, as witnesseth Mr Bull, the Queenes Maiesties Clockemaker – 'the tree bearing only one cherry, which he did eate; but myself never tasted of it, at the impression hereof'. Mr Bull might have waited.

Cornus mas, the male Cornel tree, is shown with large oblong fruits. He did not think it grew wild in England. There were some trees in the gardens of such as love rare and dainty plants: he had one or two himself. The dogberry, wild cornel or Gater tree is the dogwood (page 37). The spindle tree or English Prick-timber was common enough. The Black Aller or Butchers Pricke tree, *Frangula*, he knew at Hampstead and in most woods round about London, in particular at a small village called Hornsey, near Islington. Thus Gerard recorded, for the first time in English botany, the alder buckthorn, *Frangula alnus*.

But he carelessly tried to lump in the service tree, *Sorbus domestica* with the wild service, *S. terminalis*; Johnson comments that he has not seen the former wild in any place as yet. And Gerard knew the wayfaring tree at Cobham, Southfleet and Gravesend, on chalky ground, and on the way to Canterbury. Perhaps he gave it its name.

Botany is never brief: we are up to Chapter 109 of Book 3 before the ash is mentioned. It has lost none of its old power with serpents, and can pass on its vigour: the kite keyes 'stirre up bodily lust, especially being poudred with nutmegs and drunke'. The wilde Ash, quicke beame or quicken tree – or wilde service tree, as he admits in the heading to the cut though it remains the classical *ornus*, quite erroneously, in the text – is in most places in England, especially about Namptwich in Cheshire. The name rowan does not occur, at least to this Londoner.

Beech leaves, chewed, are good for sore gums and chapped lips. The birch has no medicinal value. It serves to beautify the streets in the 'crosse or gang weeke'. He finds the hornbeam in Northamptonshire, and in Kent by Gravesend, where it is commonly taken for an elm. The elms themselves come in for a shaking-up from Johnson, who adds a narrow-leaved species discovered by his assistant Goodyer, between Christchurch and Limmington in Hampshire. This was identified by Melville in the 1930s as a native variety of the Cornish elm. Gerard's poplars also are somewhat under-researched, but the pictures are very clear, and include the grey poplar or 'lesser-leaved white'. The white poplar itself he says is not very common, though he found many in a lane at Blackwall, London. The plane has an excellent illustration, as do the maples, great and lesser, but the honour of growing the plane is with Mr Tradescant – 'one or two young ones at this time'.

There remain many exotics which are more or less curiosities – including the banana. We will only note the Lote or Nettle tree (*Celtis australis*) from Italy, now growing in some London gardens, including Gerard's. He also describes several sumach trees, but it seems none of them are yet grown in England. Gerard has, however, a yucca, two small storax trees and some prickly pears, which he calls Indian figs. He, or rather Johnson, gives a picture of a branch from a sassafras tree in Bow.

In the Appendix is included the cherry-bay, *Prunus laurocerasus*, that we call the cherry laurel. It is, he says, 'in many of our choice English gardens, well respected for the beauty of the leaves and their lasting or continuall greenenesse'.

Gerard's lesser-leaved white poplar

Six small trees for Tudor gardens

Laburnum. Gerard's name, Stinking Hop Trefoil, hardly leads one to expect a tree, and one producing fine timber. The name *Laburnum* is a Roman one, but Pliny's description of a tree with white flowers two feet long, and hard, white timber, cannot be our Laburnum. In fact the wood is a rich dark brown within a band of creamy yellow, softer, sapwood. Elwes and Henry (1910) give a footnote suggesting that the timber was known in the time of Edward IV (1442–83) under the name awburne (Scottish *hoburn*) and recommended for longbows – with yew, wych hazel (elm) and ash. So, like the sycamore, it may have a longer history in Scotland than in England. The timber in Scotland seems to have been properly valued in more recent time – 10s 6d per foot in 1909. Large trees have been known, up to 6- or 8-foot girth, and there was even a 4-acre coppice made in 1790 at Ickleton Grange near Cambridge.

Quite rightly, one of our species is called Scotch Laburnum – *L. alpinum*, actually a native of the southern Alps, the Appenines and central Europe. This is the superior laburnum for gardens, with flowers hanging down to 15 inches, denser than those of *L. anagyroides*, also central European, which has smaller leaves on longer stalks and a more thickened pod. (*Anagyris* is a Mediterranean legume.) There are many varieties of these very popular trees, perhaps less popular now the seeds are generally known to be poisonous. Ten seeds have killed a child. A hybrid, *L.* x *watereri*, of the two species, produces seed pods less attractive to young children, with smaller seeds – just as deadly though.

[1560]

The timber is said to creep indefinitely, but I have used it for several small constructions which have a satisfactory air of permanence and a rich quality of surface. The difficulty was in sawing (ripping) when tensions released by the saw produced immediate curves. Perhaps there are secrets of seasoning I know nothing of.

[1560] **Judas tree.** *Cercis siliquastrum* – the name is a classical one, *siliqua* being pod – somehow got the reputation of being the tree Judas hanged himself on: a somewhat more informed choice than the elder which earlier had the honour. Gerard knew it as Arbor Indae, and it may have been *l'arbre de Judse* (Judean tree). It needs protection from frost as a young plant but is worth the trouble: lovely from an early age, well shaped, the prettily rounded leaves becoming transparent peachy pink in autumn. The flowers are pea-like, usually pink, and the pods which follow are up to 5 inches long, persisting through the winter. With all these distinctive characters it is not surprising that *Cercis* appealed to the Elizabethan sense of decoration.

It is said to need a lot of sun, but there is a fine small tree at Benmore, and you will find it in most arboreta and good gardens, and some parks – as, for instance, Golders Park in London. Large trees can be 40 feet high.

Cercis is represented in America and the Far East – a typically discontinuous range which suggests that its original home was not far from Benmore in the Tertiary. The eastern and American trees are redbuds, too tender for Britain. A near relative is the honey-lucust, *Gleditsia*.

[1562] **Bay.** The poet's Laurel is a true laurel, *Laurus nobilis*, not a cherry. It is well known as the bay tree, familiar as a geometrical shape in a tub; but it can be 60 feet tall. Bean (1970) describes 'primaeval' woods, thickets of 50-ft stems on rocky ground at Opatija and Rijeka. (This is one-upmanship.)

To be made into a poet's crown the laurel had to have its berries, hence *baccalaureat*; the *bacca*, berries, are black, the flowers small, round and yellow. Bay is easy to grow from a cutting in S. England, though the leaves are sometimes spoilt in hard winters.

Bay leaves, on the twig, are easily dried and stored. Dried wild thyme and bay, tied together with fresh parsley, make the basic bouquet of French meat cookery, according to Elizabeth David. I would add that a bayleaf can transform the humble fish pie. Sardines used to have a leaf inside the tin.

[1576] **Cherry laurel.** *Prunus laurocerasus* is an evergreen cherry, native of the W. Caucarsus and Asia Minor, and perhaps of Bulgaria. Writers from Evelyn onwards have railed against the pruning of this *Prunus*, wanting to see it as a tree, not a shrub. But it has been planted in many Victorian shrubberies and there it spreads, with a bad reputation for being hungry and unsociable. There are no less than fifteen varieties in Bean's shortlist, and the leaves are naturally variable. There are leathery and 'obscurely toothed', about 4 or 6 inches long: not coarsely serrated like the Portugal Laurel and on yellowish stalks, not crimson. The flowers come in fluffy short spikes, early in the year. The cherries are about ½ inch long.

[1596] **Cornelian cherry.** This dogwood or cornel, *Cornus mas* ('male'), may have been introduced much earlier than the recorded date, for its fruits. These are

Judas tree	laburnum
cherry laurel	bay tree
cornelian cherry	*Phillyrea latifolia*

large and used to be made into syrups, but are now seldom seen. It is planted for the sake of the yellow flowers in February and March, before the leaves, and unique in our grey winters before *Hammamelis* came to compete. It is a small tree. At Kew there is *C. intermedia* which is obviously very close but has made a stout bole, the bark rather shaggy. The timber is very hard – and probably very hard to get.

1597

Phillyrea. I like Evelyn's spelling, Philyrea, much better; and he especially liked this tree, explaining to everyone that it need not be grown indoors. 'The verdure is incomparable; a decoction of the *angustifolia* soveraign for sore throats.' The English name, jasmine box, is rarely used, but it reminds us that this genus is related to jasmine, privet, lilac and olive; all Oleaceae. (Box has a family of its own.) *Phillyrea decora*, *P. latifolia*, and Evelyn's *P. angustifolia* are all Mediterranean, only *latifolia*, with serrated leaves, reaching tree status, the others narrow- and entire-leaved, but all sharing the strict leaf symmetry of the olive and the ash. The trunk of *P. latifolia* ('broad-leaved') is peculiarly attractive, or so I find – the picture expresses it. The bluish-black berry seems to have no traditional uses, but the leaves were crushed for red body-paint, and hair dye in Dioscorides.

P. media, sometimes seen, is really *P. latifolia*, which has several variant forms of leaf, and *P. decora* may be a variant of *P. angustifolia*, sometimes *P. rosemarinifolia* – a greyish sort. I mention them to guard you against the splitters who make labels. Just to be confusing, there is a variety of *P. decora* called 'Latifolia', which is rounder leaved than the type, and a variety of *P. latifolia*, 'Spinosa', which has sharper serrations on a longer leaf. Such permutations are only the signs of centuries of careful cultivation: the names are expressions of love, couched in dog Latin.

[1597]

Lilac. *Syringa vulgaris* is certainly common, so it must be popular. It is never a tree. The colour, lilac, is part of our vocabulary, but lilac flowers can be any colour from white to crimson, and still *vulgaris*. Persian lilac has less heart-shaped, more oval, leaves (there is a 'cut-leaved' variety) and Rouen lilac is a cross which happened in Rouen but duplicated a Chinese species, so it is *L. chinensis*, or, perhaps more suitably, *L. dubia*. The flowers are in longer, drooping spires. The date 1597 probably derives from Gerard.

These small trees, much loved, are the oldest foreign tree inhabitants of the English garden. We must add the Turkish hazel, *Corylus colurna*, introduced in 1582. It is not small, like the native hazel and the filbert, and for much of its life not much to look at. But older trees acquire a rugged trunk and have great sweeping branches which in early spring are hung with long catkins and in autumn covered with the fantastic fruits shown on page 78. The leaves are large. There is a fine tree in the University Parks at Oxford – about halfway down the Norham Gardens side: others at Syon and Edinburgh, and the tallest, 68 feet, is at Brocklesby Park, Limber, Lincolnshire (Mitchell 1974). Leaf prints from the late Tertiary rocks of the Isle of Mull resemble the Turkish hazel.

Turkish hazel, Oxford

detail from Holbein's 'The French Ambassadors' painted in 1533. (National Gallery, London)

9 · New trees from Europe and the Near East

Trees introduced between 1600 and 1650 can be said truly to have changed our landscape. They are all quite familiar, and two, the European larch and the common spruce, have considerable economic importance.

Norway spruce   [1600s]

The indigenous forest of Norway is said to have been of Scots pine, the spruce being a relatively recent immigrant from the south. The range of the Norway spruce, *Picea abies* (spruce fir), is similar to that of Scots pine, across northern Asia and northern and central Europe. This spruce is a very variable tree, both geographically and in micro-habitats at different elevations. It avoids mild, Atlantic winters.

The spruce is mentioned in William Turner's *Names of Herbes*, 1548, but this does not establish its presence in Britain. Turner simply suggests that *Picea*, called 'rotte dan' in Dutch, could be called a 'red firre tree' in English. Gerard, even in the 1633 edition, says nothing about its growing here. Evelyn is thoroughly confusing about firs and spruces but is fairly clear that the best come from Norway and Prussia; 'unless we had more commerce of them from our Plantations in New England, which are preferable to any of them'. Parkinson states that it was found in various parts of Britain (1640). But accounts are all confused.

One aspect of this confusion is the way in which the spruce fir has changed its name since Pliny: it was then PICEA, a pitch tree. Gerard has it as *Picea major* and his woodcut is recognisable. To Evelyn *picea* was the male, *abies* the female of the species. Linnaeus called it *pinus abies* in 1753, then in 1768 it escaped from the pine genus to become *Abies Picea* (fir-spruce); in 1841 it was *Picea excelsa* and from 1881 it has settled down, at least in most works, to *Picea abies*.

Norway spruce at Batsford

It is of course our most familiar spruce because it is the Christmas tree, traditional since Prince Albert. Often it can be seen in suburban gardens where it has survived from the festivities of an earlier year. In good damp soil it can reach 130 feet, so watch out! The roots are shallow and wide-spreading.

The Forestry Commission has about 200,000 acres at a time, and plants a few thousand acres a year. Being a variable tree, *P. abies* has a record number of varieties in cultivation. Unrecognisable dwarf forms have arisen from cuttings of witches' brooms, which form in the branches, as, commonly, with the birch. The weeping form, *pendula*, includes a whole group of varieties, from the natural drooping branches of some wild trees to grotesque cultivars which grow in any direction but upwards.

Home-grown spruce timber was not much valued until well after 1900, though it supplied many needs for boxes, pit-props, posts. Now, we have ways of using low-quality timber – for low-quality houses, and for pulping, making into paper and printing with 90 per cent nonsense before burning it or burying it with the rubbish. A plank from the DIY stores, damp and bleeding from a dozen knots, will cost a good deal more than the 3d or 4d a cubic foot mentioned by Elwes & Henry in 1910 – probably about £3. But it still hardly pays anyone to salvage paper.

High quality European spruce comes from mountain trees which grow slowly, with as many as twelve annual rings to the inch – three or four would be typical of the average deal plank. Such timber, available in long lengths, was imported for ships' masts when the rest of the ship was built of native oak and elm. In our time, spruce has been used to build fighter planes, and many lighter aircraft.

The very best spruce timber, *bois de resonance*, comes from old lichen-covered specimens of *P. abies*, in the Alps, the Jura mountains and others of central Europe. Ever since viols, lutes, citterns, guitars and (later) violins have been made in Europe, and that is since at least 600 years ago, this wood has been used for the fronts – the sounding-boards. Fine-quality spruce is also used for the soundboards inside pianos. Violins, being designed as a permanent unity of curved timbers – spruce against the harder sycamore of the body – keep their tone for centuries. Pianos, whose soundboards gradually slacken, deteriorate.

The fine parallel lines of the spruce grain are clearly visible on the soundboards of stringed instruments. The wood must be knot-free: a log about 3 feet long is split into quarters or eighths, to release the tensions of the tree trunk. Then the cream-coloured, perfectly straight-grained timber is sawn into thin planks, often with considerable waste to achieve perfection.

The sort of wood we buy as deal is any sort of spruce. The frequent irregularly placed knots are the result of the tree's habit of putting out strong side shoots on a radial pattern. In pine, the knots appear less frequently and at regular (annual) intervals. Deal was used for building as early as 1629 in England, but this was almost certainly imported from the water-powered sawmills of Europe, in the form of planks.

Burgundy pitch is the material from which *Picea* gets its name. It was tapped from the trees and used in medicine and in varnishes. Spruce beer was made from the young shoots and leaves. See also page 15.

European larch, New
Forest, November

European larch

It is difficult to imagine Britain without larch, and there is no certain date
for its introduction. It is mentioned by John Parkinson as a rare tree in 1629.
Evelyn was in favour of planting larches, and knew a large one near Chelms-
ford. But the first large plantations were by the Dukes of Atholl around
1800: 10,000 acres by 1832, containing 14 million trees. Three trees supposed to have been planted about 1675 are now about 80 feet high, at Lee
Park, Lanark, but some definitely planted in 1738 are much taller, notably
at Blair Castle, and one planted in 1780 at Ardvorlich, Lochearn, Perthshire,

[1600s]

87

was 139 feet tall in 1961. A famous old tree at Dunkeld Cathedral, planted in 1738, has heavy, buttressed, horizontal limbs, and branches sweeping the ground. Mitchell (1972) describes a great tree at Kelburn, Ayrshire, only 40 feet high but with a 13-ft bole and old, thin branches reaching 30 feet from this, layering (rooting) and throwing up massive new trunks, 6 feet in girth.

As a plantation tree the European larch, *Larix decidua*, suffered from larch canker or die-back, but it has been shown that these trees were of high Alpine stock unadapted to our softer climate. A variety sometimes reckoned as a species, *polonica*, the Polish larch, is now almost extinct in the wild. There is a specimen at Bedgebury and a plot of young trees at Kilmun. The shoots are white, or pale, compared with the type, which has buff-pink shoots. The Dunkeld larch, a hybrid recognised in 1904, tends to yellow and orange: one parent, the Japanese larch (1861), has noticeably red to purple shoots.

Larch is still popular for shelter belts and planting in parkland. It is deciduous and the shrub layer remains rich under young trees. The yield of timber, though it can be of fine quality, is considered low by present day softwood standards, and no one has a use for the trimmings, which neither burn nor pulp easily.

[1616]   ### Horsechestnut

A tree with splendid blossom, then conkers and a good autumn gold, transitory though these pleasures are, clearly has won the hearts of Englishmen. The timber is not much use, and the heavy foliage, the thick, bony winter outline, the sticky fingers, though handsome in their way, are endearing only, I think, through familiarity. There are in winter, too, piles of husky dead leaves, nice to shuffle through but needing to be swept up and burnt.

Aesculus hippocastanum is a Miocene monster whose native home was tracked down only in the 19th century to a narrow, mountainous area of N. Greece and Albania. Here it had survived the Ice Ages, stunted in growth, imprisoned in the valleys. The species was discovered to science in 1576 in Turkey, by the Flemish ambassador at the Court of Suleiman the Magnificent. The ambassador was one Ghislain de Bustecq, who also gave us lilac and tulips. The Turkish soldiers fed the nuts to their horses: but everyone knows that the name comes from the horseshoe signature of the leaf scar.

Castanea Equina, as it was then called, was growing in Tradescant's garden in London in 1633, having been introduced, via Vienna, in 1616. Our suburbs and parks are full of well-grown horsechestnuts, mostly planted in the Edwardian era. They are still being planted, in towns and even villages. Edlin warns that they will not stand pollarding, but they are regularly cut back to knobbly poles in one village I know, and still produce leaves and flowers in profusion. Horsechestnuts appear not to be naturalised anywhere, though conkers germinate easily and young saplings are often seen. Damaged roots sucker abundantly.

The recommended variety, *baumannii*, is double-flowered, a natural sport in the early 19th century. It forms no fruit and therefore escapes injury by small boys. But a horsechestnut tree without conkers is outrageous, I'm sure you'll agree. There are half a dozen other varieties, mostly of different habit from the stately norm, but they do not seem to be popular. One or two with variegated leaves are now rarely seen, says Bean (never by me).

I cut a low branch, on the local common, to make a toy diesel train. I was careful to remove the bark at once, to avoid its staining the wood foxy yellow. The timber, unseasoned, was easy to saw and carve, though inclined to be fluffy here and there. The model has stood up very well to 12 months' vigorous punishment, and with one coat of polyurethane varnish has kept its pale colour. Horsechestnut is not a durable timber, lacking both tannin and resin, but it has been used in the same way as poplar – and in France for *sabots*. It is light and clean-looking. As a fuel it needs to be thoroughly dry.

Aesculin, found in the seed, is a medicine for bovine mastitis and human haemorrhoids. The seeds contain also saponin, and can be used instead of soap, just mashed up in the washing. 75 per cent of the seed is carbohydrate, and conkers are sought out by deer and cows; but pigs, they say, won't touch them.

Aesculus, with species in N. America, India, China and Japan as well as Europe (we shall meet some of them), has the wide, discontinuous distribution of a typical Tertiary tree, suggesting a once-enormous horsechestnut forest in the Northern Hemisphere. Why sticky buds, why such thick twigs, why that horny husk on the nut? (The spikes are not typical of the genus as a whole.) These characters should perhaps tell us something of the climate and the fauna (giant rhinoceros?) of 30 million years ago. But few botanists seem to ask the question 'why', and fewer have the answers.

As for beauty: the giant palmate leaf emerging from a woolly cluster, and the exquisite marking and sheen of a new conker: these are real and very transitory beauties, provoking wonder, but not questions.

[1638] Cedar of Lebanon

No conifer is more recognisable or more domesticated in Britain. Solomon built his temple of cedars out of Lebanon – there was some fir as well for flooring, but we don't know which fir. Hardly an 18th-century country house is without its great cedar, and most of them must have been planted before the massive, sculptured form of old trees was generally known. The combination of Biblical association and mothproof timber was irresistible.

The botanist Rauwolf visited Mount Lebanon in 1574, and climbed to the snowline to view the cedars. He found only twenty-six aged trees and no young ones. The woods had been the home of a Christian sect whose members had allowed their goats to eat everything growing on the ground. But there are still some cedars there. Bean reports that the largest is over 40 feet in girth.

the Childrey cedar and
Lucinda Cook

Cedars grow quickly in Britain, away from their native mountains. The oldest still alive in Britain was one of the first to be planted here. It is at Childrey, near Wantage, in the garden of the Old Rectory. It is supposed to have been planted in 1646 by Dr Pocock, who had been chaplain to the Embassy at Constantinople, and got the living at Childrey in 1642. The bole measured 25 feet in 1906 and is now 25 feet 2 inches.

The tallest (height is not everything with cedars) is at Petworth House: 132 feet. The most accessible for Londoners are probably those at Chiswick House, in a now rather sprawling line behind the lovely Palladian villa. They were planted about 1720.

Cedrus libani timber is pinkish with strong nearly parallel lines. It is lightly scented and was used for clothes chests: it may not be moth proof but it is resistant to decay. Cedar timber used for wooden houses and chalets is likely to be *Thuja plicata* from N. America; cedar for sloops, *Cedrela* from the West Indies. Pencil cedar is *Juniperus virginiana*, or was, before the Virginians cut down all their juniper forests. The timber trade calls any pinkish, scented wood cedar.

[1648] Portugal laurel

Doomed to the shrubbery and the pheasant covert, like the cherry laurel, this laurel is also a cherry, *Prunus lusitanica*. The leaf stalks and shoots are crimson, the leaves large, shiny, leathery, serrated; the flowers creamy, scented, in long spikes in summer; the berries numerous, red turning to purplish black, bitter, poisonous.

Portugal laurel is hardier than cherry laurel and it will grow on chalk. It is said not to be naturalised. In the 17th and 18th centuries it was valued as an evergreen shrub that anyone could grow: now it rather merges in with the dark, dusty leaves of rhododendrons in Victorian shrubberies and plantations.

Portugal laurel has crimson
shoots

Cotinus coggygria, **smoke tree**, **Venetian sumach**, used to be called *Rhus cotinus*, which is a lot easier to pronounce. It is all Greek for 'wild olive smoke tree', or something. It isn't Venetian, particularly, but is native in Europe eastwards to China. Introduced here in 1656, it is a rounded shrub up to 15 feet high – in July a pink cumulo-nimbus gradually turning grey.

Norway maple

[1638]

Our third most important maple after the native *Acer campestre* and the naturalised *A. pseudoplatanus*, this is *A. platanoides*. It is not particularly plane-like except that the leaves are shiny on both sides. The leaves are very sharply pointed on the five lobes whuch often have several smaller divisions, also pointed. The bark is grey, finely textured with a shallow network of lighter, greenish fissures.

Norway maple is very commonly planted and will often seed itself. The yellow, erect flower clusters, in April before the leaves, are attractive, but the gold of autumn is magnificent. There are many ornamental cultivars: one with very sharp, multi-lobed leaves is *dissectum* – this has rougher bark. 'Far too common,' says Mitchell, 'a dark, offensive purple all summer,' is the group dating from the 1930s – 'Crimson King' and others. For some reason our planners seem to feel that urban trees ought not to be green.

The London plane

[1680]

The origin of the London plane is obscure, and it was at first confused with the oriental plane. It is now generally accepted to be a hybrid between the oriental and the American plane or buttonwood, *Platanus occidentalis*. It is correctly named *P. x hispaniola*. This is because the hybrid occurred in Spain – *P. occidentalis* not being hardy in Britain, but introduced into Spain in the 17th century.

The hybrid, also called *P. x acerifolia* and *P. x hybrida*, is not only hardy

London plane

in S. Britain but extremely vigorous. The leaf is less deeply lobed than that of the oriental plane, but, more important, its habit of forming a tall trunk makes it possible as a street tree where its parent, with low spreading form would be quite impossible. In addition the London plane has proved itself able to cope with sooty air and heavily compacted soil. It leafs late, after the smogs, and the leaves, at first downy (and looking as if dusty in May) becomes shiny so that the rain washes them clean. London planes never blow down. The peeling bark, so decorative and clean-looking, probably has nothing to do with resistance to pollution.

London is a heat island, and the planes flourish in the urban warmth. But London planes are not uncommon outside London – in Oxfordshire, at Kings College Cambridge, and notably at Ely, where two great trees, over 100 feet high, near the cathedral, are originals planted in 1680. Two old planes in the grounds of the Bishops Palace are *P. orientalis*. The tallest London plane is at Bryanston, Dorset: 148 feet.

The trees in Berkeley Square are probably the oldest planes in London, with those of Bedford Square a close second. They were planted in 1789. All have great burred boles to support the tall stems. They have perhaps a hundred years more to live: we may hope that in their time Berkeley Square will cease to be a smelly, continuous traffic roundabout, though nothing will restore all its elegance. A friend recently gathered his breakfast of mushrooms in Berkeley Square. Some years before that there was a nightingale, we are told. Before the planes were planted, the dead of the Plague of 1650 were buried there.

Bean claims that there are several strains of plane in London, and who can dispute this? He says that a variety or species *pyramidalis*, introduced from France in 1850 can be seen in Vincent Square, Westminster: also that those on the Thames Embankment are 'nondescripts'.

The timber of the plane is known as lacewood – often this is imported American plane. It has a very beautiful pattern of medullary rays. It is hard, and has been much used by London piano builders for parts of the mechanism.

[1680] Dutch elms

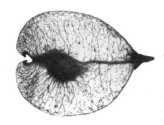

Ulmus x *hollandica*, syn. *U. major*, signifies a group of hybrids between the wych elm and the smooth-leaved elms, said by Mitchell to have been introduced about 1680. The true Dutch elm has a shallow crown supported by several ascending, sinuous branches. There are no burrs on the trunk as there are with *U. procera*, but sucker shoots form along the branches and spring from the roots. The leaves of suckers are rough, resembling the *U. glabra* parent. The best-known variety, the Huntingdon elm, was raised in 1760, but there are many forms of Dutch elm, which according to Melville, the authority on elms, is actually a triple hybrid, also containing a strain of *U. plotti*. This being so it may have arisen naturally, and it does seem to be close to the vigorous, spreading type of Suffolk elm, often pollarded, and forming hedges. Seed or plants may also have been introduced from the continent, where the Dutch elms are the most common, even in the absence, perhaps through natural extinction, of all the parents.

10 · New American trees, 1600–1700

The presence of *Thuja occidentalis*, the Canadian white cedar, in Gerard's garden in 1597 is less surprising when we learn that there were three Eskimaux living in the Palace of Westminster as early as 1504. Bristol fishermen knew their way to Newfoundland, but rarely landed and never wrote about it. Cabot, on 24 June, 1497, landed somewhere in N. America and found a burnt-out fire, tall evergreens: here and there a tree notched or felled. The grass was thick.

Raleigh's settlers in Virginia (so called after his virgin Queen) were actually in what is now N. Carolina. In 1585 they found themselves, had they known it, at the edge of the great Eastern Forest of N. America, an enormous area of deciduous woodlands 800 miles wide and stretching from the St Lawrence in the north to Louisiana in the south. It was and had been since 8000 BC the home of 'Indians'. In the immediate neighbourhood were the Susquehama, Pamunkey, Nanticoke, Powhatan, Tutelo, Pamlico, Nottaway, Catawba, Cherokee, Creek, Choctaw and others (I like the names). The Indians were not too numerous, not aggressive, and seem to have lived at one with their natural surroundings, even to the point of formally asking the deers' permission before they aimed their arrows, and punishing members of the tribe who ignored this rule.

The trees in this southern part of the Woodlands were oaks, hickories, elms, maples, chestnut, sweetgum, plane and tulip tree. Only one of these, hickory, is an Indian name: at first it was pohickory. The settlers came to call the American plane the sycamore, and the tulip tree was thought to be a poplar: these were among the largest trees in the forest. A common tree of the seaboard was the sassafras, its name a corruption of the herbalists' saxifrage.

To the south, on the wide sandy plain of the shore to Florida was an evergreen forest of exotic pines, survivors there from before the Ice Ages of the north: pond pine, longleaf, shortleaf, slash and loblolly pine; and evergreen oaks hung with 'Spanish moss'. Further south were sand pine, palmetto and swamp cypress down to the Everglades.

Inland was a band of the more northerly hardwood/hemlock forest along the line of the Appalachians; with birches, maples, beech, oaks, *Robinia* and eastern white pine (*P. strobus*).

The colonists of 1585 fortified themselves at Roanoke and gradually made enemies of the Indians. An expedition to the interior found the English deserted and short of rations. After raiding the fish traps in the river they were forced to stew their mastiffs, with sassafras. They seem to have been unable to shoot their food, perhaps keeping their powder for threatening the Indians. They were incurious and lazy; except for John White the artist, and Thomas Hariot the scientist, they were soldiers and gentlefolk. They withdrew, with the help of Sir Francis Drake, who happened by. One of his sailors wrote that Virginia was only good for fish, land turtles, nice fruits and 'saxifrage'. The Indians, who had at first been courteous, 'refused obedience to her Majesty'.

A further band of 108 colonists set out in 1587, landed, waited two years for supplies, then vanished. But expeditions to Virginia and Massachusetts continued, as we know.

Sassafras

Pocahontas, daughter of the Powhatan chief, was brought to London in 1616 by her husband, John Rolfe, who produced the first Virginia tobacco. Sassafras probably came to England as a living plant at the same time – and was growing in a garden in Bow by 1633 (Gerard). The sweet-smelling wood had been collected by expeditions to America in 1602 and 1610. It was believed to cure many human ills, including syphilis, and to 'remove the impediments that doe cause barrennesse' in women. Sassafras tea, called saloop, was still sold in London cafés in the early 1900s, supposed to cure gout and 'clarify the blood'.

The sassafras is more remarkable for its variety of leaf shape than for curing anything. A yellow powder from the leaf is used to flavour and thicken traditional sauces and soups in Louisiana – this was learnt from the Choctaw Indians. A coarse scent comes from the root-bark and the fruit. Oil of Sassafras finds its way into American 'effervescent drinks' (*A Modern Herbal*, 1976) and a spoonful can cause stupor and collapse. But these trees are rare in England. They are frost hardy but slow to grow from seed and difficult to germinate.

Sassafras albidum, synonyms *Laurus sassafras, S. varifolium, S. officinale*, is of the laurel family. Two other species are known, in China and Taiwan, almost indistinguishable from their American brother. Various extinct species are found as N. American and European fossils of the Tertiary. The Indians, the original believers in its curative powers, called it *Pavane*, and Gerard christened it the Ague Tree.

The variously lobed leaves are pale green with yellow-pink stalks in young trees and dark green, less lobed and with red stalks in older trees. The midrib is white, hence *albidum*. The twig remains green for several years. The leaves smell of oranges and vanilla, according to Mitchell (1974), and turn pinky-yellow, orange and red in autumn: it is a deciduous laurel. The flowers, without petals, in June, are yellow, and the fruits dark blue berries in scarlet cups. The bark is grey or purplish in England, red-brown in America, in

Pocahontas at St George's, Gravesend

sassafras, from the 1633 edition of Gerard

94

broad, broken ridges. The timber, permanently scented, has orange-brown heartwood. It is not very strong, but is used for cheap furniture, and, being resistant to decay, for fence posts.

Well-grown trees are broadly conic and rounded in outline. From 90 feet tall to merely shrubby, it grows along the East Coast of America from Florida to Maine and inland as far as Texas and Michigan, on rich sandy soils at woodland edges. It was perhaps the first American deciduous tree to be introduced into Britain.

Rhus typhina, **Stag's horn sumach**, succeeds remarkably well in some of the murkiest London suburbs, says Bean in 1914, and in 1976 – are they still so murky? It looks even better in the many cottage gardens where it has had a home since the early 17th century. The leaf stalk is downy like the young antlers of stags, the leaflets very regularly arranged and often hanging: they colour to rich reds in autumn. Sumachs coppice very easily and then produce very large leaves. This is a native of eastern N. America. There is a beautiful cut-leaved form, a cultivar, 'Dissecta'.

Tulip tree

Equally remarkable in leaf shape is the tulip tree of the Eastern Woodlands, which grew in vast stands of tall trees, up to 190 feet. Like the sassafras the tulip tree has a Chinese counterpart and a rich fossil history. It is closely related to the magnolias but is called *Liriodendron tulipifera*. The flowers are greenish yellow and tulip-shaped, the seeds held in a shaggy, erect oval fruit. Leaves and fruit are all rich, deep yellow in autumn.

A large tree, 95 feet high in 1745, grew at Waltham Abbey, and this must have been over 100 years old, so the tree may well have been planted in the early 1600s at about the same time as the sassafras. Tulip trees are very popular and can be found on the lawns of grand houses all over the southern half of England; not commonly in Scotland or Ireland. One at Stourhead, Wiltshire, is 118 feet high.

Evelyn described the tulip tree in his *Sylva*, 1664: 'They have a poplar in Virginia of a very peculiar shap'd leaf, as if the point of it were cut off, which grows very well with the curious amongst us to a considerable stature. I conceive it was first brought over by John Tradescant. . . .' It is still the yellow poplar in America, the timber also called whitewood, and of great economic value. Trunks may be 100 feet by 10 feet diameter. It grows particularly strongly in the Alleghenies, but is found from Nova Scotia to Florida.

tulip tree leaves

Robinia, locust tree or false acacia

Robinia pseudacacia is one of the most familiar American trees in Europe, in streets and gardens, by railway banks in France and, less well known, in very large Hungarian coppices and on sands reclaimed from the Danube estuary. It is of the pea family, like laburnum, but with white flowers; and very unlike in the bark, which in quite young trees is ridged and furrowed in a unique diagonal pattern, as of gothic tracery. The foliage is feathery looking, about fifteen fragile leaflets, roughly opposite, on each 8-inch-long

Robinia at Hatfield House

leaf, arranged alternately on the shoot. Vigorous shoots are often armed with strong thorns. John Tradescant II, who visited America three times in the first half of the 17th century, certainly grew this tree, and his father, a subscriber to the Virginia Company, may have had it in the early 1630s. The name *Robinia* is from a Parisian gardener, Vespasien Robin.

A later American visitor, William Cobbett in the early 19th century, conceived a great enthusiasm for this species. It is fast growing – it would make hop-poles in six or seven years – and he even recommended it instead of oak. He created a demand which outstripped the supply of seeds he had prudently imported. *Robinias* are vigorous, and often naturalised locally in good sandy soil, but the timber in Britain never realised its expected reputation. Many seedlings were eaten by rabbits, who specially like them.

The wood is very resistant to decay and will last eighty years in the ground as fence posts. It was important for tree nails – wooden pins used in timber ships – because it would not shrink. Being as strong as oak and as resilient as ash it had a high reputation in Europe for agricultural implements and wheel spokes. It is greenish yellow when first cut, but soon turns golden brown.

A variety with specially durable wood is the shipmast locust, var. *rectissima*, and there are many garden varieties of unusual form, or with differently shaped and coloured leaflets. The variety *tortuosa* emphasises a natural angularity which makes all *Robinias* easy to recognise in winter.

At least one London street, John Street, next to Grays Inn Road, is lined with these pretty trees, and there are of course many Acacia Avenues, not all containing false acacias. There is at least one very old tree at Hatfield House, Hertfordshire, and a considerable plantation of various *Robinia* species and varieties at Kew. The native range of the black locust is from the Midwest to the East Coast.

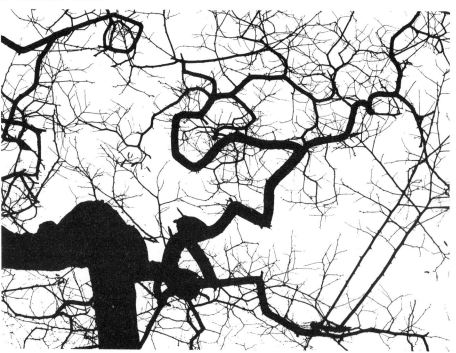
Robinia, in winter

96

Swamp cypress

A native of Mississippi and Missouri, and from Florida north to Delaware, the swamp or bald cypress *Taxodium distichum* is a member of the Sequoia family of conifers, Taxodiaceae, which includes the big trees and the red-woods of California. *Distichum* means two-rowed: *Taxodium* is a very large genus of Tertiary, and earlier, Northern Hemisphere trees, now restricted as a genus to the swamps and riversides of southeast N. America. This *Taxodium*, and, rare in Britain *T. ascendens*, the pond cypress, are deciduous, the fine leaves, often a beautiful warm red, diffused like smoke in autumn. *T. distichum* makes a tall tree commonly seen by ponds in grand gardens – but it will grow away from water. In the swamps of its native home the roots branch out horizontally in the mud, then shoot vertically downwards and often upwards as well, making a sort of podium, with ventilation shafts. Old trees also form massive buttresses. The leaves are more or less alternate on more or less alternate shoots, and this distinguishes the tree from the now more popular dawn redwood.

The timber of the bald cypress is called cypress and is highly resistant. Timber of the real cypress and *Chamaecyparis* seems to be called white cedar. Pecky cypress, especially valuable, comes from *Taxodium* trees that have been infected with a non-malignant fungus, which causes decorative streaks in the wood, but dies with the tree.

swamp cypress at Kew

Juniperus virginiana

This tall-tree juniper and the similar *J. chinensis* are those most commonly planted in this country, usually in some cultivar form. The foliage of *chinensis* smells catty (more or less), that of *virginiana* of paint or soap, that of common juniper of apple – so says Mitchell, who has a very sensitive nose. Usually they are seen as small trees: and the American *virginiana* or eastern red-cedar is typical of many trees that are moderate-sized and decorative here, but important forest and timber trees at home.

The red-cedar (note the hyphen; the western red cedar is *Thuja plicata* and the eastern red-cedar another juniper, *occidentalis*) is known in Britain as the pencil cedar, not always pencil-shaped, but one of the best trees for making old-fashioned pencils. The soft pink wood is now likely to come from a mighty juniper of E. Africa, *J. procera*. The pencil cedar is now scarce in the eastern states, where it may grow to 100 feet, a tall rough pyramid.

Evelyn knew junipers from Jamaica, Bermuda, Carolina and Virginia, and 1664, the date often given, is obviously rather late for the introduction of *J. virginiana*. It was probably brought by John Tradescant II.

Box elder

Neither box nor elder of course, but the name came naturally to the Pilgrim Fathers, who probably found the tree commonly small – and perhaps the wood was more suitable for making boxes than the hated elder. We too know it as a small tree, but it can be large, even in England. It was growing in Bishop Compton's garden at Fulham in 1688, and in 1809 it was still there, its trunk 7 feet in circumference.

box elder in flower, Alderney Gardens, Northolt

Acer negundo is a sugar-yielding maple in America, where it grows more widely than any other maple – and there are many. It is found from the Rockies to New York, by rivers of the prairies, and down to the Mississippi valley, but is rare east of the Alleghenies.

A. negundo is sufficiently unlike a maple to have been called *Negundo fraxinifolium* – ash-leaved maple is a better English name – and the species is dioecious, unlike other maples (i.e. it needs a mate). The three or five separate leaflets correspond to the lobes of most other maple leaves, and have jagged serrations quite unlike the ash.

Commonly planted in suburban streets is the cultivar 'Variegatum', a female clone, which has leaves white-margined, sometimes wholly white or cream. Flowers of this form are pink – on the type they are yellow-green, touched with pink. The wings of the seeds are acutely curved together.

[1656]

red maple, x ½. Some leaves have only three main lobes

Red maple, *Acer rubrum*

In America it is famous for its red colour in the fall – less reliable here – but is *rubrum* because its flowers are red, even forming red fruit before the leaves are out. It is a large, handsome tree, to be seen in specialised gardens, but sometimes in small ones and churchyards. The leaves are pale beneath, often only three-lobed, and somewhat narrow compared with the similar but more deeply lobed leaf of *A. saccharinum*, the silver maple. The bark is light grey, especially on younger trees.

It was introduced by John Tradescent II. The red or swamp maple is an important timber tree. With the silver maple its timber is classified as soft maple, against the equally important hard maples, the sugar and the black. All grow up to 120 feet high and 15 feet girth and are widely distributed in the eastern states which used to be the forest of the Woodlands Indians.

Honey locust

Gleditsia triacanthos, three-thorned acacia, is at its largest in damp valleys of S. Indiana and Illinois, where it was once a giant of the forest at 140 feet or more. It is widely distributed in the Eastern Woodlands as far as the east sides of the Alleghenies. It grew in Bishop Compton's garden, and is now very occasional in eastern and southern gardens, though I have heard of its being planted in Sussex as a fast-growing timber tree. The timber is hard, heavy and durable. The 'three thorns', triple spines of formidable sharpness, emerge from the trunk as well as from the shoots – effective armament against animals tempted to the tender leaves, which are like those of *Robinia* but smaller and lighter. The effect from a distance is feathery. The bark is black or purplish, the thorns unmistakable but not always present on cultivars. The twisted pods, containing 'honey', rarely ripen in England.

Linnaeus named the genus after Gleditsch, a botanist of Jena, a contemporary of his, later Director of the Berlin Botanic Garden.

Gleditsia triacanthos

[1681]

Sweet gum

The sweet gum, *Liquidambar styraciflua*, was disovered as a Mexican tree by a Spanish naturalist of Rome, but was sent to Bishop Compton by John

Banister, a missionary to Virginia. Henry Compton was Bishop of London and head of the church for the American colonies, best remembered for cultivating his garden at home – as Banister is remembered for his *Plants observed by me in Virginia*, the first American flora in English. The great American botanist-explorer, John Bartram, did not start collecting until 1734.

The leaves of the sweet gum, superficially maple-like, are alternate, regularly serrated, smell of 'lemon soap' and turn to brilliant colours, patchily over the tree, in autumn. It is for its colours that it is planted in Britain. The fruits, pretty bobbles with curly spikes, are rarely seen. But great trees of sweet gum, with tupelo, maple and oaks, grew in the original Eastern Woodlands: not only tall, but with trunks clear of branches to 80 or 90 feet above ground and 12 feet in girth. Temperate deciduous trees of these proportions are not likely to be seen again in the wild. The range extends from Connecticut to Florida and Texas, with further stands in Mexico and Guatamala. Here, in warm, drier regions, the leaves are downy below, and often only three-pointed. The timber is red gum at home, satin walnut in Europe – not satinwood. True satinwood, from two subtropical species, is a rare wood, dense and yellow. The rather poor sapwood of *Liquidambar* used to be sold in Europe as 'hazel pine'. Red gum has little resistance to fungal decay and is avoided for construction work, but is used for everything else, including plywood and pulping. The specific, *styraciflua*, refers to a balsam or resin extracted from the inner bark and resembling the incense from *Styrax* species. This sweet gum was a cough medicine, a cure for dysentery, or, mixed with lard, an ointment for children's ringworms. It smells of vanilla, and is still used in the S. E. states for manufacturing adhesives and perfumes.

sweet gum at Pusey

[1629–1689]

Hickory

One of the earliest American trees in Britain was the shagbark hickory, according to Loudon. The hickories were at first confused, quite naturally, with walnuts, and with each other. *Carya* is a Greek name for walnut. The shagbark is *Carya ovata*, from the shape of the nut, though the other hickories, discovered later, also have oval nuts.

The spectacular flaking bark of *C. ovata* is not too easy to glimpse in Britain, and none of the genus is very commonly planted. There is difficulty in transplanting saplings, because of their long taproots. But seeds can be germinated with slight warmth in spring and planted out in May. 'There is scarcely any young tree more striking,' says Bean, with the enthusiasm he endearingly transfers to any species he discusses. The giant (14 inches plus) leaves, in some species sweet smelling, certainly justify the place of *Carya* in large gardens.

The bitternut, *C. cordiformis*, is the hardiest, introduced in 1689. It is more often seen than *ovata* and *tomentosa*, the mockernut. Two others with familiar American names are the pignut and the big shellbark hickory or kingnut. The pecan, the nutmeg hickory and the water hickory are rare indeed, natives of the warm S. E. states. The red hickory, variable and merging with others of the genus, has the widest range, from New York or Florida. This is *C. ovalis*, also called sweet pignut; it has not achieved a 'stable taxonomic position' (it may be a hybrid), but you can eat the nuts.

Carya ovata, 'shagbark'

99

scarlet oak

Some of the nuts of *Carya* species are more edible than others, and the names describe them. The timbers are variable too, but apart from the large amounts that have been burnt – it is the favourite wood for smoking foods –hickory has been to the American settler everything that ash has been to the British farmer over centuries. It made the wheels of pioneering wagons, the stocks of axes to clear the wood and the tools to till those virgin soils.

The best hickory, still imported for axe hafts, is tougher than the best ash. It is recognisable by the coarse streaks in the grain – the redder heartwood is just as good. Hickory coppices produced the dog's-leg hickory hafts that distinguish the elegantly ergonomic American felling axe from the old British type with straight ash stock. By the early years of this century, hickory was no longer abundant. Supplies hardly kept pace with the demand from the carriage-building industry at Chicago.

The shagbark hickory grew to legendary heights in the Alleghenies, in Ohio and Indiana: trees of 130 feet were not rare. Its range extends north to Lake Eyrie and the St Lawrence. Bitternuts, also somewhat northern in their native distribution, are to be found in England up to 85 feet tall, with shagbark hickories not much less.

Carya was thought to be extant only in America until, in 1915, a Chinese hickory was discovered.

Scarlet oak

'There is in New England a certain red-oak, which being fell'd, they season in some moist and muddy place, which branches into very curious works' – Evelyn 1664. How different a picture that suggests from that of the hapless Virginian settlers of a century before! The scarlet oak was introduced to Britain at least by 1691 and, next to the red oak, which came from Canada in 1724, is the American oak most commonly planted here. Both have large leaves and smooth grey bark, and some red oaks have leaves rather similar to the (also variable) scarlet oak. The textures of the leaves are different: the scarlet is shiny on both sides, while the red, more stoutly shaped generally and larger, has matt leaves, greyish below. The also similar black and pin oaks, less common here, make identifying an isolated tree hazardous.

Scarlet oaks, *Quercus coccinea*, are generally rather smaller and more open than red oaks, but 70 to 80 feet is a common size in most of the great parks and arboreta of S. England. The leaves remain until November or December, colouring deep red unless released by early frost. The red oak, *Q. rubra* or *borealis*, grows quickly and forms a big, heavy crown: it has reached 100 feet at Cassiobury Park, Herts, and 110 feet at West Dean, Sussex. The largest American trees appear to be 70 feet, those of *Q. coccinea* 80 feet.

Scarlet oaks are found from Maine to Florida and W. to Missouri, red oaks (*borealis* = northern) from Nova Scotia to Texas. American oaks are a study in themselves: they are divided, perhaps conveniently, into white and black. White oaks, some of which are 'live oaks' – i.e. evergreen – have leaves whose leaves are not sharply pointed and acorns which ripen in one year, though both these conditions do not always apply. Black oaks, which include the red and scarlet, have spined lobes and two-year acorns.

All have fine, hard timber, except the common eastern black oak, *Q. velutina* and the Californian black oak charmingly named *Q. kelloggii*, which

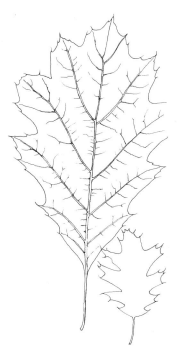

red oak

has acorns up to 1½ inches long. These two timbers are only used for fuel, or so I read. The American oak I should most like to see is the live oak, *Q. virginiana*, branching low, spreading wide, up to 150 feet, and hung all over with great fronds of moss.

Crataegus crus-galli, **cockspur thorn** (*crus-galli* apparently meaning a cock's spur) is a small hawthorn of eastern N. America not wildly different from the English midland hawthorn. The leaves are pear shaped and turn orange in autumn, and the fruit is fractionally longer than the common haw.

Canadian spruces

The **white spruce**, *Picea glauca*, which covers vast tracts of land and grows further north than any other evergreen and from Labrador to Alaska, down the eastern side of the Rockies and in New York and Michigan, was introduced to Britain nearly three centuries ago. But it has not been widely planted and older specimens have died. There are some at Bedgebury, Bicton and Crarae and other British arboreta. It has become a useful tree, however, on the North Sea coast of Denmark. The foliage has a catty smell, and in this is resembles *P. engelmannii*, at its largest in British Columbia and native to New Mexico and lands in between. This is a tree of excellent conical shape. The finest specimens here are at Dawyck, where it was introduced in 1902. Other spruces, very important in N. America but not at all commonly planted here are the **black spruce**, *P. mariana* (70 feet at Rhinefield) and the **red spruce**, *P. rubens* (Rhinefield, Bedgebury, Wakehurst, Bicton). Both these were introduced in the 18th century and both are widely distributed in eastern North America.

Eastern white pine

The handsome, tall, 5-needle *Pinus strobus* was a prolific source of lumber to the settlers in N. America. The 'white' refers to the greyish green of the foliage. Large timber is now scarce, but the species is planted for forestry in America and Europe. It was brought to Britain early in the 18th century and was enthusiastically planted by Lord Weymouth at Longleat: 'Weymouth pine' (*Pin du Lord* in France). Blister rust kills many old trees.

cockspur thorn

American States and officially adopted trees. Alaska has the Sitka spruce and Hawaii the candlenut

11 · 18th-century introductions

John Evelyn's *Sylva* of 1664, with all its intertwined learnedness and enthusiasm, was originally prefaced by an appeal to the patriotism of English gentlemen: to grow timber, to replenish our 'wooden walls'. To pay their debts landowners had been tempted 'not only to fell and cut down but utterly to extirpate, demolish and raze all those goodly woods and forests which our more prudent ancestors left standing for the ornament and service of their country'. Note the coupling of 'ornament and service'.

Evelyn was a royalist and a courtier of Charles II, who was crowned in 1661. In that year the 41-year-old Evelyn had written an invective against French clothes, which was followed by a royal proscription. He was one of the commissioners for reforming building, streets and hackney carriages in the City, and also sat on commissions for sewers and for the Mint. After Evelyn's report on tree planting to the Royal Society the King visited him at home. *Sylva* became a best-seller – though the printer made all the profits.

While Evelyn included many lesser-known trees, sometimes with strong recommendations for planting them, he treated as the primary choice the native timber trees: oak, elm, beech, ash, in that order, with the well-established aliens, chestnut and walnut. Lime was amongst his 'lesser species', and his 'Aquaticals' were poplars and aspen, alder and willows. He never gives the impression that a choice need be made between profit and pleasure – all the trees have their places.

The early 18th century was the time when English parks began to be laid out. Addison, in 1699, had written in praise of 'savage prospects' he saw at Fontainebleu. 'The horrid graces of the wilderness' supplied a magnificence beyond the formal mockery of princely gardens, wrote the Earl of Shaftesbury. Interlacing avenues and formal *parterres* in knot patterns were out. They had never really fitted in with the quirky undulations of the English ground. 'The English did not dine or entertain or parade outdoors; they did not want to stride up and down interminable avenues on a gusty afternoon' (Hugh Prince, 1967). Many parks were remodelled and often much enlarged by enclosing further waste lands – rarely it seems, encroaching on good arable. The horseback tourists of England, Celia Fiennes, Daniel Defoe, John Aubrey, observed a wonderful alteration, particularly in the home counties. Winding walks, serpentine lakes, cascades, grottoes, eyecatchers, clumps, belt plantations 'and other apparatus', were arranged in perspectives of light and shade, with classical temples, colonnades and obelisks to terminate vistas. The idea of imposing a strict geometrical plan was completely rejected by 1720. But many great avenues survive – they were tolerated, particularly for the main carriage drives: they were imposing and, since they kept the weather off, functional. To plant them, hybrid limes and Dutch elms were fashionable and available in quantities that could be expected to be uniform in growth. Oaks had their place in the open pastures which, stocked with deer or fine herds, became the epitome of English parkland.

Richmond Park oaks

But side by side with this demand for standard trees was a growing enthusiasm for new species. Miles Hadfield notes that Loudon in the early 1800s visited a model farm laid out a century earlier at Wooburn, Surrey. He found one of the largest liquidambar trees in England, a remarkably fine hemlock spruce, very large tulip trees, acacias (*Robinia pseudacacia*), hickories, pines, cedars and cypresses, and a magnificent cut-leaved alder. At Painshill, started two years later than Wooburn, he saw fine silver cedars, pinasters and other pines, American oaks, cork trees and ilex, a tupelo tree, tulip trees, acacias, deciduous cypress, Lombardy and other poplars. At Bowood, the Marquess of Lansdowne planted every kind of foreign tree that could be procured.

Such collections were daring and ambitious in the early 18th century, when few of the species mentioned had been tried. Indeed the 'silver cedar' – and Loudon was a great authority, so he would not use the name loosely – is not supposed to have been introduced at all in the 18th century.

Besides these exotic trees of the pleasure ground, spruce, pine and larch returned to the English landscape in large plantations as well as specimen trees. Sycamore, not now very typical of the landscaped park, seems to have been planted widely in the early 18th century.

While the aim of the famous landscape gardeners such as Kent and Brown was to recreate the painted 'classical' landscapes of Salvator Rosa and Poussin, Hugh Prince notes that often 'income derived from the sale of park timber, 1760 to 1880, was greater than the rent received from an equivalent acreage of farmland'. 'Ornament and service' were combined in a typically English way.

Parks were of course only a fraction of the total land area, but they could be quite a large fraction, as the map shows. Change and improvement were widespread in farming too, and the many new enclosures got the benefit of the educated landlord's ideas, so that new hedges, usually of hawthorn, were planted, with timber trees, in the pattern which has become our familiar lowland countryside. Thousands of copses and clumps of trees which now seem natural features originated as eyecatchers and ornaments, being visible through the judicious gaps in park plantations.

There were, in the early 18th century, still many large heaths and swamps, now dwindled into rare and valuable conservation areas. And in spite of the fears of the Restoration naval authorities, there were large areas of woodland, not perhaps easily accessible to the shipyards. Defoe noted that 'Kent, Sussex and Hampshire were one inexhaustible storehouse of timber never to be destroyed'. But the Royal Society of Arts offered prizes to encourage the planting of oak, chestnut, elm, pine and larch between 1757 and 1775. And Defoe, in 1720, noted waste, barren, desolate uplands in Derbyshire, Cumberland, Westmorland, Northumberland, W. Durham, W. Yorkshire and contiguous parts of Lancashire.

A survey of 1696 estimated land use, unfortunately, as Darby points out, arriving at a total greater than the actual 37.3 million acres of England and Wales:

Arable 11	Barren lands 10
Pasture and meadow 10	Houses etc 1
Woods and coppices 3	Wetlands 1
Forests, parks, common 3	

the cork oak, *Quercus cerris*, was introduced in the early 18th century or before, its bark for decoration rather than use

Parks in S. Buckinghamshire, surveyed in 1824. From H. C. Darby, *A New Historical Geography of England*

Lombardy poplars by the serpentine lake at Blenheim Park. This variety, *italica*, the black popular was not known before the 18th century: in Britain 1758

The 18th-century tree introductions are a rich and an impressive group of trees and bushes. With the addition of a handful of conifers from the west coast of N. America, discovered in the following century, they form the basis of many a large collection. It makes a long chapter.

Copper beech

Probably the best known decorative form of any tree, and certainly of the many varieties of the common beech, *Fagus sylvatica*, was discovered in Switzerland and recorded in 1680. There are even varieties of the variety – the copper, or properly purple beech, var. *cuprea*, is only one. Var. *purpurea* was in cultivation in Britain later in the 18th century, sometimes referred to contemporaneously as the American purple leaved beech: but this was some obscure error. Similar varieties may have originated in several places. The one known as *purpurea riversii*, from about 1870, a superior dark red, is the only one, says Mitchell, 'that can be occasionally excused'. All the same, that coppery tinge of all the shades of purple beeches, seen against sunlight, is permanently fascinating.

clump of purple beeches. 'From *clumps* we naturally proceed to *park scenery,* which is generally composed of *combinations of clumps*' – William Gilpin 1791

Fraxinus ornus, manna ash or flowering ash

This species reached Enfield, Middlesex, England in 1710, or Britain generally before that, according to different authorities. A native of S. European mountains, and of Asia Minor, it is planted here as the flowering ash, because of its splendid creamy, scented flowers in May to June. But the name manna ash is not an empty fancy. This is an important fodder and small timber tree in its native lands of S.E. Europe and is grown in large coppices where, at about eight years old, the shoots are lacerated and tapped, producing for a dozen summers a clear sap which solidifies into sweet (but not sugary) flakes or (inferior) syrup. As a medicine containing a sweet flavour, mild laxative properties and a Biblical name it has been very popular for children in Latin America and Italy. In the latter country its purity was controlled by law in 1927.

Do not confuse the prickly ash or toothache tree, a yellow-wood species in N. America (the bark was chewed for toothache). The name is given also to the prickly elder or angelica tree, *Aralia spinosa*. The wafer ash, swamp dogwood or hop tree is another American small tree *Ptelea trifoliata*, whose bark is a tonic. It was introduced to Britain in 1704. Perhaps the bitter, elm-like winged fruits, produced in great quantities, were used as a substitute for hops in early America. A most attractive quality of this tree is the heavy, musky scent which comes from the whole tree. For me, to sit by a *Ptelea* on a warm afternoon is bliss. Clearly the name ash for these small trees derives from the reputation of the common ash, whose sap was life-giving and whose bark was traditionally used to treat fevers.

Fraximus ornus in our parks is lovely, but often less than ornamental in winter. The trunk and branches, with smooth, dark bark often wrinkled like loose skin, are prone to knuckles and contortions – perhaps cringing from generations of manna-tappers. The tree is often grafted on to a common ash stock, which doesn't help its appearance at all, the bole of the flowering ash being often twice as thick as the common ash stem on which it grows.

Fraxinus ornus in winter

Ptelea fruits, actual size

Hop hornbeam

Ostrya carpinifolia, and *O. virginiana*, introduced in 1692 to Bishop Compton's garden, are closely related to the hornbeam but have hop-like, greeny

hop hornbeam

white clusters of scale-shaped bladders, enclosing nutlets. The leaves are darker and larger than those of the hornbeam, with up to fifteen pairs of veins. The bark is rough. There are seven or more species of *Ostrya* in a north-temperate discontinuous distribution of the pattern familiar for so many trees. *O. carpinifolia* ('hornbeam-leaved') is from the Caucasus and S. Europe. The Virginian hop hornbeam is called ironwood. It can be 60 feet high, W. Ontario to Texas. Neither of these trees is very commonly planted in Britain, but they both ought to be. Two trees of *O. carpinifolia* were recorded by Elwes as growing on the bank of the stream at Glasnevin, Dublin's Botanic Garden. They were narrow pyramids about 30 feet high. I wonder, are they still there?

[1726]

Indian bean

catalpa flowers

This southeast N. American tree, *Catalpa bignonioides*, with very large leaves and very long 'bean' pods is popular in the towns and parks of S. England. It has magnificent massed trumpets of white flowers, spotted yellow and purple, in July, when the leaves, which open late, are still fresh green. The shape of the tree is rounded and spreading. *Bignonioides* refers to the trumpet plants of Bignoniaceae. Trees commonly live only 50 to 100 years in England. They need warmth, and there are several well-known *Catalpas* in central London. One, in St James's, Piccadilly, churchyard, must be our most urbanised tree, and there are others of Palace Yard, Westminster, and in all the parks. Kew has many. The tallest, 60 feet, is probably one at Batsford. In Oxford University Parks there is a row of *Catalpa* trees, but these are *C. speciosa*. Market Harborough town centre has a *Catalpa* – further north they are rare. The timber is said to be extraordinarily durable underground.

Fossils from the Oligocene have been found in the Isle of Wight, and there are, as you might expect, oriental survivors as well as American.

The *Catalpa* was introduced from the Mississippi Valley to Virginia and thence to Britain by Mark Catesby. He was a Suffolk gentleman of some small means, interested in natural history, who visited a married sister in Williamsburg (the town settled in 1632 and rebuilt in the 1920s to the original plan). He made a second visit to America, commissioned for £20 per annum to collect plants. He sent home seeds packed in gourds – boxes, 4 pence each in Charleston, he thought too expensive. Catesby then retired to Fulham, to spend twenty-three years producing his *Natural History of Carolina, Georgia, Florida and the Bahama Islands*, mostly about birds. He learnt to engrave his own drawings and the prints were hand-coloured under his supervision, but unfortunately he had neglected to learn to draw first. At 65, he got married. Catesby also introduced and grew the *Stewartia* or *Stuartia*, of the camellia (tea, *Theaceae*) family, named after John Stuart, Earl of Bute, who helped to found the Botanic Garden at Kew. But the American *Stuartias* are too tender here.

[1730]

Weeping willow

The original weeping willow, a species, *Salix babylonica*, is rarely seen. It is a native of W. China, cultivated in Europe and W. Asia and brought from there to Twickenham Park by a Mr Vernon, a merchant whose seat it was.

The more popular story is that Alexander Pope planted some willow ropes which had tied a parcel from Spain, also at Twickenham – weeping willows were a feature of Pope's villa there.

The weeping willow we see now is a variety of *S. alba*, 'Chrysocoma', introduced about 1800 from France. *S. babylonica* has brown twigs, not yellow, and rugged bark. It does not grow well in Britain.

Bull bay or evergreen magnolia

[1734]

Bull bay seems a heavy sort of name for the most splendid of flowering evergreens, but perhaps it needs a light Carolina accent. There is another magnolia of Virginia called sweet bay – Bishop Compton had this in the late 1600s. In England there was a great frost in 1739–40 and the only bull bay to survive was at Exmouth. The tree was rented out to nurseryman at 5 guineas a layer, later reduced to half a guinea. Thus var. *exoniensis* became for a time the only British representative of *Magnolia grandiflora*.

It grows to 80 feet, a dense pyramid in the deep south, with flowers up to 10 inches across, and thick, dark, glossy leaves with yellow midribs. The leaves are felted below. Bull bay is often seen trained up a wall in our cooler climate, and only rarely more than 15 feet. The 'best' variety has the charming name of 'Goliath'. It originated in Guernsey.

bull bay

Turkey oak

[1735]

Spreading like a native and as far north as E. Ross-shire, says Mitchell. It grows quickly and makes a large tree (128 feet at Knightshayes, Devon), but the timber is poor, or has a poor reputation. It is heavier than English oak and is called iron oak for this reason and not because it is very strong. It is difficult to season properly and is permeable, so useless for outdoor work. It is called red oak in the trade, and looks pinkish, with a coarse grain. I dare say that with modern methods of handling it can be quite valuable for interior work.

The leaves are varied in size and in the way they are lobed, but there are seven to nine lobes, some at least cut deeply. The acorns are mossy-cupped and the twigs whiskery, the buds, to quote Elwes, 'surrounded by a whorl of long linear-subulate tomentose stipules'. The bark of old trees is a dull grey, rather regularly broken into fissures and rounded, close-packed plates. *Quercus cerris* (*cerris* is the classical Roman name for the tree) is a native of S. Europe and Asia Minor, not just of Turkey.

Oak marbles, the commonest of the many galls of English oak, and often mistakenly called oak-apples, are not native. They are part of the life cycle of a gallwasp which breeds in bud galls of turkey oak. The female wasp lays eggs in the bud of the common oak; the galls are caused, and only females emerge. Where turkey oaks are scarce, the wasp has adapted to reproducing only the female line, independently. Marble galls are rich in tannin – they were imported for this reason. They can be used to make black ink, simply put in a jar of water with some iron filings.

oak marble galls

Eastern hemlock

The name hemlock comes from the smell of the foliage, and the early Americans who used the name must have been familiar with the plant, *Conium maculatum*, which poisoned Socrates, and to me is indistinguishable from hedge parsley. (The hollow, smooth stem is spotted (*maculatum*) with purple, and it grows tall, by water: easy when you know.)

Hemlock spruce is a better name perhaps, for a tree which characterises a whole forest of Canada and eastern U.S.A., where it grows mostly mixed with hardwoods. The hemlock–hardwood forest area is 1300 miles wide, around and south of the Great Lakes.

There is a pure stand of eastern hemlock, *Tsuga canadensis*, at the Arnold Arboretum, Boston, which I should like to see before I try to write anything sensible about this important tree. In Britain it usually grows several stems and has a rounded crown, while at home it is described as a straight, perfect cone.

Tsuga canadensis

T. canadensis is very familiar in gardens in its many dwarf forms, easily recognised by the way the rather small, dry-looking, usually tapered leaves are seen upside down on the shoot. Cones, sometimes covering these small trees, are small pointed ovals on short stalks, which distinguish this hemlock from others.

The western hemlock (1851) is the more useful forestry tree. There are ten hemlocks in North America and S. and S.E. Asia, suggesting a once very massive hemlock forest – the theory being that the multiple species started as regional variations of the extinct parent hemlock. *T. canadensis* has a special preference for rocky ridges and river gorges, according to Henry. Its seeds do not germinate well on open or newly turned land, rather on mossy stumps and fallen logs, where the root shoot may take anything up to ten years to reach the ground. A shaded specimen of the tree, in the woods, only 10 feet high yet showed sixty-five annual rings. Such persistence, in this ancient species which once, before the spread of the Angiosperms, must have had everything its own way, invites our sympathy.

Cucumber tree

Another tree magnolia, of the eastern and mid-western states, *M. acuminata*, arrived to take a very minor place (but a good deal of ground) in the larger gardens of England. Acuminate means gradually tapering, but whether this applies to the leaf or the red, cucumber-shaped fruit, I don't know. It has a native station at Niagara Falls but grows largest and most abundant in the lower valleys of E. Kentucky and Tennessee. It is so uncommon here that to hear of the wood used for 'doors and wainscots, bowls, troughs and wooden ware' seems very surprising. There is a tree in Cambridge at the N.E. entrance of the Botanics, and a fine one at Kew: at Mote Park, Kent, 85 feet tall.

Paperbark birch

This is the Indians' birch, for canoes to jump the rapids, yet light enough to carry overland. *Betula papyrifera* has larger, broader leaves than the common birches, and its bark, very variable, is characterised by orange-pink bands

cucumber tree flower

paperbark birch at Kilmun, Argyll

below chalky white, with sometimes a touch of purple and always a fairly regular pattern of horizontal lenticels. It is very widely distributed – that's why it's variable – in Canada, New York and northern New England, rarer southwards through Ohio, Nebraska, Dakota's Black Hills and the Rockies, Idaho and Washington.

Betula papyrifera is described as uncommon in British parks and gardens, but it seems to turn up quite frequently in the arboreta that I visit. There is, naturally, a great range of different seed available and some forms are said to grow very well indeed (28.6 feet in twenty years at Bedgebury). It may have a future as a forestry tree. It is always seductively beautiful: virginal at Kew and Edinburgh, richly patina'd at Kilmun. The ghost-white stems of the young plantation at Bedgebury defy the crudities of photography.

Populus x euramericana
'Serotina', Golders Green,
London

[1751]

Populus x *euramericana*, syn. x *canadensis*, 'Serotina'

The English name, black Italian poplar, is equally useless, but 'Serotina' will do nicely. It means 'late-leafing'. This is our most common poplar, planted everywhere and doomed to celibacy, being always male. It has a distinctive, arching open crown, usually off centre; shoots always upwards, leaves reddish in late May, turning a greyish green, often large. The tree can grow to 90 feet in 30 years and doesn't mind wet clay. In France, where it was widely planted before it was much used here, the trees were supposed, in 1913 according to Elwes, to produce a franc a year per tree – not that I can work that out in real money, but it demonstrates a typically calculating attitude to poplars.

The origin of the hybrid is obscure, but it resulted from a cross between the European black poplar and *P. deltoides*, a widely distributed, enormous east N. American tree. This is supposed to have happened in France, so why is it called Italian? Perhaps black French poplar sounded too naughty.

There is a very effective golden yellow variety, 'Serotina aurea'.

Chinese tree of heaven

Or, as it was first named, stinking-ash. Peter Collinson, 1694–1768, was a rich draper of London who, without stirring from his garden at Mill Hill (now Mill Hill School), managed to be credited with the introduction of this tree to Britain. We should not ignore the ability and enthusiasm of patrons and gardener who encouraged explorers to collect plants from distant places and then, so to speak, did the spade-work, watching developments of entirely new species over twenty years or more. But it was a Jesuit father who actually discovered the tree of heaven, *Ailanthus altissima*.

The Jesuits were allowed at the court in Pekin in the 18th century only if they could offer something solid in terms of western technology in return for any souls they might win. One Father d'Incarville, who had taken a crash course in botany, was actually appointed Master Glass Maker, and he managed to interest the Emperor in some western plants. But it took him ten years to gather any Chinese plants, and even then his troubles were not over. Most of the 300 specimens that he sent to France, from country hitherto unexplored by western man, were left unopened for 140 years. Peter Collinson was one of his more appreciative correspondents, and raised the tree of heaven from his seeds – and it was also grown in France. D'Incarville died in 1757 in Pekin after catching a disease, described as 'nothing serious', from a patient.

Ailanto is a Chinese name for a sky-scraping tree, and *altissima* means much the same; *A. altissima* is 68 feet in St James's Park and, probably, by now 100 feet at Endsleigh, Devon. It is to be found as a street tree in Hampstead Garden Suburb, where it was no doubt chosen for its heavenly associations – it is close to the Jewish cemetery. It is very pretty, with very large ash-pattern leaves, the leaflets usually lobed at the base. The bark is brown with cream zig-zag stripes, the flowers greenish in panicles (the males evil-smelling) and the fruits are keys, in great quantities, each one twisted like a propeller.

Ailanthus is a genus of about nine species, confined to E. Asia and N.

Ailanthus

Australasia, belonging to the mainly tropical family Simarubaceae, which includes the *Quassia* or bitter-wood. *A Tree Grows in Brooklyn* was a well-known novel and a film: the tree was *Ailanthus altissima*. It is described as naturalised in N. America, not perhaps in Brooklyn.

Sometimes, on a dull day, the large, dark, wrinkly and shiny leaves look as unpleasant as, when crushed, they smell.

Scholars' tree

[1753]

Sophora japonica, the pagoda tree or scholars' tree, was sent to Europe by d'Incarville. Again it has ash-like leaves, panicles of small flowers, and pods. It is leguminous. It is not very common, but it is impressive. A very old one at Kew, indicated but not actually marked on the leaflet map, was planted in 1753; it is prostrate, limbs propped up and with concrete in its wounds. *Sophora* can also be seen at Oxford University Parks, very large and broad, by the Keble Gate; and at Edinburgh Botanic Garden and Cambridge. The variety *pendula* has agreeably contorted branches, usually grafted high on a stem of the type. Why it is called a pagoda or a scholars' tree I don't know. It has 'purgative properties'. And why, coming from China, is it *japonica*?

Sophora japonica var. *pendula*

In September after a warm summer it can be quite splendid: in cold summers the flowers fall off, so you will rarely see the pods, which are 3 inches long and constricted between the seeds. Thirteen species, sometimes called *Edwardsia*, are closely related in the southern hemisphere. *E.* or *S. microphylla* and *E.* or *S. teraptera* of New Zealand are kowhai trees, noted for very durable wood.

Mid-century enthusiasms

Daphne mezereon was first recorded, growing wild in Hampshire, in 1752. Unfortunately we cannot prove that this beautiful plant is a native. Linnaeus' *Species Plantarum* was published in 1753 and incorporated to some extent in William Hudson's *Flora Anglica* of 1762 and other works. There was a great rise of interest in natural history. George III's Queen, Charlotte, his mother Princess Augusta, and their closest friend and chief minister the Earl of Bute, John Stuart, were all enthusiasts. They founded the Botanic Garden at Kew in 1759.

The Pagoda at Kew was designed by Sir William Chambers and built in 1761. Chambers had visited Chinese gardens, but described their trees in terms of English landscape gardening: 'They have scenes for every season of the year: some for winter generally exposed to the southern sun and composed of pines, firs, cedars, evergreen oaks, phyllyrea, hollies, yews, junipers, and many other evergreens, being enriched with laurels of various sorts, laurestinas, arbutus, and other such plants as grow or flourish in cold weather. To give variety . . . are rare shrubs, flowers and trees of the torrid zone, with frames of glass disposed in the form of temples etc., warmed by subterraneous fires . . . [within] are all sorts of mellodious birds . . . gold and silver fishes.' The Chinese had 'plantations of deciduous trees whose leaves turn to brilliant colours as winter approaches. Amidst these were planted evergreens and fruit trees, where the flowers which blossom late grew, beside decayed trees and dead stumps of picturesque form overspread with moss

Chambers's Pagoda at Kew

and ivy. There were ruins, half buried arches, cemeteries for domestic animals, and whatever else indicating debility, etc., of humanity, co-operating with the autumnal nature and the temperature of the air, fills the mind with melancholy and inclines it to serious reflections.'

Beyond were scenes of terror in gloomy woods or dark caverns; bats, owls and vultures dwelt in their groves, wolves, tigers and jackals howled in the forests, half-famished animals wandered over plains where gibbets, crosses, wheels and instruments of torture were disposed. Or the traveller may pass through 'flowery thickets, where he is delighted with the singing of birds, the harmony of flutes, and all kinds of soft instrumental music: sometimes, in this romantic excursion, the passenger finds himself in extensive recesses, surrounded with arbors of jessamine, vine and roses, where beauteous Tartarean damsels, in loose transparent robes that flutter in the air, present him with rich wines, mangostans, ananas, and fruits of Quangsi; crown him with garlands of flowers, and invite him to taste the sweets of retirement. . .'

Chambers really did build a 'valley of the shadow of death' in a pleasure garden near Dorking. But it was Lancelot Capability Brown who got most of the work, until he died in 1783, with nearly half England not yet 'done'.

[1754]

Ginkgo

juvenile leaf of ginkgo

Ideal for Chinese-style gardens was *Ginkgo biloba*, the maidenhair tree, first described in 1690 by Englebert Kaempfer, botanist–physician to the Dutch East India Company in Japan. The ginkgo was cultivated in Japan but it is native to China – the Chinese *yin-kuo*.

The Japanese, though Kaempfer thought them 'a reasonable and sensible people', treated Europeans, officially at least, with the greatest suspicion. Visitors who wished to travel in Japan had to sign oaths in ink and blood, not to fraternise, and were closely guarded, locked in at night. When they reached the Court they were forced to perform mimes and dances for the Emperor, while his ladies watched from concealed positions. Kaempfer, in addition, contributed some western ideas on medicine, astronomy, mathematics; and perspective, revolutionary in Chinese art.

Ginkgo was not found growing wild until 1905 in China, where its indigeneity was further established by Chinese texts of the eighth century. It is first recorded in England growing at Mile End, in the nursery of one James Gordon. Layers were taken from this (male) tree: one became the large tree now to be seen at Kew. Until 1939 it was thought that no females existed in England – there are still very few – and a graft from a famous female tree at Geneva was successfully applied to the Kew tree in 1911. It fruited abundantly until someone pruned it off by mistake. Several female grafts have been made since, without issue.

Ginkgo produces two sorts of shoots – the short spur kind is illustrated. Long shoots grow on healthy, vigorous trees; they are green, with alternate spirally arranged leaves. On old Chinese trees, strange woody stalactites or hanging knuckles are produced from horizontal branches. I have no doubt that in some ancient steamy climate the ginkgos sent down vertical roots from extended horizontal branches, as some figs still do, and progressed sideways as well as upwards for indefinite distances, so that a single tree made a great interconnected forest. Conversely, in unfavourable situations

Ginkgo spur

G. *biloba* can stand still for ages, producing leaves from short spurs and wasting no energy at all on growing.

The Ginkgoales evolved separately from the conifers, but the single surviving species is usually classed as a conifer. Species preserved as fossils, particularly in the European Pliocene, are hardly different from the living *biloba*, and were, by this time, quite reduced by competition with conifers and Angiosperms. The fruit of *G. biloba* is acorn shaped with an evil-smelling and fleshy rind: but the white nut within is a Japanese delicacy and very 'yin' in China: *yin hsing*. For planters, seeds are available from S. Europe, but saplings are quite cheap if you only want one or two trees. I have one in my garden, as Gerard would say. And if it is left alone it will one day make this garden look even smaller than it is.

Ginkgo is a street tree in New York and other N. American cities, as here in Cardiff. It has withstood the Age of Smoke, as it withstood other ages. It was introduced to Philadelphia direct from Japan in 1784, by Michaux.

There are varieties – *laciniata* with deeply cut, wavy edged, large leaves, and *fastigiata*, narrow and especially useful as a street tree. *Pragensis*, 150 years old in Prague, has tortuous branches and a low, spreading crown. I have sometimes collected leaves with white stripes following the veins. All ginkgo leaves turn golden yellow, crisp-fried before they fall.

Corsican pine

[1758]

In the world of pines this one, *Pinus nigra* var. *maritima*, is only an unremarkable regional form of a European species, but it has become our fourth most important forestry tree. Apart from the 4000 acres which are harvested annually, it is a fine specimen tree in parks and gardens all over Britain. It grows well on sands and gravels and thin soils over limestones. It prefers warm summers, but is planted everywhere.

Old specimens have not reached the 120 feet, and 20-foot girth, mentioned by Elwes for natural specimens in Corsica. The oldest appears to be one at Kew, planted in 1814 near the main gate.

The Corsican pine has needles in pairs, 4¼ to 7 inches long in a sheath up to ½ inch. Cones are 2½ inches long, each scale usually with a tiny spine (these are absent from Scots pine). The bark is blackish grey, soon heavily fissured, giving a pattern of bold wavy black verticals, the raised plates between flaking in a low relief pattern of pinkish, purplish light greys – this on older trees. Mitchell points to the columnar crown, short, light level branches and pale yellow-brown shoot with long leaves as distinguishing this among other two-needle pines. But you will find it in all sorts of shapes and in all sorts of places.

Corsican pine at Westonbirt

Zelkova or Caucasian elm

[1760]

'This remarkable tree is undoubtedly one of the most picturesque and distinct of any that can be grown in this country,' says Bean with more than normal enthusiasm, and forgetting several dozen others between A and Y. It is true that once acquainted, one is always interested. It is slow-growing and many branched, with a prettily serrated oval leaf. But it has not produced fertile seed here, so far.

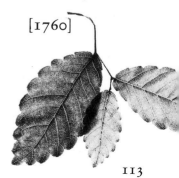

Zelkova is very closely related to *Ulmus*, but not subject to elm disease. It is a native of the S. Caucasus and Persia near the Caspian, with relations in Crete and E. Asia. It grows in oak and ash–maple–beech forests, not in pure woods. Here the bole is clear to 60 feet or more, but in England it usually looks like an old coppice tree. Some at Kew, Regents Park, and a fine one in the Oxford Parks, with suckers, have shortish trunks like hornbeams. More often the stems are very short and buttressed, breaking into innumerable branches. The largest, nearly 100 feet high and very remarkably shaped, is at Pitt Farm, just west of Chudleigh in Devon.

Zelkova carpinifolia, syn. *crenata*, was introduced via France. The name comes from the native *dzelkwa*, which means stone wood, and it seems that the timber is a superior sort of elm, heavier and stronger, reddish and beautifully marked. Even the white sapwood equals ash in strength, according to Michaux, quoted by Elwes.

Huntingdon elm

A form of Dutch elm of fine form and rapid growth was raised about this time at Wood and Ingram's nursery at Huntingdon, from seed supposed to have been gathered from some old trees at Hinchingbrooke Park near by. The Huntingdon elm grows tall with long, ascending branches covered with sucker shoots. It was not recommended for avenues by Elwes, but it is chiefly remembered from some beautiful avenues, as at Hidcote, Gloucestershire. The forking habit produces a kind of Gothic arch, but there is some loss of timber because of moisture entering the trunk. It is *U. x vegeta*.

U. x vegeta Lindl. is *U. carpinifolia* Gled. x *U. glabra* Huds., while the Dutch elm, *U. x hollandica* Mill., is *U. carpinifolia* Gled. x *U. glabra* Huds. x *U. plotii* Druce, as published in 1975 by Melville (*Hybridization and the British Flora*, ed. C. A. Stace). But we shall not see these elms again for some time, if at all. The Huntingdon elm does not come true from seed, so it is to be hoped that some young plants are kept alive until the present epidemic of elm disease is worked out.

avenue at Hidcote

Sweet buckeye

Aesculus flava, syn. *Ae. octandra*, also called the yellow buckeye. Not very common and not very often large in Britain, but another great tree of the Eastern Woodlands; a straight bole to 60 or 70 feet in Tennessee and Carolina river valleys and mountains. It is found as far north as S.W. Pennsylvania and west to Texas.

All American horsechestnuts are buckeyes. The European horsechestnut was not established in Britain in time for the common name to be on the lips of the new Americans, so they invented their own. The lustrous red-brown seed is likened to the eye of a deer. The blossom is very attractive, a subtle yellow (*flava*), and the whole tree, though obviously *Aesculus* in every detail, is much less coarse than *hippocastanum*. Buckeyes in fact used to have a separate genus, *Pavia*: the name is retained for the group of *Aesculus* species whose buds are not sticky. The flowers can be red, pink, or cream, the last from West Virginia (White Sulphur Springs). There is even a purple variety in cultivation. *Ae. pavia* is one parent of the familiar red horsechestnut.

sweet buckeye,
Regents Park, London

The Californian buckeye, *Ae. californica*, is said to be perfectly hardy here but remains a bush (a broad, low tree, 30 to 40 feet by Californian streams), with white or pink flowers. It was introduced in Victorian times. The Ohio buckeye, *Ae. glabra*, is rare here. Introduced early in the 19th century it seems to have been neglected, or mistaken for the sweet buckeye: it also has yellow flowers.

Buckeye timber is not specially good, but it is useful. It can be pulped, and it was used for artificial limbs, and piano keys. Buckeye sugar-toughs traditionally cradled the infants of poor immigrants in the 19th century.

Lucombe oak

This is a hybrid between the cork oak and the Turkey oak which occurs naturally in Europe, hence the name *Quercus* x *hispanica*. The Lucombe oak also occurred naturally near Exeter, among seedlings of Turkey oak in the nursery of a Mr Lucombe. When he died, aged 103, the tree was used to make his coffin. Seedlings are variable: in the true Lucombe oak the bark is not corky. The leaf is lobed, with points to the lobes, nearly evergreen. A variant has leaves with triangular lobes. Two varieties have corky bark, including the Fulham oak, of separate origin presumably in Fulham; this has pendulous shoots.

Koelreuteria paniculata,
Kew

[1763]

Pride of India or golden rain tree

Mu-lan-tse in Chinese, *Koelreuteria paniculata* in Latin, and nothing much to do with India, it was grown from seed sent by d'Incarville, the Jesuit at the Court of the Emperor at Pekin. It has probably the most complicated leaf of any of our trees, small yellow flowers in the panicles of the specific name, and fragile-looking pink bladders each containing three black seeds. It is hardy in Britain.

Koelreuteria is of the soapberry family, mainly tropical and once stretched to contain the horsechestnuts, now separate in Hippocastanaceae. Sapindacea includes *Nepheleum litchi*, or *Litchi chinensis*, the precious white fruits of which are really the pulpy aril of a brown seed, the whole contained in a globular, prickly, pink rind. The rambutan of Malaya is similar, but with soft, hairy spines. *Koelreuteria* is only useful for necklaces, but a black dye is got from the leaves.

Professor Joseph Gottlieb Koelreuter, 1733–1806, was a pioneer of plant hybridisation. The tree was first introduced to St Petersburg in 1752 and grown under glass: d'Incarville sent material there overland from China, by caravan (which left every three years).

Rhododendron ponticum

This is the common rhododendron, invasive, sprawling, and the rootstock of many hybrids, whose suckers always revert: corolla a light purple, or rosy, with greenish or brownish spots on the upper wing. *Pontus* = Asia Minor. The plant was first described by the great J. P. de Tournefort, professor of Botany at the Jardin du Roi (Louis XIV), who was sent in 1700 to discover the plants of the Ancients. His party travelled in Armenian dress because west Europeans were treated with suspicion, but wore leather boots instead of Turkish slippers, and 'Callicoe Drawers'. Tournefort brought home 1356 different plants, but the King forgot to pay him and he died, in a low state from overwork, after being crushed by a cart.

Rh. ponticum has several native stations in S. Europe, as was discovered later. It was growing in Ireland in a comparatively recent interglacial, and it grows now from its own seed in the woods of Lake Killarney, as fresh and lovely as, in town shrubberies and the shrub layer of plantations, it is sooty and undesirable.

Rh. ponticum reached Britain in 1763.

Grey alder

I found it in Wigan, on a bank smoothed over from a railway that used to penetrate into the centre of the town, and saw it in S. Wales by a trunk road. At Kilmun there is a small wood of the dark silver stems astride a stream. A native of Europe and the Caucasus, it is a dull, retiring small tree which will grow anywhere, wet or dry, from the Alps to the Arctic circle in Russia. But specimens of 70 or 80 feet are recorded. The leaves are pointed, and shaped and veined like the hornbeam's, but grey and downy, with coarse serrations. There are cut-leaved and golden-leaved forms, and a pendulous-branched variety which can be impressive – a tall pyramid in outline. The timber appears to be slightly superior to that of the common alder. It is *Alnus incana*; meaning grey.

An eastern American shrubby tree, the speckled alder, used to be known as *A. incana* var. *americana* but is now *A. rugosa*.

Cricket bat willow

Once known as *Salix coerulea*, the blue willow, this is a *S. alba* variety, narrow in shape, with bluish leaves. One of the fastest-growing trees in Britain, it is not planted only to make cricket bats. It can reach 100 feet.

For bat-making, however, trees are planted about 30 feet apart in good soil by streams in Essex and Suffolk. Buds are removed from the stem up to 12 or 15 feet. After about 15 years' growth the bole can be cut, and sawn into 30-inch lengths. These are then split radially. There is about 9 years actual growth in the best bats, the oldest wood being at the front.

Cricket is older than var. *coerulea*, some form of the game having been played since the 11th century. The first cricket club was formed in 1750 and MCC in 1787.

cricket bat willow

Willow-leaved pear

Pyrus salicifolia is a species of S.E. Europe and W. Asia, and no doubt, like many others, only prevented by the peculiar mountain structure of the Alps from recolonising N. Europe after the Ice Ages. It is easily recognised and commonly planted, a small and very decorative tree, especially when the rich white blossom is seen amongst the young, whitish leaves.

Irish yew

Taxus baccata, the common yew; but a variety, *fastigiata*, *stricta* or *hibernica*, which was found in Co. Fermanagh about 1780 by a man called Willis. His two trees, which were both female, are the parents of all Irish yews, about the commonest tree in British churchyards; but some males have been found in England, it is said. The recognizable characters of the Irish yew are the numerous vertical spires and the radial leaves. Trees are sometimes tied to keep their shapes in snow, and often cut into urn shapes: or, as Alexander Pope suggested, 'for a politer sort of ornament in the villas and gardens of this great city ... Adam and Eve in Yew; Adam a little shattered ... Eve and the serpent very flourishing.'

Irish yew, one of several exactly similar on the *parterre* at Bowood House

Aucuba japonica

Also for villas and gardens, in this great year for little trees; the spotted laurel from Japan. It was described in 1712 by Kaempfer of the Dutch East India Company. There was by 1780 a flourishing export trade in plants from Yokohama, supplying the gardening and 'stove plant' craze in Europe. *Aucuba* was known in England only by the female, and there was speculation as to whether the male was 'blotched' also, not resolved until, in the early 1860s, Robert Fortune brought home the male plant: 'Only fancy all the *Aucubas* which decorate the windows and squares of our smoky towns covered during winter and spring with a profusion of red berries!' Such a result was worth the journey. The spotted form is a variety of *Acuba japonica*, an Asiatic evergreen with leathery leaves, allied to *Cornus*. It will grow in shade, under trees, a fact which has not been ignored by those in charge of public gardens. Perhaps it became too common. But one variegated leaf can be an object of fascination, even of meditation – a well-varnished map of botanical indecision, a speckled thought in a dappled shade. But in dusty town plots it can look as if splashed with cream distemper.

Chinese privet

Chinese privet. Below, wingnut thicket at Cambridge

Ligustrum lucidum: no hedge bush, it can be 50 feet high, a splendid tree with really beautiful, shining (*lucidus*) evergreen leaves and a lot of white, scented flowers in autumn. 'It is devoid of down in all its parts' (Bean), but a tree at Kew has a rough pattern of warts on the shoots. Its geometry is excellent, the leaf elegantly tapering to a point and curled as if to show off its polish, the shoot straight and symmetrical. It is the commonest evergreen in parts of Hupeh, China.

Ch'ien Lung, the Emperor who had employed the Jesuit fathers to such purpose was still on the throne when the British, in 1793 sent Lord Macartney as Ambassador. He refused to kowtow the prescribed nine times, or even once, and the Emperor graciously accepted a genuflection. A Fellow of the Linnaean Society, Sir George Staunton, was Macartney's second in command, and by the time the Emperor had seen enough of the British, Staunton, with the help of the official gardeners, had collected over 200 plants, including Macartney's Rose, *R. bracteata*, and *Ligustrum lucidum*.

Caucasian wingnut

To end the century, after all these lesser, pretty trees, are two giants. The wingnut, *Pterocarya fraxinifolia* (*ptero* = wing, *carya* = nut, *fraxinifolia* = ash-leaved) was brought from Persia to France in 1782 by Michaux the elder, but it is not clear whether it was planted in England before the Napoleonic wars made communication difficult. It is a large deciduous tree, up to 100 feet high, wide-branching. The female catkins (see page 16) are up to 20 inches long, followed by strings of winged nuts. The leaves have often twenty-one leaflets. The bark is an unremarkable grey, but with broad, sinuous ridges which are sometimes polished in trees exposed to the weather. In the wild, in damp ground of the Caucasus, it grows both as a large tree and as a bush with miniaturised leaflets. Trees planted near Vienna are said to be particularly fine, but *Pterocarya* flourishes in S. Britain. At Cambridge Botanical Garden there is a thicket which grew up from an old tree blown down in 1886. This is interesting and inspiring for botanists studying our prehistoric flora, for under the soil are fossils of the same tree dating from the late Tertiary. A small stream runs through the middle of the thicket. There are specimen trees in most botanical gardens and arboreta.

The leaves can be used by lazy Caucasian fishermen for intoxicating fish, the bark for making sandals and roof tiles, while the timber, which resembles lime, is only used for packing cases. A tree about 110 feet high is at Melbury, near Evershot, Dorset.

well-formed *Araucaria* at Benmore House, Argyll

Monkey puzzle

[1795]

Most people can recognize this mighty conifer of the Andean forests north of Lat. 41°S. Ideally, a large tree is egg-shaped with the pointed curve at the top and the lower branches sweeping the ground, curving left and right in majestic rhythm, a rich deep green patterned with the lighter green of the spiny shoots. Each shoot, thick as the paw of a leopard, has the leaves close-packed in a vigorous spiral pattern. The cones are as big as a human head. The trunk is elephantine, toes and all, and banded regularly, as if mechanically. The bark of old trees in the Andean valleys is described as broken into a gigantic jigsaw pattern of five- or six-sided plates.

As cedars of Lebanon were planted by Georgian mansions, so were *Araucarias* by Victorian ones, and in many smaller gardens too. Few are of the ideal shape described – but nor are the forest trees of Chile; they vary, flat-topped or domed, and often bare of branches below the top, as are most specimens in towns. The Chile pine – a better name – grows best in the west of Britain, away from smoke and cold winds.

Araucaria araucana was named after the local Indians and discovered by a Spaniard with the excellent name of Don Francisco Dendariarina, who explored the territory of the Araucanos for timber trees.

The Indians not only ate the nuts, boiled or roasted; they made pastry from them and distilled liquor. Resin from the tree made all sorts of medicine, internal and external.

Archibald Menzies, the surgeon–naturalist with the explorer Vancouver, on a visit to Chile, pocketed some seeds from the Governor's residence and, back on board, sowed them in pots, rearing six plants on the voyage home. Five were sent to Kew and one lived until 1892. A large supply of seed came in 1844 from William Lobb, who was sent to Chile by the Exeter nursery firm of Veitch.

A. angustifolia of S.E. Brazil provides the well-known Parana pine, a hardish, smooth-grained softwood. There are ten or more species of *Araucaria* in the Southern Hemisphere, which with twenty-one *Agathis* species make up the whole family of Araucariaceae, conifers of archetypal antiquity in the history of the world's surface.

The introduction of this amazing tree marks the end of the 18th century and the start of the 19th. It is a plant that must be appreciated for itself and its ancestry – it doesn't 'fit in' to the view, but it certainly had to fit in to any concept of evolution. And evolution was to occupy people's minds a good deal in the 19th century.

The landscaped park in the mid 18th century opened vistas on to the surrounding scenery and educated people began to explore their countryside, as, philosophically, they explored the meanings of Beauty, Sublimity, Natural and Scientific. A school of picturesque artists followed, rather than led, the movement, which was inspired first by poetry. With Turner and the English watercolourists English landscape painting became great. Gentlemen and their ladies toured, looking for viewpoints, and landowners planted trees and ruins. What was emerging was a recognisably modern attitude to the countryside, quaint and pastoral or savagely awe-inspiring, as in Snowdonia and the Lake District – both regions being then 'discovered'.

Landscape was there to be enjoyed, for inspiration and for philosophical and historical reflection. Where the landlord controlled the arable fields and the meadows, he planted or encouraged picturesque trees, not forgetting their future timber value.

Avenues, if they had ever quite gone out in the 'serpentine' period of the landscape gardeners, came in again. The favourite tree was, as always, the hybrid lime. The only reasons that can be advanced for this choice are availability and fashion, or vice versa. Elwes says that the fashion was started by Le Nôtre, the designer made famous by Versailles.

Common lime

Tilia x *europea*, syn. *T. vulgaris*, the common lime, is a cross between the two native species, possibly itself a native. Certainly there is no date for its introduction, but it is our most commonly planted broadleaf as a decorative or 'amenity' tree – common to the point of monotony. The great avenues which remain date from around 1700 and around 1840.

Mitchell, who positively hates this tree, makes a case for its being the least suitable of any tree for streets and avenues (but there it is). He points to the nail galls on the leaves (the large-leaved lime gets these too), and the drip of honeydew from the aphids which swarm on them; it sticks to anything (cars) beneath and then goes black with sooty mould. The boles are frequently 'sprout-infected' – a peculiarity of the hybrid and not of either parent. All this is true of course, and it may be that Le Nôtre and his followers never intended their trees to get old. The spray of young leaves gives a pretty effect at eye level, and this is lost in a great old avenue, where in summer the shade is too dense. Autumn colour, however, can be very attractive, especially in the late stages, when the black limbs are almost naked and autumnal rays light up the scatter of leaves. I cannot accept Mitchell's verdict: 'Autumn colour usually nil.'

The most famous avenue is at Clumber Park, near Sherwood Forest. It is nearly 2 miles long (the National Trust says 3 miles), 1315 trees in two rows. It is impressive by any standard. You can drive through – take the Rolls – and the park has patches of modified heath between new conifer plantations, and many other attractions. The serpentine lake is the work of Capability Brown: the house has gone.

Clumber Park, Notts

Prunus serrulata, the first oriental flowering cherry, introduced from China in 1822

12 · Trees for gardeners, about 1820

'Here is a wood, never touched by the finger of taste'*

The planting and management of great estates continued, 'for the ornament and service of the country' and for personal pleasure and profit. Squire Mushroom, with his stagnating serpentine river, his bridge (partly in the Chinese manner) and his groves 'perplexed with errors and crooked walks' (Francis Coventry, 1753) may have been scorned by the intelligentsia and the hereditary landowner, but he and his kind were pioneers of a sort and not too preoccupied with yield per acre.

By the early 1800s the classical, the oriental, even the Picturesque were being swept aside. Romanticism, obscurely revolutionary, demanded the natural – usually, confusingly called the Scientific or Utilitarian. (Natural Beauty conformed to rules, like Hogarth's 'S' line; serpentine, man-made lakes were 'natural'.) Repton was the prophet of the new rustic simplicity, with his before-and-after views appealing to sense and sensibility. Often, the reform consisted of little more than trimming, thinning and re-shaping trees and shrubs that had become overgrown since the clumps of the mid 1700s had been planted or arranged. A more scattered effect was obtained in parkland: the informal was seen to be capable of more informality without sacrificing a sense of design. Repton, except when forced, was not destructive: he was a sensitive worker and something of a conservationist in landscape gardening. In any case, people did not always follow his suggestions.

But the true Romantics, Wordsworth, Cowper, Scott, disapproved of 'improvements' and with the pre-Raphaelites and Ruskin there was a move towards nature-worship. Wild scenery, even if its wildness was kept at a suitable distance, became the ideal in landscape – the opposite, then as now, of urban 'ugliness'. Gardens, therefore, might as well be formal, or Gothic, or Persian, Indian, even Elizabethan. Some stalwart English gentlemen and ladies still had their Tudor and Jacobean gardens, unaware that tastes had changed and changed back again. Now – and we may be thankful – such gardens could be preserved. There were plenty of new plants to put in them.

*Thomas Love Peacock, *Headlong Hall*, 1816

Fonthill Abbey deities

In the 1820s and 1830s there were many new estates of about two acres, and enthusiasm grew, along with industrial prosperity. The Horticultural Society was founded in 1804. Curtis's *Botanical Magazine*, begun in 1787, could be subscribed to. (It has since that date published over 10,000 colour plates.) J. C. Loudon, author of the great 8-volume *Arboretum et Fruticetum Britannicum, or the Trees and Shrubs of Britain, Native and Foreign*, 1838, produced many helpful books for amateur gardeners – they were formidable works in hundreds of pages of small type. People usually seem to have ended up with (a) an evergreen shrubbery, (b) some flowerbeds on a lawn with (c) some accessory such as a summer house.

In *How to Lay out a Garden*, 1850, we find instructions for 'Proposed Greenhouse or summer house', three yards including a stable yard, house yard and garden yard, a kitchen garden and a 'Terrace with Vases and Pedestals'. There are to be Irish yews, kept equal in size and shape,

Golden blotched hollies
Andromeda floribunda and standard roses (*Andromeda* = *Pieris*, an American evergreen shrub).
Laurustinus

these in neat lines, then

Mass of Rhododendron and specimen Rhododendrons
Hodgins Holly (Hodgins was a nurseryman near Wicklow. His holly is a cross with the Madeira holly. It has large, leathery leaves and no berries, being a male clone; it is said to resist smoky atmospheres. It can grow to 50 feet and is very vigorous.)
Aucuba japonica
Masses of Evergreens, chiefly Rhododendrons
Masses of Azaleas (or Roses)

Another plan has Laurustina, 'black leaved' sometimes, *Cotoneaster microphylla*, 'leather-leaved' holly, a *Yucca gloriosa* and 'masses of hollies'. You can see the way it is going.

There was a variety of much more exciting and attractive small trees (and large) available, and from 1820 or so many more. Of course, as with all the dated introductions in this book, time was needed for the plants to be widely available, and for their virtues to be widely recognised. But gardeners with taste and imagination, though not rare, are in a minority. For a long time, also, interest centred on the greenhouse with its tender camellias and orchids, and other fascinating exotic plants.

Form and texture

From the Himalayas, by post to Hopetoun, near Edinburgh, in 1818, came cones of a splendid spruce which was named after the first president of the Linnean Society, Sir James Smith – or after the Hopetoun gardener of the same name. The Californian Brewer's spruce, with its even more graceful and feminine shape, was not discovered until the end of the century. Neither can be said to be well-named, but *P. smithiana*, the West Himalayan spruce, was also called *P. morinda*, a native word something to do with flower-honey, and **morinda** has stuck. Mitchell describes it as frequent (1972) and

Morinda spruce, *Picea smithiana*, young cones

123

infrequent (1974) and it is not exactly common, being sensitive to frost when young, and hating lime. The morinda spruce has the longest leaf of any spruce, 1¾ inches, sharp pointed and square, or round according to different authorities (not flat). It can grow to 200 feet, but may be expected to be 50 feet in British gardens. One of the original trees at Hopetoun has reached 90 feet, and the tallest, 124 feet, is at Taymouth Castle near Kenmore.

An incredibly fine textural effect, but one not available everywhere in Britain, is provided by the gorgeous **silver wattle** of Australia and Tasmania. Some hundreds of plants had been imported from Australia, and Brisbane, founded in 1823, had a Botanical Garden by 1827. There had not been the usual trouble with natives, even with Captain Bligh of the *Bounty* as Governor from 1805 to 1808. The leaflets of *Acacia dealbata* ('white-powdered') are ⅙ inch long by ⅟₃₀ inch wide, says Bean, who has a very good ruler, and are in thirty to fifty pairs. The flowers, imported from France as 'mimosa', ought to qualify this tree for colour rather than texture, but they rarely appear even in mild Cornish winters. Naturalised in India, the tree changed its flowering season by one month per year until it reached June, but it does not achieve this reversal in the temperate zone. It is leguminous, a member of the large sub-family Mimosae, very widely distributed south of the equator. The golden wattle, *A. longifolia*, is the national emblem of Australia, and *A. melanoxylon*, sometimes grown in England since 1808, produces the hard, close-grained timber called blackwood. *Dealbata* itself is a poor-quality timber tree, not without its uses of course. It reaches 100 feet, more usually 50.

The **weeping wych elm**, so familiar until the disease epidemic, appears to have been unknown until 1816 when it appeared in a bed of seedlings of *Ulmus glabra*, in Perth. All the weeping elms in all the gardens and churchyards of Europe came from this one tree, we are told. It is usually grafted at 6 feet or more, has a domed, wide-spreading, usually lopsided crown, ribbed by the curving branches, and it bears masses of seeds after the manner of wych elms. This is var. *pendula*. The other weeping variety, *camperdownii*, emerged in 1841: it is tortuous. Another variety of the wych elm, *exoniensis*, from Exeter in 1826, is densely bunched in leaf and upright in form, but old trees may have long hanging shoots. This is probably now extinct.

The weeping elm is a truly 19th-century tree — 'admirably adapted for particular situations', as Loudon puts it — monumental, sober and decorative, and not too large, not too extreme.

The **weeping beech** is much more ostentatious. Introduced from Europe in 1820, it is a variable form which has been found several times in France (Moselle) and once in Northamptonshire (Milton Park). Usually it is seen now as a mature tree, an elegant monster which really needs a grand setting. *Fagus sylvatica* var. *pendula* is described as tent-like. Var. *miltonensis* is extremely pendulous. Weeping beeches frequently surround themselves with layered offspring — great fountains splashing vegetatively up again.

Another variety of the common beech frequent in large gardens is the **cut** or **fern-leaved beech**. There are several named varieties probably not correctly called *laciniata* — Mitchell suggests the sensible 'Heterophylla' to cover the variable shapes of the varieties. Var. *laciniata* proper seems to have originated in a hedge in Bohemia in 1792. Var. *asplenifolia* ('fern-leaved') was listed in Loddiges catalogue in 1804. (Conrad Loddiges started his nursery in Hackney in 1771 and remained supreme until the mid 1900s.)

silver wattle in a S Cornwall garden

There are indeed many varieties of the common beech, but it may be most fascinating in its 'normal' form, for it responds in many different ways to its surroundings. In woods it is a very straight tall tree – the unique character of high beechwood is well known. Open grown, as the foresters say, it forms a fine round shape. As a cut hedge it retains its red leaves in winter – a protective habit of juvenile trees carried over into stunted adulthood. In exposed, damp situations its branches have often grafted themselves together (mastomosis) and even joined to the branches of other trees – to an oak in the New Forest, and with a pine, trunk to trunk in a copse on Crichel Down. Pollarded beeches in Epping Forest are as picturesque as the hornbeams, and at Burnham Beeches famous for age and grotesqueness. More correct in form, a famous hedge at Meikleour, Perthshire is 90 feet high and $^{1}/_{3}$ mile long; planted in 1746, they say.

The beech was not always in favour. William Gilpin, the authority on the Picturesque, wrote: 'its skeleton, compared with that of the Oak, the Ash, and the Elm, is very deficient. Its trunk, we allow, is often highly picturesque; it is studded with bold knots and projections, and has sometimes a sort of irregular fluting about it, which is very characteristic. . . . In full leaf it is equally unpleasing: it has the appearance of an overgrown Bush.' In fact he is in two minds about it; anyway, his opinions carried no weight with the great planters, who needed no guide to their trees. There are many English and Scottish roads shaded by avenues of superb beeches, in spite of the more than tenfold increase in traffic. One of the best is at Badbury Rings, between Blandford and Wimborne, Dorset.

Weeping Willows are usually now *Salix* 'Chrysocoma', also called *S. alba* 'Vitellina Pendula'. This is usually said to have originated in France in 1815, but was not named until 1908. It is easily recognized by the yellow, hanging shoots. Weeping willows were widely planted after 1823 which had been raised from a tree by Napoleon's grave in St Helena. (He died in 1821, and his body was moved to Paris in 1840.) These were *S. babylonica*, already introduced in 1730, but were called, by 'uncrupulous nurserymen' (Bean), '*Salix Napoleonii*'.

'Chrysocoma' is probably a hybrid of *S. alba* var. *vitellina*, the golden willow, with *S. babylonica*, and is now included under *S.* x *sepulcralis* (1889), of obscure origin in Hungary. It comes into leaf early, a livid pale green, and with the flowering cherries of mid-April makes Thames-side and Cam-side gardens much more cheerful than anything by the waters of Babylon. There are usually pale gold leaves still hanging in December: and that makes winter only three months long.

Rarities

Winter's bark, *Drimys winteri*, of the family Winteraceae (very close to Magnoliaceae) was discovered by William Winter, one of Drake's captains, in the Magellan Straits. There it is a tree; further north, in other regions of coastal S. America, it is a widespread shrub. Capt. Winter deserves his fame for his practical approach to what must have been a miserably predictable hazard of long sea voyages, scurvy, before the value of fresh fruit and vegetables was known. He may have been led to the bark by its slight fragrance: it is pinkish too. The evergreen leaves are narrow, light green and,

weeping beech, Batsford Arboretum

in hardier varieties introduced in the 1920s, blue below. *D. winteri* does not mind chalk, likes damp, but is not altogether hardy here. The shrubby form was introduced in 1827.

A relatively small tree of great formal beauty is the **Italian alder**, *Alnus cordata*, introduced from Italy or Corsica in 1820. It is greyish, but beautifully shaped, dense in foliage and superior in every detail. You can buy one for the price of three gallons of petrol, yet it is quite uncommon – not showy enough, I suppose. 'Cordate' is heart-shaped – this applies to the leaves.

leaves and fruit of the Italian alder. The leaves turn to grey

Even rarer is the obscure **Osage orange**, *Maclura pomifera*, introduced in 1818 – understandably rare, because you need both sexes to produce the green 'oranges' which are anyway useless. The leaf is ordinary – wavy, oval and pointed – and the bark, orange-brown, is ridged like a crack willow. However, the timber is unusually hard, heavy and flexible: it is the 'bow-wood' in its native Wild West, where the Osage tribe lived. The wood was used for wagon wheels and the trees are planted for tough hedges. It is related to the mulberry. Autumn colour is clear yellow.

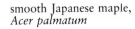
smooth Japanese maple,
Acer palmatum

Colour

It seems strange to me that gardeners should plant a tree just for the sake of its unusual colour in autumn. It will be green for months and red for days only, and even then you may be cheated by a sudden frost. But I must admit that the colours of the **Japanese maple**, *Acer palmatum*, are brilliant, subtle and long-lasting. As a tree it is small – some varieties are no bigger than a bedding plant – and can be most attractive in summer as well. The many varieties resulting from a long history of active admiration by the Japanese include red, purple, variegated and golden leaved forms of infinite degrees of 'dissectum'; five or seven lobed, large and small leaved.

In spite of its long domestication, there is a wild form of *A. palmatum*, growing to 40 feet. A native variety, 'Senkaki', the coral-bark maple, has red bark when young, and pretty, light green leaves which turn to orange rather than carmine. *A. palmatum* likes a sheltered position, some shade and some sun. The specimen, photographed at Batsford, is an old, sprawling tree which has a little clearing all to itself. In autumn afternoon light its colours are magically varied and luminous against the surrounding shadows.

Aesculus x *carnea* trunk

The **red horsechestnut**, *Aesculus* x *carnea* ('flesh') is a cross between the common tree and an American shrub, *Ae. pavia* which has red flowers. Nobody knows how the cross occurred, but it was about 1818 somewhere in Europe. Botanically x *carnea* is interesting in that spontaneous doubling of the chromosomes provides the means for reproduction true from seed – it behaves as a species (and has perhaps duplicated an extinct form). Awful things, however, sometimes happen to the trunk – eruptions – for no known reason: and the flowers' colour, I feel, appeals more to the carnivorous eye than to the vegetarian.

The hairy and attractive **Oriental thorn**, which you must call *Crataegus laciniata* instead of the simpler *orientalis*, was introduced in 1810. The fruits are yellowish – can be coral – the leaves a nice dark green, grey below, downy all over, as are their stalks, and there are few thorns. It is much the nicest hawthorn for a lawn.

In related light grey-green colour key is the **tree cotoneaster**, *C. frigidus* ('of the cold') introduced in 1824 from the Himalayas by the great Dr Wallich.

Cotoneaster frigidus in a
Cotswold garden

Amherstia, 'the most beautiful plant in the world'. from Wallich's *Plantae Asiaticaie*

The Danish surgeon Nathaniel Wallich was the first of the 'hardy Himalayan' collectors. After the Danish settlement of Serampore was taken over by the British forces he was released to help the Scot, William Roxburgh with the Botanic Garden at Calcutta, founded in 1786 by the Government and the East India Company as a sort of trading post for plants. He became its director in 1815 and proceeded over the next thirty years to turn it into a sort of paradise, with groves of teak, mahogany and *Cinnamomum* trees, an avenue of sago palms, and the rare *Amherstia*, named after Lady Amherst. Wallich travelled to Katmandu in 1820. Tibetan pilgrims brought him specimens from the high valleys, and among these were *Cotoneasters microphylla, rotundifolia* and *frigidus*, as well as the magnificent pine, *P. wallichiana* (page 135) and *Rhododendron campanulatum* (white to purple, 30 feet high at Benmore). He discovered also *Geranium wallichianum, Lilium wallichianum* (and *L. giganteum*). He went down with fever on his return to Calcutta and took a long sea voyage to Singapore and Calcutta, collecting more plants. He travelled to N. India, and to Burma by steamboat (wood-fired). He brought an enormous collection of herbarium specimens to London in 1828 and published his *Plantae Asiaticaie Rariores* in 1830–2. Wallich was host at Calcutta to many botanist explorers, some of whom, like William Griffith, who took over the gardens, 1842–4, in Wallich's absence, were opposed to his liberal and genial approach to botany. Griffith cut down most of Wallich's trees to make 'scientific' open beds, which the sun baked hard.

Amherstia became one of the glories of the Duke of Devonshire's stove houses but *Cotoneaster frigidus* remains to decorate more humbly many thousands of large and small gardens. Cotoneasters, mostly small or prostrate shrubs, are a study in themselves. Nearly all are natives of the Himalayas and the mountains of China, but one *C. integerrimus* ('most undivided') was found wild at St Orme's Head in 1783 – it appears to be virtually extinct now – and the closely related *C. tomentosa* of Europe was introduced to Britain in 1759. Many of the eastern cotoneasters were discovered at the end of the 19th century.

After the miseries of the English January and February, early blossom is a reasonable preoccupation of gardeners. Two American cherries introduced in 1773 probably only slightly augmented the effect of our cherry-plum and blackthorn (March) and *P. avium* 'Plena' (May). Long cultivated, the almond also shows its delicate pink in late March or April, and there was in the late 18th century a hybrid between almond and peach raised by the great horticulturalist Thomas Andrew Knight, which is still planted as *Prunus* 'Pollardii' – like a large-flowered almond.

The first **Japanese cherry**, *Prunus serrulata*, was sent from a garden in Canton, China, in 1822. Semi-wild in Japan as the hill cherry, *Yamazakura*, it has been venerated and even worshipped for centuries, says the collector and authority Collingwood Ingram. It is the national tree, but, it appears, not a true native – it was found wild in W. China by Wilson in 1900 – there it grows to 40 feet high. Since the double-flowered cultivar was found first and given a specific name, the wild hill cherry is *P. serrulata* var. *spontanea*.

The many later introductions, of various parentage, (*Sato Zakura*, flowering cherries) are classed under *P. serrulata*, but many are said to derive from *P. speciosa*, Oshima cherry. (O Shima is an island south of Tokio). *P. serrulata* is a convenience heading.

Serrulata itself is usually quite small, with a flat top, small white or pink-tinged unscented double flowers in short-stalked clusters of two to five in April to May: shoots smooth, leaves 3–5 inches, taper-pointed, opening with the flowers.

Now almost naturalized as an escape from suburban shrubberies, the American **Snowberry** was introduced in 1817. The berries, pure, luminous white, ripen in October and are ignored by the birds. This shrub *Symphoricarpos racemosa* (in bunches or racemes) is deciduous, can grow to 10 feet and reproduces by suckers, the seeds being rarely fertile. A cultivar 'White Hedge' is now the most popular form. The Indian currant or coral berry, *S. orbiculatus*, has been in cultivation here since the early 18th century but is not often seen: berries dark red. Early in the 20th century Wilson discovered a Chinese snowberry with dark blue berries.

[about 1820]

snowberry

Patterns

The cabbage palm, *Cordyline*, was introduced from New Zealand in 1823. The fan palm, *Chamaerops*, native of Europe (and extinct on the Riviera) was already here in 1731, though not much heard of. *Trachycarpus fortunei*, the Chusan palm of China, is hardy in Britain and was sent as seed from Japan in 1836 – it was cultivated there – by Siebold (Jongheer Dr Philipp Franz von Siebold, a Bavarian, later of Siebold and Co., Leyden. His *Flora Japonica*, 1835–42 was illustrated by Japanese artists.) Many palms in Britain look rather sad, but remarkable exceptions are a nice clean fan palm at Oxford Botanic Garden (with a much taller brother under glass); a row of really impressive cabbage trees, branching and leafing with great vigour, in the public park at Penzance, and some fine, hairy-trunked Chusan palms at Minehead, also in the town park. This palm grows well in the west of England, Ireland and north to W. Ross (Scourie), but it needs to be under glass at Kew to gain any height. Bean recommends top dressings of cow dung. The flowers, tiny, white, scented, are in erect 4-foot panicles.

the fan palm *Chamaerops*

A mighty creeper, *Wisteria sinensis*, was introduced from Canton in 1816. It is a godsend to gardeners with pergolas (large ones) and it also climbs walls as everyone knows – it needs assistance. While it contributes impressive (light purple) colour I have put it under the heading of pattern because of its habit. For the stem, see the picture. The leaves are long, ash-like with about eleven leaflets. It is leguminous.

Also Chinese, and called japonica, is the shrub *Chaenomeles speciosa*. This was introduced in 1796, followed by *Ch. japonica* in 1869. Hybrids ensued. The quince japonica is allied to the true quince, *Cydonia*, but the fruits have none of the quince aroma; mostly decorative. Those of *speciosa* are yellow green, spotted and pear shaped; of *Japonica* not spotted, yellow blushing red. The flowers of both in early spring or even before Christmas, are orange or red. A much-loved plant, and the persistent fruit make a charming pattern.

Camellia japonica was known in Europe in the 18th century. It can be 40 feet high, so it is a tree. It was much cultivated in greenhouses in the 19th century, then went out of favour. Now it is grown outdoors in sheltered places, an evergreen with almost black leaves, and, of course, beautiful flowers. There are many varieties.

Wisteria sinensis, Hill Gardens, Hampstead

Flavour: apples and pears

The Blenheim Orange, a revolution in eating-apples, originated obscurely before 1818, a tree of unknown parentage in a cottage garden in Woodstock, the small town which flourishes beside Blenheim Park. It became the favourite, and remained so for a hundred years. One of its parents was perhaps a Golden Pippin, known as the best dessert apple in the previous century – or the Golden Reinette, a russet-orange tinted apple from Europe which gives its name Reinette to the group which includes Blenheim's and Cox's. The Cox's Orange Pippin – the name pippin implies that it grew as a seedling – was reared by a retired brewer, Richard Cox, before 1850: the female parent was a Ribston.

Thomas Laxton was born in 1830. His nursery's Fortune and Superb took over most of the market in the early 1900s. Fortune derived from a Cox's cross. Before Laxton, Thomas Andrew Knight had made apple breeding into a science. His *Treatise on the Culture of the Apple and Pear* was published in 1797. There are now 3000 named varieties of apple, of which, sadly, none are Varpneys (four-a-penny's) or, not so sadly, Leatherhides, known to Shakespeare.

Blenheims keep until Easter or later, as the owners of many an old tree are aware: not only in England but in Europe, America and, I believe, Australia – where, presumably, they are harvested at Easter.

Apple timber has been used for cogwheels, wooden screws, shuttles, golf club heads, carpenter's planes and mallets.

A separate line of evolution has produced, over the centuries, cider apples and perry pears. The Saxons made cider, but perry pears probably came in with the Normans. The origins of these cultivated varieties, as with the domestic apples and pears, are in the distant past in the wild, variable *Malus pumila* and *Pyrus communis* – both with more or less green fruit. Cider apples and perry pears are of many shapes and colours but have in common a high tannin content, small size and hard texture. The expressed juice of either will produce alcohol, usually within 24 hours.

old pear tree at Little Comberton, Worcs

Pears, wild or cultivated, are usually large trees which can live at least 300 years. A smaller tree, a wild pear of Europe, *P. cordata*, was found to be also wild in S. W. England in 1853. The fruit is small and brown. Perhaps there is a strain of this tree in the several perry pears which are coloured brown, such as the Rock or Madcap, from a smallish, wide-spreading tree without the strongly upward-thrusting branches of most pears. Some perry pears are yellow, some green, some red. The Blakeney Red or Painted Lady pear is from a large tree, heavy-cropping – well known in Gloucestershire for perry and for stewing and pickling. During the First World War a special factory was set up to can these fruit. Khaki dye was a by-product.

Of eating-pears, only two English varieties, both from the late 18th century, have added anything to history; but they are still important today. They are Williams's Bon Chrétien, known to us all as a William and to the American canning industry as a Bartlett, after the man who introduced the variety to the U.S.A.; and Conference, raised in Berkshire. This tree, widely grown, is said to produce fruit without fertilization, like a hen does eggs.

Pear timber, known as fruitwood, is an especially valuable timber for furniture. The best artists' easels are made of pear wood.

Bhutan pine

13 · The Pinetum, 1822–1861

Oaks, ashes, elms, and, in spite of Gilpin, beeches continued to be planted by large landowners with, now, European Larch. Scots pine, reintroduced to S. England, spread from the gentlemen's parks to the increasingly neglected heaths of Sussex and Breckland. Walnut trees fell for very high prices – the wood was the favourite for gunstocks in the Napoleonic wars. But the great period of tree planting was yet to come.

The Commissioners appointed to study the neglected Crown lands, woods and forests were able to report in 1793 that 'Private property, happily for this country, is in perfect security; but the property of the Crown in the forests is open to daily encroachments.' Perfect security continued, in spite of fears of a Napoleonic invasion. After the war, in 1803, plans were made to restock the forests, and by the middle of the century, 33,000 acres were in production. But the great private estates supplied the bulk of the timber market until well after Britain's wooden walls had changed to iron. Import duties on all foreign timber were removed by 1866, and, says Hadfield, 'there was no incentive to plant timber to meet the changed needs of the next century'. Also, 'a body of prejudice was built up against homegrown timbers', which Hadfield attributes to clever publicity organized by 'financial interests'.

The early years of the century, however, were a hopeful and exciting period for arboriculturalists (as in other sciences and arts), and many of these men put their ideas into effective practice. The Dukes of Athol, between 1783 and 1826, brought their already large plantations of pine and larch to 10,324 acres, much of the land useless for ordinary agriculture. Others followed this great example, and all were aware that the fast-growing, tolerant larch was virtually a new tree to Britain. Other foreign trees, especially the fabulous giants of the west coast of America, were of great interest, and this was focused by the publication in 1803 of the important *Genus Pinus* by A. B. Lambert of Boyton, Wiltshire. (*Pinus* was taken at this time to

cone of *Araucaria* from The *Genus Pinus*: original is full size

David Douglas

include all conifers.) Archibald Menzies, exploring with the tireless Captain Vancouver, had described, in the early 1790s, some of those giants: Sitka spruce, Nootka cypress, coast redwood; and *Pinus taxifolia*. This last was *Pseudotsuga menziesi* which was to be called the Douglas fir; our living, very tall monument to a most extraordinary and determined Scot.

David Douglas

He was born in 1799, the son of a stonemason, and apprenticed, aged 11, to the head gardener at Scone Palace. By ability, enthusiasm and physical energy he advanced himself so as to become the brightest student under William Joseph Hooker, who was then Professor of Botany at Glasgow – later the great Director of Kew. On Hooker's recommendation he was sent by the Horticultural Society to collect fruit trees and plants in America. In 1823 he was commissioned to explore the area now Washington and Oregon with the assistance of the Hudson's Bay Company, based on the Columbia River. In his short life Douglas introduced 254 new plants to Britain. His more important tree finds are reviewed under their own headings later in this chapter. After the long sea voyage round Cape Horn he stepped ashore at Cape Disappointment, the ship fogbound. *Gaultheria shallon*, the first plant he took in his hand, delighted him. 'Menzies correctly observes that it grows under thick pine forests and would make a valuable addition to our gardens.' It is one of his introductions of 1826. (You can cut it back in April to control its growth). When the fog cleared, the ship proceeded 8 miles up river, then Douglas set off to the new Fort Vancouver, 70 miles on, in a boat with one Canadian, six Indians paddling. They made only 40 miles the first day against the very strong current. Douglas was quick to observe the habits of his Indians: 'They sat round the fire the whole night roasting sturgeon . . . on sticks. . . . They ate a fish weighing 26 or 28 lb from ten o'clock till daylight . . . they had young shoots of *Rubus spectabilis* [a yellow currant, one of Douglas's introductions] and water.'

At base he was first given a tent, then a lodge of deerskin, but these were too small for his growing collections. By August he was settled in a hut made of the bark of *Thuja plicata*. On his expeditions he soon got used to sleeping with no protection but one blanket, under the shade of a pine.

In June 1825 he went up river with the canoes bound for different outposts. Below the Grand Rapids the river with the wind against it made waves so large that the canoes were often invisible to each other. At the rapids the Indians caught 'incredible numbers of salmon' using scoop nets on 12- or 15- foot poles: the hoops were of *Acer circinatum* (like *A. rubrum*), the pole balsam pine,* which is light when dried, the net of a species of *Apocynum*, very durable. Two salmon of 35 pounds or so he bought for ½ ounce of tobacco, value 2 pence.

The Indians called him *olla piska* – 'fire' in Chenook – because he drank foaming Epsom salts, and lit his pipe with a lens – and they were astonished at his spectacles. They also respected him as an excellent shot.

*The balsam fir of western N. America is *Abies lasiocarpa*, difficult and rare in Britain. The eastern balsam firs, *A. balsamea* and *A. fraseri*, very widespread in eastern Canada and U.S.A. are also rare here. *A. balsamea*, the source of 'Canada balsam' was introduced in the 17th century, and has usually failed.

With neither time nor space for comforts, tea, sugar and two or three biscuits were Douglas's usual travelling rations, and, essential currency, tobacco. Shortage of food was a common problem in the western forests. In 1826 he was exploring the middle Columbia. 'Reached the old establishment at Spokane at eleven o'clock, where I was very kindly received by Mr Finlay. He regretted exceedingly that he had not a morsel of food to offer me. He and his family were living for the last six weeks on the roots of *Phalangium quamash* [camass, a Chenook name for a bulb of the lily family] and a species of black lichen which grows on the pines.' Douglas on this occasion was able to offer him the best meal he had enjoyed for some time.

At one camp, rats devoured all his collection of seed in the night, cut a bundle of dried plants through and carried off his razor and soap-brush. One was about to make off with his ink stand when he woke up and shot it. He shot another, more carefully so that he could preserve the skin for the Horticultural Society, not then too specialised.

In October 1826 he was in relatively unexplored country seeking a large pine. A humter had given him a cone 15 inches long, and he had seen the seeds with the Indians' baggage. Marching 17 and 18 miles a day through thick woodland he passed a night of terrible storm, immense trees falling round him every 15 minutes. His horses put their heads close to his and whinnied for protection. ' . . . indulging myself with a fume of tobacco, the only thing I could afford . . . started at ten o'clock, still shivering with cold though I rubbed myself with my handkerchief before the fire until I was no longer able to endure the pain.'

A sketch of the cone inspired an Indian to point the way to the sugar pines. The cones were very high in the trees, two-thirds of the trunk being bare of branches. He was shooting down some cones with his gun when eight Indians appeared, wearing war paint and with bows and arrows, spears and knives. They sat down to smoke but at the same time sharpened their weapons. Douglas tried to stare them out for ten minutes, then they asked for tobacco and he indicated that they should have some if they would fetch more of the cones. As soon as they were out of sight he retreated to his camp and sent away his guide, in case the Indian betrayed him.

(The pine, *P. lambertiana*, was named after the author of *Genus Pinus*. Many old specimens growing in Britain have died, infected with white pine blister rust. Young trees, however, grow fast and healthy.)

The next day, Douglas's Indian returned with a trout to be roasted for breakfast. A grizzly bear with two cubs threatened them. 'I levelled my gun at the heart of the mother, but as she was protecting one of the young keeping them right before her and one standing before her belly, my ball entered the palate of the young one and came out at the back part of the head. It dropped instantly, and as the mother stood up a second time I lodged a ball in her chest, which on receiving, she abandoned the remaining live young and fled to an adjoining hummock of wood. The wound was mortal, as they never leave their young until ready to sink. With the carcase of the young I paid my guide, who seemed to lay great store by it. I abandoned the chase and thought it prudent from what happened yesterday to bend my steps back again without delay.'

In January to July 1827, he travelled overland and by river and lake to York Factory in Hudson's Bay. He kept his journal all the way. 'Strangers in this quarter appear to be few; scarcely a house I passed without an invitation to enter, more particularly from the Scottish settlers, who no doubt judging from my coat (being clothed in the Stewart or royal tartan) imagined me a son from the bleak mountains of Scotland, and I had many questions put to me regarding that country, which now they only see through ideal recollections. Appear to live comfortable and have the means of subsistence by little exertion.'

He sailed for England in September, and in London found he was famous. But he soon became irritable, refusing the help of his employer Sabine, Secretary of the Horticultural Society, and the distinguished Dr Lindley (who misnamed so many plants) in editing his journals for publication. His eyesight was failing, and his deportment left much to be desired. Visiting a large garden he disconcerted his hosts by flinging himself into a bed of dwarf juniper, to show how he had so often slept.

In 1830 he went back to the Columbia River, on a surveying expedition. On this tour, lasting until 1834, he collected the noble fir, *Abies procera*: 'I spent three weeks in a forest composed of this tree, and day by day could not cease to admire it.' He also visited the redwood forests of coastal California, but no seed reached England from him. In the winters he based himself at Monterey in California, adding *Pinus radiata*, the Monterey pine, to his collection.

Trying to walk back to Europe via Alaska, he had to give up, and then lost everything, including all his notes and journals for the four years, in a canoe accident on the way back to Columbia. He spun in a whirlpool for 100 minutes, it is said. He then explored the Sandwich Islands and called at Honolulu to wait for a ship home. Here he fell into a wild bull trap and was gored to death, aged 35.

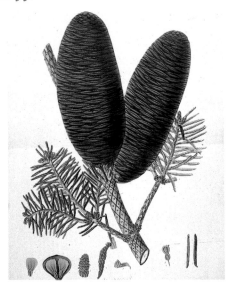

Abies Webbiana (now *A. spectabilis*), the Himalayan fir, from *Pinetum Woburnense*, published by the Duke of Bedford, 1834

Conifer collections

Douglas was followed in N.W. America by William Lobb in 1849, sent by James Veitch and Sons. Earlier, in 1840, Lobb had collected a quantity of Chile pine, *Araucaria*, seed for distribution in Britain. In 1853 he sent large quantities of *Sequoiadendron gigantea* seed. The two most noticeable and least useful Victorian trees thus owe their ubiquitousness to Lobb. A much more useful, as well as beautiful, introduction of his was the western red cedar, *Thuja plicata*. He also sent marketable quantities of most of Douglas's discoveries. Lobb was not required to keep a journal, and nothing is known of his adventures.

The *Gardeners Magazine* of 1838 listed 69 conifers and 18 pinetums where the trees were grown and observed, including Kew, Edinburgh R.B.G., Glasnevin, Woburn, Chatsworth. In 1849 a group of arboricultural gentlemen at Edinburgh formed a society, the Oregon Association, for the botanical exploration of N.W. America and the introduction of trees, especially the Coniferae. They sent John Jeffrey in 1850. He did splendidly at first, but after three years his despatches diminished and he then disappeared, never to be heard of again. Perhaps he struck gold, and changed his name. Botanical explorers were usually worked to death – and for a pittance.

Pinus jeffreyi is big-coned, needles bunched in threes, allied to the western yellow pine, *P. ponderosa*, and resembling *P. coulteri*, the big-cone pine. There are specimens at Batsford, Scone Palace (118 feet) and Powerscourt (108 feet) of *P. jeffreyi*, and at large arboreta of *P. coulteri* – but one at Kew is low and accessible, near the Isleworth Gate.

In 1854 the Royal Scottish Forestry Society was formed – originally as the Scottish Arboricultural Society. The English Arboricultural Society, formed in 1882, became the Royal Forestry Society.

East Himalayan fir, *Abies spectabilis*. This was first called *Webbiana* after the Captain Webb who sent seeds to Wallich at Calcutta. *Spectabilis* (with the accent on the *a*) apparently means spectacular, and the coloured plate from Woburn is surely that. As the first 'exotic' silver fir in Britain it must have been admired, but it was soon overtaken by the W. American firs discovered by Douglas. In Britain it is limited by late frosts, though it grows above 8000 feet in Afghanistan, Sikkim and Bhutan.

The leaves are longish and appear square ended, with dense white bands below, on a stout brown shoot with deep grooves like a spruce. The second year shoots are paler. The bark is pinkish grey, shredding when young and irregularly fissured in age with distinctive horizontal pattern on the raised sections between the fissures. Cones, grey, turn to purple in winter.

The shape of the tree is broad, irregular, even flat-topped, with side branches and epicormic shoots – that is, produced after the main crown is formed. Old trees thus have a cedar-like appearance. It is an important tree, forming large forests, where mosses, ferns and even bushes grow upon it. The timber is white and used for constructional work in India. There are trees of 80 to 90 feet at Inverary, Pencarrow (Bodmin) and Powerscourt – and lesser specimens at Benmore. In its native mountains it can be 200 feet. *A. pindrow*, introduced in 1837 is closely related with stout but smooth shoots and large, notched leaves. It is rare in Britain, but looks very healthy in a plot at Kilmun.

Bhutan pine or **Himalayan blue pine**. Still in Wallich country, this is *P. wallichiana* Jackson, or *P. excelsa* Wallich, or *P. griffithii* McClelland, and was introduced by Lambert at Boyton. Even without all these gentlemen it

cones of the Bhutan pine

is one of the more approachable pines, not remote in the sky above a massive pole, but with low sweeping branches and attractive bunches of long shiny needles. The leaves are triangular in section with one face bright green and the others bluish white, in fives. The cones, as you see, are banana shaped. The bark is thin for a pine, becoming orange and fissured, but not deeply so.

Bhutan pine timber is reddish and is valued next to that of the deodar which grows beside it at some levels, with spruces, firs and birches. The wood is resinous and the trees are tapped for turpentine.

[1824]

Greek fir

The **Greek fir**, *Abies cephalonica*, named after a Greek island, is close to the Spanish fir, with which it crosses as x *vilmorinii*, and has similarly spiky foliage, smooth shoots and resinous buds. The bark is brown-grey, somewhat smooth up to 100 years old, then breaking into a crackle-pattern of squarish plates. It grows above Athens and north to Albania, covered with mosses and lichens among the rocks – 'The forest of Puck and Titania,' remarks Hugh Johnson. Over-grazing and frequent fires, perhaps from the wrath of Zeus, are reducing its numbers.

One of the original introductions survives at Barton, Suffolk, and there are old trees in most arboreta. Spring frost can kill. Young trees at Bedgebury grow with birches which invaded the plot, protecting them. Birch is not usually a protective tree: in the windy Highlands its wiry twigs can whip off the young shoots of conifers.

[1827]

Douglas fir

Douglas fir. The dominant tree of the western forest, from Canada down the Rockies to Mexico. A 300-year-old was recorded as 340 feet high and 42 feet round. Such a tree might contain 8000 cubic feet of timber; and this species has produced more timber than any other American tree. The wood is called Oregon pine, Columbian pine, Oregon fir, red fir, yellow fir and red pine. The yellow, harder sort comes from crowded forest trees. The timber dries well, works well, is strong and moderately resistant to decay. Some old stands still remain in the American National Parks, and the finest are on Vancouver Island. Douglas mentions a stump at Fort George, the old establishment of the Hudson's Bay Company. It was 48 feet in circumference at 3 feet above the ground, without its bark. 'The tree was burned down to give place to a more useful vegetable, namely potatoes.'

Pseudotsuga menziesii, originally *Ps. Douglasii*, was *Pinus taxifolia* (yew-leaved pine) to Lambert. The names tell its history and nature, though 'pseudo-hemlock' is hardly a happy concoction. The typical form in Britain is the Oregon, green or coastal Douglas fir. There is a southern, blue form, the Colorado, and an inland, grey one from the Rockies. Thirty trees or more in Britain are 150 feet high, and one, at Powis Castle, Welshpool, was temporarily the tallest tree in the country at 181 feet. A tree from Douglas's seed is at Scone Palace.

The bark of older trees is unmistakably rugged and corky, but young trees, which are regularly conic in outline, may not be easily recognisable. They have dark grey-green shiny bark with resin blisters, and this changes to purplish brown with vertical cracks. Often a tree in woodland may be recognized by the prominent pointed buds, which are reddish brown. Mitchell notes a fruity aroma in the leaves: others are reminded of pineapple. Well-drained mineral soil, not chalky, good rainfall and moderate shelter suit the tree best. It may grow 100 feet in 30 years. Some rather shapeless old trees at Westonbirt, in the meadow, have witches' brooms hanging from the branches. The flagstaff at Kew, 214 feet, is a Douglas fir trunk, a present from British Columbia.

cone of Douglas fir

Western yellow pine, *Pinus ponderosa* Douglas. Widely distributed, and thus variable, from S. British Columbia to N. Mexico and from W. Texas to the Pacific; tall, up to 230 feet, it grows on sunny mountain sides and in dry valleys. One of Douglas's original trees grows at Bowood, the great bole majestic with coarse orange and black stripes in the gloom of the Pinetum. The top is lost to sight above the other trees.

This is the most important pine in western America. Douglas found it on the Spokane River in 1826. The early settlers called it the bull pine, and the wood is hard and strong, light red, and useful for heavy construction work.

The shape of mature trees is variable, with forking branches forming a cylindrical tower; or short-trunked with an uneven, rounded head. The leaves are long, usually in threes (sometimes twos or fives), the cones 3 or 4 inches, green, brown or purple, closed for three years.

Deodar, *Cedrus deodarus*. The cedar of N.W. India, where it grows from 4000 to 10,000 feet with oaks, morinda spruce, Bhutan pine. Pure forests of this cedar are rare in nature, but the genus is so distinct that the three species, Atlas, Lebanon and Deodar, each separated by 1500 miles, can be visualized as surviving sections of a great continuous cedar forest of the Tethys shores.

[1830]

deodars at Blenheim

Of the three, the deodar is the most graceful and at the same time the most useful timber tree. It is a 'sacred Indian fir' and a 'tree of God', and is used to build temples as those of Lebanon were used by Solomon. Also it has made miles of railway sleepers, being durable. Logs can be split, which is not usually the case with the other cedars, so that straight-grained boards can be made, and long-lasting roof shingles. The wood has a strong smell which is said to be overpowering indoors.

The needles are longer, thinner and sharper than with other cedars. The leading shoots at the top as well as on the branches droop elegantly. There are yellow varieties and blue varieties, and a form, *pendula* that is completely collapsed, only occasionally rising from the ground, somewhat menacingly.

Seeds came to Britain from the Hon. Leslie Melville and were planted at Melville, Fife, and elsewhere, notably Westonbirt House, where, when the grounds are open, you can see an original tree. The Commissioners for Crown Lands tried it as a commercial softwood, without success.

Noble fir, *Abies procera*. If *procera* means tall, that is right, for it reaches 240 feet and is already over 150 feet here, very healthy and widely planted in the W. and N. of Britain. Douglas discovered it in 1825 and sent seeds from W. America on his second visit.

The bark is purplish grey or silvery, with a pattern of wandering cracks crossing the frequent 'eyes'. The leaves are grey green to blue grey, white below, flat, grooved and lightly notched. They lie close to and concealing the brown shoot and then curve away; as if combed out, says Hadfield. The cone

part of the cone of the noble fir

is splendid, barrel shaped and up to 10 inches long on specimen trees – less in the wild. It well justifies the name of noble.

There are fine trees in most large gardens and arboreta, and congregations in Scottish policies and at Westonbirt. In Scotland the tree regenerates naturally. There are original trees of 1835 at Chatsworth and the unfortunately inaccessible Dropmore.

The timber in America is red fir, of high quality, light, strong and close-grained. *A. procera* formed large pure forests in the Cascade Mountains of Washington, and it grows with *A. amabilis*, the red silver fir or Cascade fir, which it resembles. *A. magnifica*, the red fir of Oregon and California, is also somewhat similar.

The **grand fir**, *A. grandis*, or **giant fir**, also introduced by Douglas, is the tallest of the great silver firs of the western American mountains. The finest trees are 300 feet, on Vancouver Island, and the range extends to central California and inland to Idaho. This fir grows best in the wet, and has been planted as a forestry tree in Britain. One grew to 167 feet in 53 years. It is conical in shape, an archetypal fir tree, with flat leaves in two ranks on an olive green shoot. The bark is brown grey, later dark, dull grey with a few cracked plates here and there and a tendency to horizontal folds more common with Old World firs. The cone is a simple, large oval, green or brown, with no bracts visible.

One of Douglas's original trees is known for certain, at Curraghmore, Waterford, but there are many bigger ones planted in the 1860s to 1880s. Some of the tallest are at Glamis Castle, Angus, and Dupplin Castle, Perths, but large trees can be seen at all arboreta: the tallest tree in Britain is a grand fir: over 182 feet at Leighton Hall, Welshpool.

The timber is coarse grained, but perhaps this can be forgiven.

To the south, *A. concolor*, the Colorado white fir takes over, with an intermediate form var. *lowiana*, very distinct, with elegantly spaced leaves, growing with *A. grandis*. It was introduced in 1851: not common, but it may yet have a future in Britain.

Sitka spruce, *Picea sitchensis*, was described by Menzies from Sitka in Alaska and introduced by Douglas in 1831. A larger quantity of seed was sent to the Oregon Association by Jeffrey.

This spruce is known to us all as the most common forestry species of modern Britain. It did not reach this status without the benefit of the early experience of 'curious' persons who planted it in the mid-Victorian period: 50 to 70 years on, and even in poor soils and exposed positions, *P. sitchensis* towered above its neighbours, spruces, firs or pines. By 1920 its reputation was made and the new Forestry Commission had its most useful battalion in the fight to change grouse moors into forest and maybe supply a quarter of our timber needs. Sitka has everything: the thinnings have a ready market for paper pulp; the trees resist most diseases, deer, voles and human beings (nobody likes the sharp needles). There were over 600,000 acres in 1965 and 30 million are planted every year. Only in frost hollows is Norway spruce the better tree.

The old specimen trees survive in a graceful and impressive style, very

Sitka spruce

different from the tough commercial atmosphere of the plantations, and reaching heights that might be unwieldly in an industrial context: 170 feet at Murthly Castle, Perths, planted in 1846.

The bark, with round peeling plates, and the woods, full of the dead inner branches, are distinctive. The cones have papery, crinkly scales, and are pale brown, squashy and about 3 inches long. Epicormic shoots and root suckers are common, and some old trees in the open have large, low branches which form layered roots.

Good-quality Sitka spruce is straight-grained and strong, and if not up to musical instrument standard, was good enough to build fighter planes in the last war. In the trade it is whitewood.

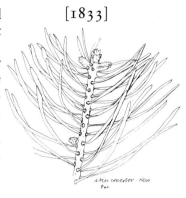
[1833]

Monterey pine, *Picea radiata*. Douglas found this in the Monterey Peninsula where it has a limited native range and grows to extravagent shapes in the Pacific winds. The warmth of California is only approached in S.W. England and this very distinct pine is not generally hardy, though it will be found in most arboreta. It is very commonly planted by the southern shores; easy to recognize with its very coarse nobbly-ridged bark and squarish outlines. The cones, asymmetrical and fat, stick to the branches for years. Needles are straight, in threes, a mid green colour. Like *P. wallichiana*, it often has low branches and is one of the more human pines, climbable by small children.

P. radiata grows very quickly and there are many specimen trees of more than 100 feet. It is now an important forestry tree in Australia, New Zealand and S. Africa.

The **bishop pine,** *P. muricata*, found by Coulter in 1832 at San Luis Obispo, is rather similar, more massive, and greyer. It was not introduced until 1846. It has a scattered coastal Californian range, a two-needle pine slightly hardier than *P. radiata* but not very commonly planted here. A narrow, blue, northern form has grown 6 feet in a year at Muckross in Co. Kerry, and there are specimens of the more sprawling, heavy-limbed type in the large arboreta. The cones sometimes stay on the tree for 70 years, waiting for forest fires which, killing the roots, would open the scales and release the seed to ensure the survival of the species.

Monterey pine, *P. radiata*

Oriental spruce, *Picea orientalis*. No trouble with names, except that it is Caucasian and only as oriental as Turkey. Recognition is easy too, for it has the smallest of all spruce needles. The bark is attractive, brown to grey with a homespun texture of leaf scars, horizontal in emphasis, later breaking into small curling plates. But old trees in the open are immense bulging cones with dense foliage carried to the ground on pendulous branches, no trunk being visible. This spruce was introduced in 1839.

At about 100 feet they seem to stop growing in Britain. As a late Victorian conifer it seemed the most promising spruce and is in large gardens everywhere. Young trees are less common, but there is a group, nicely spaced, N. of the Lily Pond at Kew, which gives some impression of the sober calm that must have prevailed in the spruce forest above Trebizond, discovered in the early 18th century by Tournefort. There is a plot at Bedgebury, planted in 1949, which reached 20 feet in 15 years – but so did the beeches.

Oriental spruce, Batsford

Monterey cypress,
Cupressus macrocarpa,
Gower coast

Cupressus macrocarpa. The **Monterey cypress** is almost better known as the 'macrocarpa'. The fruit in fact is not quite so large as with *C. sempervirens*, the Italian cypress, long resident here and the only other well-known 'true' cypress in Britain. Macrocarpa was cultivated in 1838, from seed supplied by Lambert, in the Horticultural Society Garden at Chiswick, and called *C. lambertiana*. Its native habitat was not discovered until 1846. Soon there were probably more trees in Britain than in their narrow coastal home in California, but many were killed in a severe frost in 1860. The species is however hardy to a degree, and wide cultivation has enabled it to grow tall and to diversify in ways that nature had discouraged. On the Monterey coast the trees grow raggedly, but in some sheltered English gardens they are already up to 120 feet, taller than in the wild and of perfect symmetrical shape – sometimes assisted by pruning. In damper Ireland they grow broad as well as large. Though variable in habit, their tendency to fork low down into many upward-thrusting branches is constant, and the stringy, yellowish bark is easily recognized.

Typically, this is the shore-line tree of south-western resorts, not always lovely, but growing where other trees would not.

> Those macrocarpa still survive the gales
> They must have had last winter. Still the shops
> Remain unaltered on the Esplanade. . . .

of Betjeman's childhood holidays in N. Cornwall.

The timber is fragrant, yellowish; of good quality, according to Esmond Harris; coarse and knotty, according to Elwes and Henry; hard, durable and close-grained, according to Sargent.

[1839]

Spanish fir, *Abies pinsapo*. 'Hedgehog fir', because of its spiny, outward-pointing needles set all round the shoot, but also, I think affectionately. The needles are not really sharp, and it is nicely shaped as a young tree in spite of a tendency to form several trunks. It will grow on chalk, which few firs will, and is planted in eastern England, where firs are few. The bark of old trees is a clerical grey broken by zig-zag, linear fissures into irregular plates which seem to emphasize the excellent cylindrical form of the trunk.

Discovered by a M. Boissier in 1837, who built its local Spanish name into the Latin specific, it grew, and I hope still does grow, in three small forests near Ronda in southern Spain. These, with a few isolated groups nearby suggest a former large forest, which once must have extended eastwards to join the Grecian fir. After the Ice Ages its spread northwards was restricted by the east–west barrier of the Guadalquivir valley, and its habitat south-wards to the Mediterranean limited by dryness. It clings to the north-facing slopes of hills, where moisture can be retained. It has a Moroccan cousin, *A. marocano*, across the Strait of Gibraltar.

In England it needs warmth – it is not a fir for Scotland. Young trees can be seen in the Forest Plots at Bedgeberry. Old trees are 90 to 100 feet at Rhinefield, New Forest – others at The Frythe, Welwyn, and Dropmore are surrounded by high wire fences and security guards, and one of the two original trees at Dropmore is dead. If you have a bit of downland to spare, please plant *A. pinsapo*.

leaves of the hedgehog fir

Atlas cedar, *Cedrus atlantica*. Native of Morocca and Algeria – the Atlas mountains – this is almost too familiar in its blue or silver form, var. *glauca*, and rather difficult to separate from *C. libani*, as a single tree in the green or typical form. The bark is a lighter colour at first, the outline is usually pointed at the top, and the trunk usually taller before the first branches. The shoot, and this is the botanist's telling point, is grey-green with dense, blackish curly pubescence (hair), as distinct from *C. libani* whose shoot is fawn to coffee brown, slightly ribbed, with short, greyer brown pubescence usually in the ribs. I have used A. F. Mitchell's words becuase no one could improve on his observation. With a lens you can distinguish a transparent spine at the tip of the leaf of *C. atlantica*.

blue Atlas cedar at Batsford

The original tree at Bowood is 132 feet by 18 feet (1968) and there you can also see the blue form, as at Eastnor Castle where it was first introduced in 1841 by Lord Somers from seed gathered at Teniet el Haad. There are other varieties too – and there *are* blùe forms of *C. libani*.

Coast Redwood, *Sequoia sempervirens*. The world's tallest tree, 370 feet, grows in the northern part of a coastal fog belt in California, north of the San Francisco smog belt, 500 miles by 10–35 miles wide. Both this and the more massive Big Tree, *Sequoiadendron*, are called redwoods by the Save-the-Redwoods-League and other Americans, and have in common their great size, red brown compacted fibrous bark and egg-shaped cones with laterally arranged flat diamond-shaped scales. They are included in the family Taxodiaceae with the 'bald cypresses' of the southeast States and the *Cryptomeria* or Japanese cedar, and are clearly the remains of a worldwide forest (once including the Isle of Wight) of unimaginable proportions in the Cretaceous. Fossil trunks in American yellowstone show annual rings of phenomenal thickness. Lucky for the redwoods and for us that the Pacific was not 30 miles wider: nowhere else could the redwoods have survived.

[1843]

Sequoia produces two kinds of leaves: spirally arranged scale-leaves on growing shoots and two flat rows of yew-like leaves on side shoots. At human height, the scale-leaves are rarely in evidence. The bark is thick and a bright orange brown, old trees forming massive vertical ridges which meet and cross at 10 or 15 foot intervals like a mighty Gothic architecture made of fibre matting. The bark is unusually fire resistant, but are forest fires common in the natural state, in areas subject to sea fogs?

Redwoods coppice, that is, they sucker from the root or stem, or from a cut shoot. For this reason, trees in the natural forest grow very close together with a shared root system. Small burrs from the trees, put in a bowl of water, produce indoor gardens of green shoots.

By 1900 large sawmills in Mendocino and Humboldt counties had cleared 215,000 acres of the original 1,454,000. 'Since that year cutting has been going on at an accelerated pace and the quantity now felled annually is enormous,' wrote Augustine Henry in 1908. Natural redwood forest contains more cubic feet of wood per acre than any other, and that includes the tropical rain forests. Whole Californian cities (including Redwood City?) have been built of redwood timber. The California Redwood Park, 50 miles long by about 5 miles wide, was constituted in 1901, between Eureka and Crescent City. Now 26 coastal parks contain 48,383 acres of redwoods.

Sequoia, named after a Cherokee half-breed chief who invented an Indian

bole of a large redwood in the depths of an early Victorian plantation, Fonthill

Cryptomeria japonica cone

lacebark pine at Kew

alphabet, is clouded in the literature, not by sea fogs, but by its rarer and mightier relative, *Sequoiadendron*. In Britain the trees are less often confused. Redwood has reached 165 feet (1970, Endsleigh near Milton Abbot, Devon, planted 1859). There are small groves of large trees in most arboreta, and an impressive grove is at Leighton Park, Welshpool. At Bedgebury, where they have less than half the rainfall of N. California, no fogs – and are subject to frost as late as May and dry summers – they have grown 63 feet in 37 years.

Japanese cedar, *Cryptomeria japonica*. A sort of Japanese redwood and the most important softwood tree of that fortunate country. It grows to 180 feet. It was introduced to Kew in 1842 and seed was sent in quantity by Robert Fortune from Shanghai, with various forms brought from Japan later. It has been cultivated as a forestry tree in Japan for centuries and this has resulted in a wide range of varieties. The wood, *sugi*, is used for everything from laquered ware to rafters. *Crytomeria* has bunched, bright green foliage, conforming roughly to a tall pyramid, and dark brown bark, soft and fibrous with deep vertical fissures and some peeling strips. Older trees in Britain are necessarily var. *sinensis*, less dense and lighter green. Var. *lobbii*, which William Lobb sent from trees cultivated in Java, is narrow, with foliage markedly bunched and upturned. Var. *elegans* has permanently juvenile foliage – thin soft leaves – blue green in summer and red or purple in winter; bullet-shaped or sprawling. *Cristata* has compacted fists of foliage reminiscent of cacti, and suggesting, as much as all the Taxodiaceae, a vegetable world of the distant past that we can explore only in imagination.

Cow's tail pine, *Cephalotaxus*. Not a pine, and not like a cow's tail: *cephalo* is something to do with a head. *Taxus* = yew. This is a far eastern group of yew-like trees with olive-like fruit. They are quite hardy in Britain but never grow large – 'useful evergreens' say the gardening books. The specific name of the Japanese *Cephalotaxus* is *harringtonia*, and var. *drupacea* is the one we have here, the type species being rare here and unknown in the wild. It, *C. h. drupacea*, was brought to Leyden by Siebold in 1829 but did not reach England until 1844. Henry describes 'an old specimen at Kew, about 10 feet high and 15 feet through, and clothed to the ground with luxurious dark green foliage'. It is much the same today, 70 years on, and last time I saw it there was a rich crop of fruit. The bark is also luxurious, described as greyish in the textbooks but actually full of purplish tones and flaking picturesquely. A variety *fastigiata* behaves exactly like the Irish yew.

This tree grows throughout the Japanese mountain forests, sometimes reaching 40 feet, and is also found in China. It reaches 25 feet at Wakehurst and Bicton. See also the Chinese cow's tail pine, 1848, opposite.

Lacebark pine, *P. bungeana*. Bunge, Alexander von, Professor of Botany at Dorpat (Tarsu), Estonia, found it by Buddhist temples near Peking, cultivated for its milk-white bark. Fortune introduced it. The bark in Britain is patchy, the palest patches greyish yellow, and very beautiful, if not lace-like. Specimens may be seen and admired at Wisley and at Kew – a group near the Isleworth Ferry Gate (sadly, you can no longer cross to the London Apprentice) and one, the oldest, N. of the Palm House. It is perfectly hardy, says Bean. British Buddhists and others please note.

Chinese cow's tail pine, *Cephalotaxus fortuni*. Robert Fortune, who collected in China for the Horticultural Society – and later in search of tea for the East India Company – got his material from mixed seeds, and plants labelled *C. fortuni foemina* are really, usually, *C. harringtonia* var. *sinensis*. These plum yews are very similar anyway, and both have lovely shiny leaves – down-curving with *fortuni*, thrusting forward and upward with *harringtonia* var. *drupacea*. Before blaming Fortune we should remember the difficulties under which he worked, dressed like a Chinese and with his hair in a pigtail, having his clothes and his collections stolen more than once or twice, and travelling in country quite unexplored by westerners. He spent 19 years in China. He was not merely courageous (on £100 a year) but resourceful. Lying aboard a Chinese junk, in a fever, he was roused by the attack of a pirate junk armed with deck guns. Forcing his captain at gunpoint to sail on he fought the pirates single-handed with his shotgun, so effectively that their leader knelt to beg for mercy. Robert Fortune was a Scottish gardener well in the Douglas tradition, but exploring, not a primeval forest but a very ancient civilization.

Fortune's equipment was made bulkier but much more effective by the Wardian Case, invented by a London G.P., Dr Ward, who had noticed that his fern collection did very well under glass. It is a portable greenhouse which employs the now well-known plastic bag principle, by which the imprisoned plant creates and maintains its own atmosphere. This invention, added to the speed of steam-assisted and schooner-rigged ships, made collection of far eastern plants easy, once the plants had been extracted from the jealous or suspicious natives and sufficient coolies assembled to carry the equipment.

Caucasian fir, *Abies nordmannia*. 144 feet at Cuffnells, Lyndhurst, and 134 feet at Powerscourt: aphid infected at Bedgebury. Like *A. alba* it would have a future as a highly productive timber tree but for *Adelges*, the aphid species which attack these trees in Britain.

Torreya californica, **California nutmeg**, was discovered by William Lobb. It is not a common tree even in its native Santa Cruz, Sierra Nevada and Coastal Range mountains. Another plum-fruited, yew-like tree but distinctive and interesting: you can see it at Edinburgh B.G., Batsford, Benmore and other great gardens: 67 feet at Mells Park, Frome, Somerset. *Torreya* is represented in Japan by *T. nucifera* (Wakehurst; Bicton) and in China by *T. grandis* (Kew, and Borde Hill, Haywards Heath, Sussex).

General Grant, Colonel Stewart and 'Wellingtonia'

[1853]

Wellington had won the Battle of Waterloo, which at least released large quantities of spare teeth to the dentists of Europe. But, considering that we already have Wellington boots, the naming of the biggest tree in the world after the Duke seems both unnecessary and inexcusably parochial. After all, the biggest of the Big Trees was large before the birth of Christ. I have therefore used the American vernacular name, or **giant sequoia** in this book. The Americans used also to call the giant sequoia a redwood, a Washingtonia (in answer to Wellingtonia, but *Washingtonia* is a palm); Sierra redwood is still accepted. It is botanically *Sequoiadendron gigantea*.

bark of *Cephalotaxus harringtonia* and leaf of *C. fortuni*

General Grant of Sequoia Lake, General Sherman of Giant Forest, Kings Canyon, and Grizzly Giant of Mariposa Grove, Yosemite Valley, are three of the mightiest of all living creatures. Gen. Sherman is estimated to weigh 2145 tons, though I hope we shall not know the truth in our lifetimes. It, or he, is 272 feet high, 79 feet round at 5 feet and 101 feet round the base: alive and healthy and over 3000 years old, with roots occupying over 3 acres.

It was not long after their discovery by European man that five workers armed with pump augers, working for a fortnight, in 1853, began to destroy the work of millenia. The fallen Father of the Forest was converted into a tube for horse riders to divert themselves in, no doubt at a nickel a time. The Mother of the Forest was spared, but others were to follow.

'When a large tree is felled,' wrote Elwes, 'its immense weight breaks a great part of the top into useless fragments, and crushes many other trees in its fall; whilst the usual means adopted to break up the logs into pieces which can be handled is by *blasting* [my italics], and this destroys another large part of the timber. When the best is removed, a mass of broken branches, lumber and bark, often 5 or 6 foot deep, is left on the ground, and is later destroyed by fire. . . . It is said that owing to various causes, the lumbering of these forests has often been quite unprofitable to their owners.' The timber, soft and brittle (a tree of 250 to 300 feet *has* to have fairly light-weight wood), had no market except locally, and was used for vine stakes, shingles, fencing and some building. Vine stakes indeed! It was estimated in the twenties that only a fifth of the trees cut down was actually used.

What we do not destroy, we preserve, and the Big Tree is great enough to survive even this. The Sequoia National Park was created in 1890, most of the initial acreage being owned by the first white man to set foot there, in 1858, Hale Tharp. 'There were about 2000 Indians then living along the Kaweah Rivers . . . the Indian chief was named Chappo, and he was a fine man . . . . Few of the Indians had ever seen a white man prior to my arrival. I shot many deer for them, as they had no firearms. . . . There was then abundance of game. Deer were everywhere, with lots of bear along the rivers and occasionally a grizzly. Lions, wolves, and foxes were plentiful. There were a great many ground squirrels, cottontail and jackrabbits; quail were seen in coveys of thousands . . . there were plenty of fish in the rivers below the rapids. . . . I carved with my knife on the big hollow redwood log my name and the year, on the same day that we got there. When we arrived at Log Meadow there were a great many deer and a few bear in the meadow, and the animals paid little attention to us. The deer came around our camp, and some of the bears sat upright in order to get a good look at us. I shot a small buck for camp meat. This shot did not seem to frighten the other deer or any of the bears.' Tharp later 'occupied' the place by leaving some horses to graze at Log Meadow. He made a cabin out of the fallen tree – a curiously shaped room 56 feet long and 8 feet high, tapering to 4 feet.

Colonel Stewart was the editor of the Visalia *Weekly Delta*, which campaigned for conservation of the giant sequoias. In 1885 when proof-reading he found that a large number of applications for 'quarter sections' of land, which had to be advertised by law, were fraudulent and would have put the whole Forest area into the hands of a syndicate of three men. He got the Land Register Officer to suspend the applications.

It was soon realized that mere suspension might not be permanent. 'We wrote letters to every person in 1890 in the United States, in and out of Congress, whom we knew to be in favour of forest conservation and to every magazine and newspaper we knew to favour the idea. Their name was not legion in those days.' The *Delta* got yet another military person, Congressman General Vandever, to introduce a bill to create a National Park of the Giant Forest. Another bill later in 1890 created the Yosemite and General Grant National Parks and enlarged the Sequoia National Park to 252 square miles. This was increased to 604 in 1926. The General Grant N.P. is now included in Kings Canyon N.P. (1940) immediately to the N. of the Sequoia N.P. George Stewart is remembered: a peak is named after him.

The finest groves are among 3500 trees of the Giant Forest and Muir Grove, 1800 trees on the North, Middle and Marble Forks of the Kaweah River; at Redwood Canyon, 3000 trees; at General Grant Forest, Mariposa Grove and Yosemite N.P., at North Calaveras and 7 miles south, Stanislaus – 1100 trees. North of General Grant is Converse Creek, with the ghostly remnants of a forest cut down and hardly used; also at Indian Creek, S. of Converse Mt. There are many more named groves: I note Lost Grove, 10 trees, and Eden, 8 trees, 'very inaccessible'. Surely the Pontiacs and Buicks can now drive to Eden? Young trees are at South Fork and there is regeneration elsewhere. A mix of the original yellow pine and sugar pine remains at Squirrel Creek, 90 acres at the centre of Sequoia N.P.

The great age of the Big Tree is the result of many aspects of its structure which are beyond my understanding – why don't they die of old age? The tree survives because of its wide, deep roots, which tap available moisture in dry seasons and provide a stable base. As a young tree its branches sweep downwards and its shape is conic – the whole structure, as with most conifers, designed to avoid snow damage as well as to reduce moisture loss in summer. The snow slips down the cone, pinning down the lower branches to form a rigidly braced structure. At about 600 years the lower branches are gradually sloughed off and the crown becomes round with ascending branches, at the top of the now massive trunk. The pointed top of the tree is lost, sometimes after fire has damaged part of the roots and stem, sometimes in a storm. Old British oaks usually undergo a similar load-reducing process. Thus the mature tree is redesigned for survival as a tower-tree.

The bark, 2 feet thick in age, is very resistant to fire. Even if it is charred it will not carry the fire round the whole tree. A large tree can be destroyed only by direct lightning strike (one is on record as reduced in one flash to an immense heap of cinders) or by erosion of the mountain gravel from the roots on one side; or by earthquake.

The tree is self-pollinating, the flowers, in early spring, being male at the top and female below. Cones, sometimes 400 on one branch, are green the first year, ripened the second. Each one may contain 200–300 seeds, and these can be held in the cone for 30 years – slightly longer than the frequency of severe forest fires, which clear the ground otherwise unreceptive to seed. No seed germinates in the thick dry humus of fallen leaves under the trees. *Sequoiadendron* does not coppice: it reproduces entirely by seed.

Big Trees in the native Sierra put on less than 1 inch in diameter in 17 years: in Britain they often add 2 inches in 3 years – but growth may be slower in maturity. Our trees will still be more or less juvenile for the next 300 years at least.

Big Tree, Rhinefield,
New Forest

[1853]

Big Tree cone

At Endsleigh, Devon, is the largest Big Tree in Britain, 165 feet. There is a tall avenue at Benmore. In 1853, seed came by steamship, from the Calaveros Grove by J. P. Matthew, and more by Lobb. It arrived fresh, and Wellingtonias, I mean Big Trees, found their way to every gentleman's seat and to many farms and churchyards. They never blow down.

Some of the best of the conifers, even after this, were yet to come – certainly some of the most useful to the gardener. Many a lifetime has been spent in the culture of these wonderful trees. Like me, you may have been put off at first by walls and spires of very dark green against suburban skies of grey. But only sniff them, only examine in close detail their magnificent colours, their intricate geometry. Why were they given these heraldic reds and blues, these coppers and silvers, these throbbing strawberry pinks and tender mauves, lustrous browns and dull, gleaming orange yellows? They needed no insect to pollinate them; no birds or small animals that we know of distributed their seed. And if you find no colour, to handle their leaves is to explore a tactile world very different from (and much older than) that of the tender, sappy, sometimes leathery but very destructible tissues of the Angiosperm leaves.

But there are always too many trees to describe. Anyway, my purpose is not to bring every conifer, or every broadleaf, before you, its freshness debased by words and inks, but to get *you* to the trees. Let us accelerate.

Libocedrus or, properly, *Calocedrus decurrens* ('running down' – the leaves run down the stem) the **incense cedar** of Oregon and California mountains. Colonel Fremont, an Army 'Topographical Engineer' sniffed it out in the drier uplands – later on he struck gold. Jeffrey sent it to the Oregon Association. The branchlets are set sideways, getting the sun both sides, and the form, shape or habit in cultivation is narrow, strikingly columnar: 97 feet at Westonbirt, 100 feet at Eastnor Castle, 88 feet at Bicton, 82 at Fota, Co. Cork (where it is one among many perfect conifers). It smells, not of incense but, according to Mitchell, of boot polish.

Western red cedar, *Thuja plicata* ('in plaits'). A really inspiring spire and a very nice smell this time, fruity, balsam-like: 'cooked apples, peardrops', says Mitchell: it is better than any of these, more dreamy. This is the best of the thujas or 'arbor vitae' – Gerard knew the almost as common *T. occidentalis* – it is also used in sheltered sites here as a forestry tree. This is the cedar for cedarwood cabins by the sea and roofing shingles for the well-insured. Trunk fluted, with red dark peeling in strips. Male flowers black, female yellow green turning to green ovoid cones which open into miniature Ove Arup architecture. The cones of *T. orientalis* are even more intriguing: a thinner tree, uncommon, but easy to see at Cambridge or Kew. It has been grown here since 1752, the **Chinese thuja.**

Thuja plicata, Bedgebury. The tree was introduced in 1853

The several dwarf cultivars tend to be dumpy, with foliage hardly recognisable except by smell. One, in winter the colour of a red cabbage, has prickly 'juvenile' foliage: *'juniperoides'*.

Lawson's cypress, *Chamaecyparis lawsoniana.* Yet another of the riches of botanical Oregon, named after Lawson of Edinburgh by W. Murray whom he sent to search for such things. Tell it from *Thuja* by the touch of parsley in the scent – it is closer to that species than its different-sounding name suggests. In practice – and it is above all practical – it takes the forms of numerous varieties. Most are narrow spires or columns and only some show the drooping leading shoot and frond-like foliage of the species type. It is interesting, in view of *lawsoniana's* talent for disguise, to seek out this 'type', or typical native form, which is 90 feet or more at most large arboreta and some small ones – 100 at Penjerrick near Falmouth, 102 at Endsleigh, 121 at Doune House (N.W. of Stirling), 108 at Rhinefield (a double bole). Fine big boles in S. central Ireland, says Mitchell. For cultivars you'd need a separate book: try Hilliers, Ampfield, Romsey, Hants. And see the Cypress Glade at Bedgebury for tree cvs. Timber: Port Orford cedar, important in N. America, for, among other things, boat building and mothproof clothes chests – a faint cedar-like odour.

Lawson's cypress. Below: Nootka cypress

Nootka cypress. Another pointed cone-shape, another *Chamaecyparis*, another Oregon beauty – and north to Nootka, Alaska: branches more or less pendulous; cone spherical but emphatically horned; habit more, I think a perfect geometrical conical shape than any other tree, but frequently, with large old trees in well-planted surroundings, shaded off below to leave a gigantic pixie hood on a stalk – broader and short pointed in W. Ireland. Leaves smell oily when crushed. 90 feet at Westonbirt (in the Loop). Not at

golden larch

Japanese umbrella pine

Podocarpus trunk

all rare. Golden and heavily pendulous forms. Timber: called yellow cedar from British Columbia. Easy-working, resistant to decay, smells of potatoes; for boats, engineers' patterns, surveyors' poles, furniture.

Golden larch. Rare, lovable *Pseudolarix amabilis*, by Fortune from Chekiang and Kiang-si. Unique. It really is golden, turning to red in autumn, deciduous. Cones artichoke-shaped. Hard to miss at Wakehurst and Kew.

Thujopsis, a single species, *dolabrata* ('hatchet-shaped'), **Hiba** for short, from Japan via Java. Died, reintroduced 1859 and 1861. Distinguished from *Thuja* by larger, flatter leaves with white-marked undersides only shared with the rare, later (1918) Korean thuja. Tree often many stemmed, bark finely shredded and curling. Female flowers blue grey preceding ridiculously complicated woody cones. In large arboreta and 1868 at Scorrier House, Redruth.

Japanese umbrella pine, *Sciadopitys verticillata* ('spindle whorled'). Another single species which also died, reintroduced in 1861. With no relations left, it represents a line of coniferous evolution which can be traced only dimly in the (N. European) fossils of the early Tertiary rocks. 'Pines' with leaves like umbrella spokes and terminal bunches of flowers and cones were not necessarily poor survivors in that distant world. The habit of this survivor is broad-conical.

Plum-fruited yew. Not that again – this one is different: *Podocarpus andinus*, of the Andes. Collected for Veitch by Richard Pearce and now rare even in Chile. Hardy if sheltered and happy on chalk; I would grow it for its muscular trunk, not for the rather muzzy foliage. The tallest is 71 feet or more at Bicton; usually it is 35 feet. There are a lot of other *Podocarpi*, least rare of which is *salignus*, elegant as the willow podocarp with in this case peeling purplish bark. The totara of New Zealand, *P. totara*, is an important timber tree there (which means they've cut most of them down). Rare here: leaves yellowish below, brownish, coarsely peeling bark. In N.Z. 100 feet, a massive head of thick foliage on a stout trunk. Fruit, yew-like not plum-like, cherry red with the nut sticking right out of the receptacle.

Sawara cypress and **Hinoki cypress.** The first, *Chamaecyparis pisifera* ('pea bearer' – the small round cones), is most often seen in the var. *squarrosa* ('scurfy'), a rather rude name for a fluffy, blue-rinsed tree of juvenile foliage. (Cypresses have seedlings with needles and scale-leaves thereafter.) Bean recommends a trim now and then. A specimen at Wisley is 60 feet high. One of Fortune's introductions, but also of J. G. Veitch in the same year, 1861. It was cultivated for ages in Japan as *shinofuri-hiba*. The form *filifera* is *hiyoku-hiba*, with long pendulous, cord-like branchlets, not juvenile but attenuated. *Filifera aurea* is an especially glamorous blonde cypress.

Hinoki is *C. obtusa*, 'blunt' (leaved). It sounds more masculine and is very useful but looks soft and feathery from a distance, bright green. There are several varieties for small gardens, notably *cripsii*, squat, shaggy and golden. The type has fanned-out, flat foliage, but in most of the cultivars it is bunched – all are very attractive close to. Hinoki is valuable timber in Japan, white, straw or pink, in ⅛-inch threads for sewing cherry bark rice containers and in satiny blocks for interior walls it plays up to the Japanese genius for design. Whole Mikado's temples have been built of it, and the red bark is stripped, not more often than every 10 years, from growing trees to make a perfectly waterproof roofing felt. Native trees can be 150 feet in two centuries. Hinoki is 83 feet at Bedgebury House and about 70 feet at Killerton, Bicton, Westonbirt (Loop) and Petworth House, Sussex.

[1861]

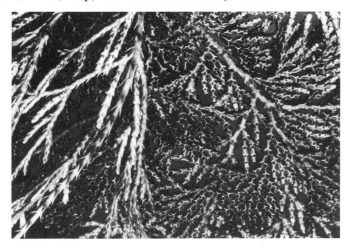

left, leaves of Sawara cypress
right, Hinoki cypress

The smallest conifer of all is *C. obtusa minima*, a ball of minute fern-green foliage, like a large sponge after 50 years' growth. For some idea of all these Japanese wonders see Harrison's *Ornamental Conifers* (1975).

Lodgepole pine or **shore pine**, *Pinus contorta*, named by Douglas and introduced by him, 1831, but lost. 'Contorta' refers to the twisted leaves, bedraggled and thick on the shoot. 'Lodgepole' because the Indians used the straight, tight stems for wigwams. Seed was sent by Jeffrey from the coastal-to-Cascades form, called var. *contorta*. Its importance was not realised at the time. Now it is planted at the rate of 15 million trees a year (second only to Sitka spruce), on peaty moorlands that would support nothing else. Cones are small with a longish prickle on each scale; bark in var. *contorta* is reddish with darker squares, deep, close fissures in old trees. Fairly large specimens can be seen at the important English arboreta and old ones at Bodnant and Ashford Castle, Cong, Co. Mayo. Var. *latifolia*, looser, longer leaved and a neater conic habit, is the inland form – Rockies and E. to Idaho. Tallest here at Borde Hill (Haywards Heath) and Bodnant.

lodgepole pines

Japanese larch. Not the least of our benefits from arboreal Japan is *Larix Kaempferi*, syn. *leptoleptis*, a timber tree more resistant to canker and more tolerant of acid soil than the European larch. The hybrid of both is the important Dunkeld larch, 1900. Japanese larch also is very decorative, and has shoots reddish (orange to purple) not yellowish, cones more squat and rounded than other larches, with strongly decurved scales. A tree 93 feet in 1957 was planted as late as 1916 at Drumlanrig, Dumfries. There are large plantations in Western Britain, some on the poor soil of reclaimed pit tips. Japanese larch has a dense crown and heavy leaf fall suppresses (cleared) rhododendron and fire-hazard underbrush. Veitch introduced it, 1861.

14 · Victorian beauties

Rhododendron
'Victorianum',
Trengwainton, Cornwall

The pure young queen crowned in 1837 and her brilliant consort, who joined her in 1840, were unusual in the British monarchy in attaching great importance to the new and the worthwhile in the arts and sciences. *Britannia victoriana* var. *saxe-coburgensis* soon flowered; her colours, early and late, were white, black and gold. In the middle years more florid and exotic hues were to be seen. Nature now began to imitate Art, and even, a little, Science.

Deep fissures became evident in the ever-expanding bark of the great tree, which had its roots in the fields of England and its branches far and wide in the world. There was often a rift between intention and practice. The Corn Laws, intended to help the farms, actually put the price of bread beyond the means of the working people. The Poor Laws, no doubt intended to relieve poverty, separated men from their wives and children from their parents, placing them all in institutions calculated to punish misfortune. Legislation to end the hardships of young children, forced to work at screaming looms six days a week, was resisted by men whose new mansions had the appearance of monkish abbeys or Early English churches. Reform of Parliament admitted the moneyed to the stronghold of the landed. Cobbett reviled the MPs who thought we could not run the country without the labour of 300,000 little girls in Lancashire, and was contemptuous of stockbroker architecture: 'Of all the ridiculous things I ever saw in my life, this place is the most ridiculous. The house looks like a sort of church. . . . I suppose he is some honest person from Change or its neighbourhood, and that these Gothic arches are to denote the antiquity of his origin.'

Parkland, under the influence of Repton and then of Loudon, began to open out in ever wider vistas, dotted with the arboreal magnificence of the Americas, the Orient and the Antipodes. The new conifers with their dark, pointed geometry, fitted in very well with the Gothic taste. (The Chile pines didn't fit in with anything, but they hinted at the wider study of natural history and the mysteries of Creation.) But in the great, old estates the new conifers were planted and assessed, with due consideration for future generations, as forest trees.

Trees generally were freed from the formality of clump and belt, and could now be seen as individuals. The age of the specimen tree had arrived: some large 'collections' still have an uneasy air of being displays of rarities, but the impression is dispelled by the magnificent waywardness of the exhibits and the unifying effects of English weather, Scottish vapour, and native algae, lichens, mosses and scrub. Some great gardens, such as Sheffield Park, unrivalled for the splendour and variety of its trees, yet contrive to be perfectly composed. They look natural. The most extraordinary trees of the temperate world are at home by an English lake (itself a fake) full of perfectly natural water lilies and familiar, domesticated, ducks.

The imposition of a pattern or design on the parkland sward and timber began to seem unnecessary; even, as the century progressed, undesirable. More and more the landscapist aimed to achieve a natural, airy effect.

Cottages, summer houses, even farms which appeared in the view had to look natural too, and were covered with suitable materials – tiles, rustic woodwork and trellises with ramblers, and ivy.

While at home gardeners aimed to re-create all that was best in the English rural scene, the great Joseph Dalton Hooker had set out, with a party of 56 in 1848 to conduct a thorough campaign in the foothills and passes of the Himalayas, where he found 43 new species of rhododendron and collected many of them. But nature imitated art, and the invention in 1856 of the first synthetic (aniline) dye, mauveen or mauve, followed by many more, gave the decorative arts a clear lead over the rhododendrons at least, which could not be expected to flower before the sixties. There were, by 1841, dahlias to the incredible number of 1200 named varieties, but these owed as much to art or science as to nature – and are no business of ours in this book.

Early in Queen Victoria's reign, while she still adored her sweet and clever old tutor and P.M., Lord Melbourne, two or three new trees appeared which were to occupy special niches in the affections of arboriculturalists and which seem symbolic of these times: the Pacific dogwood and the southern beeches.

Cornus nuttallii, the Pacific dogwood of N. America; Kew

Cornus nuttallii, **Pacific dogwood**. The purest white and very large flowers (the 'petals', so limpid, are really bracts surrounding a tiny flower) decorate this tree with the most perfect regularity of spacing, as can be seen from the

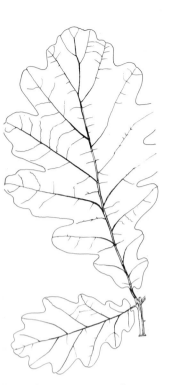

The Hungarian oak, *Quercus frainetto*, was introduced in the 1830s. It is fast-growing and makes large trees. Leaves are up to 10 inches, many-lobed

Nothofagus antarctica at Benmore, Argyll

[1836]

photograph. To quote from Curtis's *Botanical Magazine* of a much later date (1910): 'In the most favourable conditions, and especially in the Redwood forests of Northern California, it attains a large size; one tree is recorded as reaching a height of 100 feet. Prof. Sargent and Miss Eastwood speak of it as one of the most beautiful of trees, gorgeous in autumn with its red fruits and brilliantly coloured foliage; a recent writer in the *Gardeners Chronicle* says that on this account the tree is spared even by the settler. The involucre is at times 6 inches across, with individual bracts 2¾ inches wide. The first botanist to discover the species was Mr David Douglas, about 1826; at that time it was believed to be only a form of *C. florida*, and it was not recognized as distinct until it was discovered by Mr Thomas Nuttall, some ten years later, during a journey to the Pacific Coast.'

Nuttall, who started as a printer apprenticed to his uncle in St Helens, somehow got to America to follow his developing interest in botany, and achieved an amazing series of journeys, adding hundreds of new species to the American flora and eventually being appointed, in 1822, Curator of Harvard University Botanic Garden. In 1841 his uncle left him the printing firm and he returned to cultivate his garden at Nutgrove, St Helens, Lancashire, where many first-time introductions from America had been planted. His full story is probably as interesting as Douglas's, whom he preceded as a pioneer, travelling much more widely in N. America.

Southern beeches, *Nothofagus* spp. Early explorers in the Tierra del Fuego found themselves struggling, not far from the shore, through wide belts of low beech or thicket, so heavily intertwined at thigh level that walking was almost impossible. One exhausted party was forced to leave two sailors entangled in the thicket, to make their peace with their Maker.

This otherwise innocent and pretty tree, *Nothofagus antarctica*, grows to more respectable heights further north, where it forms pure forests with *N. betuloides*, an evergreen otherwise similar – together they are the dominant trees of Patagonia, which, from what I have read, isn't saying much. *N. antarctica* is found with *Araucaria*, and it reverts to the prostrate form on the Andean slopes.

The leaves, ½ to, rarely, 1½ inches, have the miniature fascination and fine detail of the foliage in a glass paperweight, or of Nottingham lace. Their edges are wavy and decoratively serrated – the leaves can be delicately scented too. *N. betuloides* has evergreen leaves, hard, shiny as if damp, nearly black, small, but regularly toothed; only slightly like the *Betula* of their name.

The Antarctic beech is supposed to grow up to 50 feet. Low, spreading trees with prostrate branches at Kilmun and Benmore produce considerable crowns of the tiny, glittering leaves, and have polished bark, like a birch but grey, broken by creamy coloured lines of lenticels. Older trees have dark grey orange-fissured bark with papery plates. The trees, if not wholly or partially prostrate, usually lean.

Some plants of both these species reached Kew in Wardian cases in the 1840s. It is not known whether they succeeded in adapting to the reversal of the seasons. It was a topsy-turvy world.

The **Jersey elm or Wheatley elm**, which is a hybrid, *U.* x *sarniensis*, of the Dutch elm with the Cornish elm, emerged, apparently, in Jersey. It is, until old, a narrow, well-behaved elm of regular conic shape with straight, ascending branches, and was very popular as a park and street tree. The original tree at Kew, mature and broad, still kept the regular outline of youth. It was a lovely rich green (Hooker's Green Dark, in watercolour boxes). The leaves were not very different from those of the Cornish parent.

A fine tree called 'Guernsey' stood in the middle of the green in the University Parks, Oxford. It was shaped almost like a cypress. It was injected with fungicide, but could not be saved, in spite of being surrounded by advanced laboratories where something, surely, could have been thought out to protect it, even if only a large polythene bag.

'Guernsey' elm at Oxford University Parks

Paulownia tomentosa ('woolly'): named, the generic part at least, after Princess Anna Paulowna of the Netherlands, by Siebold. Very few trees are named after women, you notice, but plenty of climbers and herbaceous plants. *Paulownia* is a native of China. Only one plant was raised from seeds sent to Paris from Japan in 1834. This flowered in 1840 and two years later had a progeny of between 20,000 and 30,000 in Europe. Flowers, resembling the (related) foxglove, in erect panicles, only rarely appear in any quantity in Britain, pale purple, to be followed by sticky green fruits of a sort of pointed egg-shape. The leaves, like the nearly related Catalpas, are very large, and, on juvenile trees, slightly lobed. Most of the woolliness of the specific name appears on the leaf stalk. Juvenile trees are often grown as decorative plants about 12 feet high with leaves often 2 or 3 feet wide. A young tree is coppiced and a strong shoot selected, the rest being discouraged.

At Kew, map reference F5 will find you some Paulownias.

Paulownia coppiced

Cappadocian maple, *Acer cappadocicum*. Never large but sometimes massively trunked, always round-crowned and unfailingly golden yellow in autumn. The leaves are five or seven-pointed, not serrated, the bark smooth pale grey. Cultivated varieties have yellow leaves or, commonly, red leaves in spring. Regional varieties are Chinese, with broader, or much narrower, lobes to the leaves and a Himalayan one with hard, only five-lobed leaves; but these varieties merge into the type, which is Caucasian or Turkish, Cappadocia being an ancient name for the central, mountainous part of Turkey. The wings of the fruits, curved inwards in the picture, later spread outwards.

Cappadocian maple

The **silver pendant lime** is the pretty *Tilia petiolaris*, of unknown (Caucasian) origin, with smallish leaves dark above, white below, and white flowers in July, strongly scented and inclined to knock out bees. Habit compact and pendulous, but may reach 100 feet.

[1840]

In this year of the Queen's marriage to Albert a superior red-purple plum was found in a Sussex wood and named **Victoria**. All plums and damsons are hybrids, *Prunus domestica*, of ancient origin, which interbreed, sometimes doubling their chromosomes and producing larger, superior plants.

Persian ironwood

Herr Parrot, from Russia, ascended Mount Ararat in 1829, or 1834, and perhaps discovered *Parrotia persica*, the **Persian ironwood**, introduced from St Petersburg to Kew in 1841. *Parrotia* was first called *Hamamelis persica* and it is of the family of witch hazels. Besides, no doubt, very hard wood, this tree has everything for the large garden. It is not large, it has lovely brown flowers in March, decorative, peeling, patchy bark and amazingly red and yellow leaves in autumn.

In the wild it sometimes grows in thickets as a shrub. There are nice trees at Syon, Kew, Wakehurst Place, Oxford B.G. and a huge bush at Saltram, Plymouth. It is 50 feet at Abbotsbury (telephone 228 for subtropical garden and nesting swans, 14th-century stone barn and Iron Age fort).

The **Camperdown elm**, *Ulmus glabra* var. *camperdownii* came, as you might guess, from Camperdown House, near Dundee. It was described as creeping along the ground, but is grafted onto stems of the type and forms a round head of large leaves and tortuous, pendulous branches, an arbor or bower of an elm – up to 35 feet. The picture was taken at Westonbirt at the S.W. end of Broad Drive in autumn 1977.

Colletia cruciata

[1846]

Colletia cruciata perhaps has no place in a chapter entitled 'Victorian beauties', since it is one of the most fiercely armed of all trees, every shoot redesigned as a rigid triangular thorn and carefully angled to be most wounding. These prongs can be as much as 1½ inches thick. But it *is* a beauty, for its engineering and its thoroughness and its indestructibility. Stephenson's Tubular Bridge of 1850 looks unoriginal compared with this constellation of tapering monocoque tubes, gently corrugated for extra rigidity, and reinforced at every junction. From these junctions appear very small yellow flowers; and leaves, but not necessarily any. Sometimes it produces a few extra, needle-shaped prongs. The one drawn was at Lostwithiel Church. I fear it is now dead after a hard winter in 1979-80, but it may have revived. Two large trees are at Sharpitor, Bolt Head, Salcombe (N.T., open daily) unless they also got frostbitten. As a bush it may be seen at Kew and Cambridge. It is a native of Uruguay, introduced from Chile, Bean says, as early as 1824, but it is here placed in 1841. It is related to the purging buckthorn.

Cider gum, *Eucalyptus gunnii*, was discovered in Tasmania by J. D. Hooker – a forest of small trees in a swamp. It grows up to 5000 feet in S.E. Australian mountains. In Tasmania the sap was drunk and called cider. This is the commonest – and it was the first – of the 300 (to 500?) species of

Eucalyptus to be seen in Britain, and is especially useful in the eastern counties. Frost may nip the young growing leaves, which form without a bud and simply pause for the duration of a cold spell.

Juvenile leaves are elliptical, opposite; adult leaves alternate, blue grey above and yellow green below. Flowers are dusters of male and female organs waving out of triplicate cups with lids and knobs – the cups expand to contain the seeds. Shoots are described as yellow-white bloomed grey with perhaps a pouch of pink or blue; or just grey. (The pigmentation of eucalypts is often on two levels, neither definable.) The bark peels massively, sometimes audibly cracking in the sun – orange-brown-pink revealing light grey. Most of the older trees came from one at Whittingehame, E. Lothian, and are known, improbably, as var. *whittingehamensis*.

Gum trees cast little shade: they are either very open or turn their leaves edge on to the sun. The cider gum is fast growing and light-looking, until very old – see the old ones at Wakehurst, 77 feet. Cider gums coppice. They are planted all over the warm temperate world.

Indian horsechestnut. Lovely smooth and flecked bark – it peels from old trees – and wrinkled, shiny black chestnuts inside round, not spined, cases flecked like the bark, a pleasant dull, pale brown. Seven leaflets, often very large, pointed, from a geometrically perfect spoked hub. Flowers not unlike our ordinary horsechestnut, but a month later. Introduced by Colonel Bunbury to Barton, Suffolk, in 1851, it flowered aged seven. *Aesculus indica*.

Ulmus glabra var. *camperdownii*, Westonbirt

[1851]

Indian horsechestnut

cut-leaved alder

Acer japonicum, downy Japanese maple, var. *vitifolium*

Alnus glutinosa var. *imperialis*. Deeply 'cut' leaves have a strange fascination: these are almost skeletal, but as elegant as the normal form is blunt. The tree is small, a feathery thought of a tree, by lakesides in grand gardens. Var. *laciniata*, known before 1819, has leaves more oak-like and makes a larger, stronger tree.

The **hawthorn 'Paul's Scarlet'**, a variety of *C. oxyacantha*, 'the best of all double flowered red hawthorns', originated as a sport near Waltham Cross. William Paul cashed in.

The little **snowbell tree**, arching and curving in the shade and rooted in the humus of greater trees, a native of Japan and Korea, made its entrance to the soil of Kew in this year, 1862. The shiny leaves are very lightly toothed: *Styrax japonica*. The wood is used for carving in Japan.

Another Japanese maple, this time called *japonica*, was introduced in 1864. In its most familiar form, 'Vitifolium', it grows to tree size.

The **katsura**, *Cercidiphylum*, is a single species, *japonica*, which Hutchinson places in a separate family, Cercidyphillaceae, close to Magnoliaceae and therefore very ancient. It is commonly planted in good gardens and in arboreta, popular for its autumn colour, which is variable from gold through pink and scarlet to purple. It is sometimes mistaken for the Judas tree, *Cercis siliquastrum*, but not when it grows bigger. The foliage is distinctive in the mass, very regularly patterned. The drawing shows the curious contracted ('obsolete') twigs at each joint, and the harmless terminal spines. So incidental, a curiosity here, it is in Japan the largest of their hardwoods (100 feet), and a producer of the very best timber: not showily grained or very hard, but even-textured, medium light brown, plain but lustrous. It can be carved to fine detail and therefore is used for foundry patterns – the crankshaft of your Datsun was probably evolved in katsura. (Jelutong, *Dryera* spp., from S.E. Asia is preferred here.) Being lightweight, katsura is used for Japanese shoes and drawing boards, mouldings, cabinet work generally, and veneers.

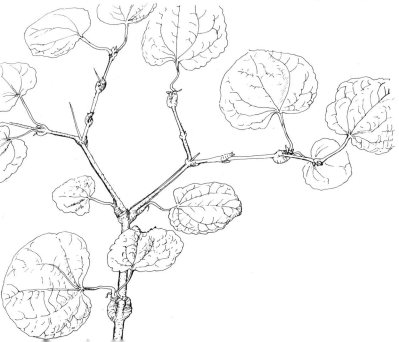

Magnolia kobus, a small tree-magnolia of vigorous constitution, but not highly considered by gardeners because believed slow to flower, was introduced from Honsu, Japan by Maries in 1879, perhaps the second introduction. A variety *borealis* – northern – from Hokkaido makes a larger tree and is probably the one I photographed. I found it impressive, but if it takes 40 years to flower properly, as is reported, its reputation is understandable. Few of us can wait so long. *M. stellata*, probably a dwarf form of *kobus*, is less hesitant in flowering. It was introduced in 1877, found wild in the mountains N. E. of Nagoya. 'For small gardens this is the most desirable of all magnolias' – Bean.

Charles Maries was a native of Stratford on Avon who collected mostly in China for the firm of Veitch. He travelled 500 miles overland through Japan to discover an, at first, unattainable fir on Mount Hakkoda. He exhausted himself trying to reach it through dense bamboo, then, failing had to walk back 34 miles in a thunderstorm. The next day he took a horse. He collected cones of his fir, *Abies mariesii*, and another, *A. sachaliensis*, and returned to the town to find it had burned down – but his gear had been saved by his host. Sir Harry Veitch put on record that Maries was enthusiastic but lacked staying power.

Magnolia campbellii – 'perhaps the most magnificent', says Bean, never sparing where praise is due – came from the Himalayas, 6000 to 8000 feet, Nepal to Assam, found by J. D. Hooker. Hooker's work in N. India was by no means officially sponsored, though he was helped by the British government agent at Darjeeling, Dr Archibald Campbell. They had native trouble in Sikkim in the form of an unscrupulous Prime Minister.

Hooker sent home 80 coolie-loads of plants in 1844. This was botany on the grand scale. He had hired collectors, but he himself worked sometimes as high as 13,000 feet. Then Campbell was kidnapped and held to ransom by the Sikkim forces. The guards, wrote Hooker, who was hovering nearby in the rhododendrons, were starving, and he and Campbell had to buy food for them. A ransom letter in Tibetan, sent to Darjeeling, went to Campbell's office and was put aside for his return. Eventually, Hooker was allowed to write in English, but he addressed the letter to the Governor General. Military intervention was threatened and the prisoners were released.

M. campbellii grows to 100 feet tall in the wild. The flower buds are large, and hairy as if close-cropped. The flowers, in early spring before the leaves, 10 inches wide with 12 to 16 tepals (Magnolias are Angiosperms too primitive to have divided the corolla (petals) from the calyx (sepals). A tree in Ireland flowered in 1885. One at Kew, planted in 1904, had over 500 pink flowers in 1959. White flowers are said to be common in the wild, and a tree in Darjeeling had wine-coloured flowers; graftwood from this tree provided Hilliers's 'Darjeeling'. Others, 'Lenarth' among them, have deep purple flowers. The bark of *M. campellii* is described by Mitchell as elephant-grey – a good description of this magnolia's slightly folded skin.

M. campbellii is one parent of *M. x. ritchii*, a modern (1907) cross which grows to an enormous size in Britain and flowers with 'amazing profusion'. The other parent is *M. denudata*, a Japanese favourite, called the Yulan and cultivated there for 13 centuries (and eaten – the flower buds flavour rice). It was introduced here in the late 18th century but is not quite hardy. It had

bark of Campbell's magnolia

served us well, however, by producing, when fertilized by *M. lilliflora*, our most successful and popular early-flowering magnolia, *M. x soulangiana*. This occurred at Soulange-Bodin near Paris and first flowered here in 1826. Flowers of most varieties have large (up to 4 inch) tepals, white, stained purple or pink outside and spoon-shaped. The bark is mid grey with raised lenticel patterns of horizontal dots and dashes.

Magnolia kobus in flower, Kew Gardens, April

Other tree magnolias are *M. salicifolia*, 'willow leaved', from Japan in 1892 and the loveliest of all tree flowers, *M. sieboldii* (or, ridiculously, *M. parviflora*). This is said to be a shrub, but the flowers are well out of reach in woodland at Westonbirt. Too poetic to bloom in a crowd, they appear in ones and twos throughout the summer: porcelain-white shell tepals with a yellow centre of carpels surrounded by crimson stamens, against the background of light green leaves. Siebold kept a Japanese mistress, Sonogi, but I suppose her name would have been no better for this Japanese beauty, introduced about 1880.

'John Downie', a crab apple with flowers opening pink to white, and fruit 'bright orange and scarlet, slender stalked, produced in wonderfully profuse clusters', was raised at Whittington, near Lichfield, in 1875, and named after a Scottish nurseryman. The object of crossing the Siberian Crab, *Malus baccata* (1784 or before) or its derivatives with domestic apples, *M. domestica*, was first to produce a more hardy apple for long cold winters in American continental states. Some decorative varieties emerged, and *Malus* 'John Downie' is the best known of several dozen with brilliantly pigmented small fruit. Such a range of pure colour in the perfect form of living, shining apple skin is to be valued, I think, above jewels.

Malus 'John Downie'

Cornus controversa, of China and Japan and the Himalayas, has alternate leaves like the American *C. alternifolia*, and is confused with *C. macrophylla*, which has opposite leaves as do most cornels: perhaps the controversy was about this. It could be called *C. tabuliforma*, because it puts out a clutch of new branches every year, each forming a distinct flat layer of foliage. Flowers, numerous, in June and July. Rare, rather, but there's a good specimen at Kew by the Lily (or *Taxodium* tree) Pond – and better ones at Westonbirt and Nymans, Sussex.

Snakebark maples. From Japan *Acer rufinerve* was introduced by Maries for Veitch & Son and *A. capillipes* by Professor Sargent of the Arnold Arboretum, who sent seeds to Kew. *A. davidii*, the best known, Père David's maple, was sent from China by Maries (he was the one with no staying power, you remember). It is named after Armand David, who went to Pekin as a missionary in 1862. He was released from religious duties to pursue scientific studies in Mongolia. He was often very ill, but made many arduous journeys in W. China, discovering 250 new species and 10 or more new genera – good staying power: Père Delavaye, who followed him, discovered 1900 new species, however, and this proved too much for the Natural History Museum in Paris to cope with, so that some of his work was neglected. Among trees, David has his maple, and the beautiful *Davidia*; Delavaye his fir.

Cornus controversa

subtle difference in snakebark maples: left, *Acer capillipes*, right *A. davidii*

159

Western catalpa, University Parks, Oxford

Populus trichocarpa

Poplar, 'Robusta', at Bowood

The **Western catalpa**, *C. speciosa*, differs little from *C. bignoniodes* in the slightly more showy (*speciosa*) flowers with less purple spotting – a creamy effect – and a longer leaf and possibly a taller habit. It is not so inclined to the mushroom or even sprawling shape of the Indian bean, *C. bignoniodes*. The timber has been found to be remarkably durable in the ground and the tree has been planted by American railway companies for a future supply of railway sleepers. The wood is soft, coarse grained, light brown. Its durability was only discovered when several acres of trees had been inundated for 67 years after an earthquake of 1911, and the catalpa trunks were perfectly preserved. Perversely, perhaps, I feel envious of a country where a large tract of land can remain under water for 67 years.

C. speciosa grows to 100 feet: for 'western' read mid-western: west of the Appalachians. It is 30 feet at Radnor Gardens, Twickenham and a bit less in a row of excellent trees in the University Parks, Oxford. (See our jacket.)

Populus trichocarpa, the **western balsam poplar** or **black cottonwood** grows by streams in California and up to 8000 feet in the Sierra Nevada, Oregon, Washington and British Columbia, to Alaska. It is the largest deciduous tree in the northwest, to 200 feet. Leaves yellow-green in April, typically clothing each shoot, and then dark above, white or yellowish below, heavy. Bark pale greenish ochre with heavy dark streaks on branches and the upper part of the trunk, the bole soon dark grey, ridged variously. Stem and branches are subject to cankers which are absent in hybrids, commonly with *P. tacamahacca*, syn. *balsamifera*, the eastern balsam poplar or tacahamac, and widely distributed over the northern U.S.A. and Canada. One result of this unison is called romantically, T.T.32 (presumably T. for tricho and T. for tac). Much planted 'in odd corners of rich moist soil' – Mitchell. Belgian crosses of *trichocarpa* with *P. deltoides* are U.N.A.L.7 and U.N.A.L.8 and Dutch ones are 'Barn' and 'Donk'. U.N.A.L. arose from Fritzi Pauley, which used to be called S.P.126, so they do get humanized, when proved successful: and success is trouble-free timber production in double-quick time.

Populus x. *euramericana* '**Robusta**' arose at Plantières. It is a male clone from varieties of *P. deltoides*, the eastern cottonwood and *P. nigra* var. *plantieriensis*, a broader, downy, type of Lombardy poplar. 'Robusta' is important among the vigorous hybrid poplars of the x *euramericana* or x *canadensis* group (which excludes the balsam poplars and includes the European black poplar as parents). It has been much used in forestry and shelter belts since the last war. It is decorative, not just robust, with fulsome sea green foliage which is orange tinted at first, in April; a regular broad conic crown becoming like the picture (100 feet at Bowood). It is one of those newly planted trees which can make roads a pleasure to drive on, and is highly productive of soft, white wood, which is a lot better than no wood. The sawdust, used in stables and sties, makes the best manure for beetroots. Of course, sawdust now goes into the furnace, not back to the farm.

P. x *euramericana* I.214 is a particularly successful Italian production, a female clone which grows so quickly that it needs careful control. It is grown all over the world but not in cooler N.W. Europe. Another, I.45/51, is much liked in France because of its pleasant appearance, in spite of susceptibility to canker and rust. *Vive la France!*

Late Victorian conifers

I can do little more than list these: space, time and colour are running out.

Spruce: blue or **Colorado**, *Picea pungens* f. *glauca*, 1877, can be large, native of the Rockies, many varieties properly called selections; some remain small. 'Pungens' refers to the sharp pointed leaves and not to the disgust which some people feel for blue trees. **Brewer's**, *P. breweriana*, 120 feet, stupendously elegant scarce native of Siskiyou Mountains of California – Oregon. Discovered at 7000 feet, by, you guessed, Brewer (W.H.); 1897 to Sargent, 1911 to Dawyck, Peebles. **Serbian**, *P. omorika*, flat-needled survivor of pre-Ice-Age Europe, relict in Upper Drina, Yugoslavia. Fairy-tale spire with those pointed, curving branches difficult to describe, shared with Sitka with which it is sometimes hybridised. 1889. The rare *pendula* form photographed merely emphasizes the typical (and fits the margin). Bark brownish, squarish flakes on older trees. Slow-growing but frost-proof as it leafs late.

Spruces, *Picea*, can be divided botanically into two more or less natural sections:

Section *Picea* has four-sided leaves with rows of microscopic stomata on all four sides.

Section *Omorika* has flattened leaves, stomata on the underside showing white or paler green.

These sections do not harmonize with geographical divisions. The second, beside *omorika* itself, includes the Sitka and Brewer's spruces of N. America and the Asiatic *P. jezoensis* and others. There are fewer species in this section than in the first.

P. jezoensis is known here by its regional variety *hondoensis*. The Hondo, now Honshu, spruce of Japan is frequently grown in large gardens. It has dark brown, later grey bark, often speckled with white and deeply cracked into small squarish plates – a rougher effect than is common with spruces. It is a narrow tree – it can be 90 feet tall – with stiff leaves very white below on white shoots. A straight, handsome, rather forbidding tree.

Veitch's silver fir, *Abies veitchii*, was discovered by J. G. V. on Mount Fuji, 1860, introduced by Maries in 1879. It is a small, short-lived tree as firs go, with unusually fluted, wrinkled bark which does not become fissured. Leaves well-silvered below, dark and glossy above, pointing outwards and curving upwards, buds purplish, shoots buff to grey, flowers red, cones blue to purple to brown, bracts visible. In all a delightful tree if you don't need a giant. Growth is rapid in early years, form conic to columnar or flat-topped. The shade is dense.

The **Dunkeld larch**, *Larix* x *eurolepis*, arose about 1897, but was not noticed until 1904. Now you can hardly miss it, but identification is confused by obvious variability of trees in plantations and I must admit that the detail is beyond me. Alan Mitchell, who has measured and assessed every worthwhile tree, conifer or broadleaf, in these islands, has one in his garden, says Bean. It was planted in 1963 and was 27 feet in 1969. An original tree can be seen at Blair Athol, in the Bishop's Walk near the Cathedral.

Leyland cypress. Neither a true cypress nor a quasi-cypress but a hybrid between the two and a most amazing tree, originating in our soil. The soil, to be exact, of Leighton Park, Welshpool, in 1888 and again in 1911. Another, of 1955, a grey-leafed form, is likely to be much planted soon, says

Serbian spruce, *Picea omorika* var. *pendula*, 40 feet at Batsford

Cupressocyparis leylandii

Mitchell, and there are other forms of the hybrid, which was described in 1925 by W. Dallimore. The shape of a Leyland cypress is as distinct as a Mini, and, in the ninety years of its existence so far, large, solid, dark and emphatic, but nicely sculptured, almost aerodynamic. Live, not shaded out, branches sweep upwards from the base, as the picture shows. In fact, this tree retains the good shape of the Nootka cypress and the thrusting vigour of the Monterey cypress, with hardiness and vigour combined and an additional narrow grace. The 1888 Haggerston Castle seedlings have leaves 'dark yellow green' above, greyer in summer, grey green beneath: from cones Nootka cypress. The Leighton Green variety, 1911, has leaves in a flatter spray, dark grey green above, paler at base beneath: from cones of a Monterey cypress. Naylor's Blue, 1955, is bluest and near to Monterey cypress.

'Leyland cypresses must be propagated by cuttings from side growths in March, or in late summer from half-ripened growths, 3 inches long – in sand, give slight bottom heat' (Bean). Planted in 1935, Leyland cypresses in Cypress Avenue at Bedgebury averaged 70 feet by 1970.

To end this chapter is a great elm, typical of about 10,000,000 field elms that have died. The cause of their death (and of several million of other species) was the so called Dutch Elm Disease, always present but this time virulent in a strain introduced during the 1960s on the bark left on logs of Canadian rock elm – imported for work which some of the lost 10 million would have done almost as well. In any case the bark should have been removed before the logs were moved, even if that would not suit the wet-seasoning process required for most of this timber. The disease is a fungus carried by the elm bark beetle (*Scolytus* spp.) which nests in elm dead up to 2 years. There was a lot of this about, because we don't use up dead wood; and trees like this one, though planted 200 years or so ago for use, had become merely ornaments, expensive to remove. Not enough people wanted the lop and top for fuel – they couldn't cope with it in fireplaces designed for coal – and furniture makers found imported exotic veneers more saleable. Even coffins were cheaper and more impressive in blockboard veneered with oak.

Trees like this were typical of late 19th century arable scenery and home-steads, where they were 'immemorial', like the Gothic Revival – not so by hindsight. Before the Age of Steel they usually would have been lopped (shredded) and every bit of wood made use of, if only as fuel. You can take the telephone pole as a memorial cross or as a symbol of the Age of Communication which has followed the Age of Steel. It is all that remains on *this* skyline, apart from a few suckers, which the Ministry of Agriculture will probably pay the farmer to remove, by subsidy.

Elm disease, 1960–198?, is by no means the isolated or irrelevant occurrence that it might seem, as we flash by in our costly cars: 5p a minute on petrol and about the same on rust and rubber. We can afford that, but we cannot afford to harvest and store the fine timber of 20 million homegrown trees.

A correspondent in Kai Iwi, Wanganui, N. Island, New Zealand, has sent me photographs of English elms there, apparently a smooth-leaved type and flourishing. Thirty-three were planted, with other English natives, by a road-man along his stretch of road, 50 years ago.

the fastigiate hornbeam, *Carpinus betulus* 'Fastigiata', here in N. Oxford, was introduced from Europe at the end of the last century Opposite: *Ulmus procera* in North Oxfordshire, 1978

Flowering cherries

Not really Victorian but Edwardian: some important ones were introduced about the turn of the century. One benefit of the Age of Communication must have been the ease with which seed of *Prunus sargentii* was received at Kew via the Arnold Arboretum, Boston, from the Agricultural Institute of Sapporo in the N. Island of Japan. Bean says that **Sargent's cherry** is close to the wild hill cherry, *P. serrulata*. So be it. It certainly has all the charm of a wild tree and none of the slightly fervid atmosphere of some of the cultivars; the colour is described as blush pink. This pretty and distinct cherry, with leaves red when new and deep crimson in autumn – and black fruit – has two or three varieties and also is crossed with *P.* x *yedoensis* to produce *P.* x *juddii*. Sargent found it on the Island of Yezo in 1892.

The craze for double-flowered Japanese cherries seems to have been started by Sir James H. Veitch, who, around 1891, arranged for a Tokio nurseryman to send a collection of cherries to England. All turned out to be useless except one, '**Fugenzo**', deep pink and very double, which he called *P. pseudocerasus* 'James H. Veitch'. The Japanese name is used however: serves him right. This tree flowers in late May.

P. x *yedoensis* (Yedo was the name of Tokio before 1868) is **Yoshino**. White or pink, sprawling or neat, this is not certainly a hybrid but is a traditional and worthy object of Japanese love and care. The picture may speak for itself. The Yoshino cherry came here in 1910.

Kanzan, even later in the Age of Communication, was one of the cherries observed by E. H. Wilson, of the Arnold Arboretum, who, in contrast with earlier collectors, took his wife and little girl and stayed at a hotel – in 1914. But Wilson had had his own share of adventures. Kanzan is that purple tree with sure-fire, ice-cream-pink flowers, along streets and in front gardens.

Tai Haku was discovered by Captain Collingwood Ingram in Sussex, not Japan, in 1923. It had languished in someone's garden since 1899. This lonely tree was the Great White Cherry of Japan, there famous but extinct. Ingram assembled a large and esoteric collection by paying in advance for cuttings to be taken in the winter of trees he selected in spring, in Nippon and Kiu shiu. All were duly sent to him in Kent, and he grafted them to *P. avium* stocks. He was much luckier than Veitch: by 1929 he had nearly 60 fine cherries in bloom, and some of them, now cultivated in Britain, are lost in Japan. Tai Haku has large saucer-shaped single flowers, and young leaves red-bronze, large and handsome in summer, yellow to orange in autumn. The bark has prominent brown lenticels. I have used Bean's words, lacking personal experience of this tree. It sounds lovely. '**Cheal's weeping**', of 1915, seems to signal the end of the show of performing cherries; with its bare crinoline-frame full of lingerie-pink bunches it hints at a past taste in prettiness. But I must mention the **winter-flowering cherry**, *P. subhirtella* var. *autumnalis*, deservedly popular in dull, dark towns and gardens for its incredible little flowers in November and December, of all months. A tree from Japan was planted at Borde Hill about 1900, the variety distributed after 1910. *Subhirtella* means 'less than minutely hirsute'.

The gorgeous bark of *P. serrula*, **Tibetan cherry**, is well known. The tree does flower of course, but no one notices (prolific, May, lost in the leaves – fruits bright green all summer – Mitchell noticed).

Tibetan cherry

To bring us well into the 20th century, here is a quotation from Neville Shute, an early novel called *Stephen Morris*, closely based on Shute's personal experiences as recounted with utmost readability in his autobiography, *Slide Rule*.

> He turned to his wife. She was several years younger than he, hardly more than a girl. 'I say,' he said, and munched steadily for a moment or two. 'We ought to have a double cherry somewhere. We had one at school — it was just outside my bedroom window. Great.'
> 'M'Yes,' said the girl doubtfully. 'I don't know whether it would do in this soil.'
> 'It would have a damn good try,' said Morris firmly.
> 'We'll look it up in the book of words after dinner and see what it says.'

Whitebeams

Also much planted these days are whitebeams, from *Sorbus aria*, through *S. intermedia*, the **Swedish whitebeam**, to *S. aria* 'Lutescens', 1892, a favourite compact street tree, leaves greyish-yellowish in summer, and the **bastard service**, *S. x thuringiaca*, a hybrid between the whitebeam, *S. aria* and the rowan *S. aucuparia*, and, as you see from the leaf, looking just that. Lots of these in Victoria Park, Glasgow, where the fossil *Lepidodendrons* are, and in the back streets of Minehead. *S. hybrida* is the same thing, usually 'Gibbsii': hardy, and fruiting cherry-red. There are also many exotic whitebeams in special collections, notably, and very impressive, *Sorbus* 'Mitchellii', actually found among the native Himalayan whitebeams, *S. cuspidata*, with leaves 8 inches by 6 inches. One tree among several at Westonbirt is over 60 feet tall, with leaves like dinner plates.

bastard service leaf

15 · New trees of the twentieth century

To continue the story it would be necessary to go into a great deal of detail which is beyond my scope. In gardens, this is the age of the individual, creative or not, and not of styles imported or applied in accordance with fashion. The recent history of each Botanical Garden, each arboretum, each private garden, large or small, and every plantation in our own century is of absorbing interest. But we are too close in time to make generalizations, and too much in need of every acre, 'open Wed. Sun. Apr. – Oct.', to be able to criticize.

As for forestry trees, these are subject to laws of economics and administered by a government department. Certainly *they* are not beyond criticism. But since its formation in 1926 the Forestry Commission, we can say, has done its work well and responded where it could to public comment. Can more be said for any other department? There can be hardly any criticism of the two great arboreta run by the F.C.: Bedgebury and Westonbirt. I for one am grateful that these have been taken over and handled well. The Scottish F.C. should learn from the south, and then decide whether people want or need the same sort of access and facilities as are provided by the English and Welsh plantations. Personally, I'm not keen on picnic areas, weary forest walks, and woodland loos, but I realize that the visiting public has to be handled somehow.

The trends in 20th-century garden planning have followed largely the precepts of Gertrude Jekyll. Owletts, Cobham, Kent, was her work – with the owner – and her style is perpetuated in parts of Nymans, Sussex and Hidcote Manor, Gloucestershire: and everywhere, for she invented the herbaceous border and inspired many rich and enthusiastic gardeners, the results of whose labours are now, largely, accessible to all. Here is a query from Miss Jekyll, quoted by Tunnard:

> Should it not be remembered that in setting a garden we are painting a picture – a picture of hundreds of feet or yards instead of so many inches, painted with living flowers and seen by open daylight – so that to paint it rightly is a debt we owe to the beauty of the flowers and to the light of the sun; that the colours should be placed with careful forethought and deliberation, as a painter employs them on his picture, and not dropped down in lifeless dabs, as he has them on his palette?

This begs a lot of other questions, does it not? But so far, only the avant garde has thought of using a few acres of nothing but grass variegated with chemical fertilizer. We may have learnt something from the sensitive minimalism of the Japanese, but we have no real ideas better than Miss Jekyll's, and no real architectural style to inspire them.

Among modern gardens the most impressive perhaps are such assemblages of yews as at Packwood House, or the herb garden and the 'white garden' at Sissinghurst Castle.

In 1924 Richard St Barbe Baker formed the Society of Men of the Trees.

Gertrude Jekyll

I think that I shall never see
A poem as lovely as a tree.
A tree whose hungry mouth is prest
Against the earth's sweet flowing breast;
A tree that looks at God all day,
And lifts her leafy arms to pray;
A tree that may in summer wear
A nest of robins in her hair;
Upon whose bosom snow has lain
Who intimately lives with rain.
Poems are made by fools like me,
But only God can make a tree.

Joyce Kilmer (1858–1918)

Silver birches

A number of exotic birches came on to the scene about the turn of the century. None has achieved anything like the popularity of the native *Betula pendula* and its varieties. Of these *B. pendula* 'Youngii', **Young's weeping birch**, 1900, has a special appeal for smallish gardens. As Lancaster points out, it is the birch equivalent of the Camperdown elm, but it can take two forms: a tortuous head grafted to a high standard, or a tree which rises a few feet, then dips, while thin branches spread on the ground – a curtsey from 'the Lady of the Woods'. 'Youngii' has leaves smaller than the type.

A cut-leaved variety, *dalecarlica*, from 18th-century Sweden, has branches sweeping down, or tortuous. A fine specimen can be seen at Cambridge.

B. utilis and *jacquemontii* are important, sometimes large, trees native to the Himalayas – their territories overlap; *B. jacquemontii* is more westerly, and has jaggedly serrated leaves, while *utilis* has very regular teeth. Neither has always white bark in nature, but it is for this that they are planted here. Hooker introduced *B. utilis* in the early 19th century, but *jacquemontii* came from St Petersburg in 1880. Victor Jacquemont was a young French botanist who explored N. India in a gentlemanly way in 1829–32. He was offered the Vice-regency of Kashmir; which he ought to have accepted, because soon after he returned to the plains he died of cholera, aged only 31.

Betula albo-sinesis, perhaps not typical

B. albo-sinensis, Chinese red barked; *B. ermannii* and *B. costata*, both east Asiatic; *B. maximowicziana*, the monarch birch of Japan; and *B. medwediewii*, a tongue-twister from the Caucasus and shrubby to boot, are all rarely planted. All can have exquisitely white, pink or orange bark, smooth and peeling. Most of them can be seen at Kew and Edinburgh. All have large leaves, for birches, and *maximowicziana* has the largest leaves, 6 inches long, of any birch.

Populus lasiocarpa ('hairy fruited'). 'Chinese necklace poplar', it is called, but I refuse to put that in bold type. Its value is as yet unknown, for timber or breeding, and its chief virtue is its very large (12 inches) catalpa-like leaf on a red stalk. It was discovered in China by Henry and brought to Britain by Wilson for Veitch & Son. It roots easily from cuttings in China, and should do so here in time, says Bean. There are two largish trees at Westonbirt, about F23 on the 1978 map leaflet, and one at Bath B.G. The bark is light and stringy, unusual for a poplar.

Populus lasiocarpa

Chinese *Stuartia*, peeling
gracefully. Below,
paperbark maple, peeling

Acer griseum, the **paperbark maple**, was introduced by Wilson from Central China in 1901. It is now up to 45 feet in cultivation and probably is going to be rather more than the decorative miniature it so far appears in most gardens. The leaf is trifoliate, like the box elder's but with teeth, and greyish, as the specific name says. (No specific name since *Betula alba* concerns itself with the bark of the species, however remarkable). This beauty rarely produces fertile seed and cannot be grafted, so is rather rare. The picture was taken at Oxford B.G., where you can see the tree, in the front plot, even after the place is locked up (at the ridiculous hour of 4 pm).

Stuartia sinensis and *S. pseudocamellia* are not at all common — they are rather tender. It may be that the last to be introduced (of five species including the American one originally named by Catesby) may be the hardiest. This is the **Chinese Stuartia**, which has paler bark than the Japanese *pseudocamellia*, stripping to the pink even more enthusiastically. The flowers are especially interesting in bud; two green bracts edged with red, opening in July. The leaves colour red in autumn, usually.

Davidia involucrata ('bracted'), **Dove tree, handkerchief tree**. This was discovered by David in Szechwan and Hupeh in the form *vilmoriniana*, introduced in 1899. Wilson, after a long and anxious search, sent home a lot of seed of the type species in 1903, and this tree is hairy-leaved, *vilmoriniana* being smooth. The large white bracts hanging all over the trees in May to June are familiar in all large gardens in the south, the egg-shaped fruits less so: they turn from green to dull purple, with flecks of light brown. The bark is inclined to shred, brown with vertical oracles. The tree looks like a lime.

Wilson had to wait for weeks for the seeds to ripen, with the Boxer risings going on all round him, when he found some trees 1000 miles east of David's original. But Wilson, not troubling with disguise and not bothering to learn the language, took with him about 25 coolies and assistants, a large plate camera and a sedan chair for when he wanted to look important. His last journey in China ended heroically. He broke his leg in two places in an avalanche of rock, splinted it with his camera tripod and had himself carried the three days' march to hospital. On a narrow mountain track he had to lie on the ground while nearly 50 mules stepped over him. None touched him. His leg had to be reset when he got back to Boston, and remained shorter than the other. Wilson was born in Chipping Campden. He introduced 1200 species of trees and shrubs of which 400 were his own discoveries, among them four new genera.

Rhus verniciflua, a tree up to 60 feet high in China, is the source, by incision, of the traditional Japanese lacquer. The tree was collected by Wilson and there are examples in most botanic gardens. The 7–19 thick, shiny leaflets are on a long smooth stalk, or rachis, which is striped at the base. The bark is grey with vertical fissures — like many another tree. The berries are poisonous and the sap can cause blisters.

Cornus kousa var. *chinensis*, from Hupeh — Wilson found it in 1907 — seems to flower more perfectly than the Japanese type-species. In fact, it is the flowering tree, or bush, which has most impressed me — but I am no judge.

Eucryphia

Delavayes fir. Var. *forrestii*, Forrest's fir, is the most widely planted of the several regional varieties of *Abies delavayi*. Var. *fabri*, closer to Delavaye's type perhaps, is rare but most attractive. The type itself is almost unknown. The characters common to all varieties are: buds red, purple or brown, shoots stout, brown/orange; leaves all round the shoot with a double 'parting' above showing the very clean white undersides; blue green or bright cool green above. Cone barrel shaped, dark purple or blue purple with bracts more or less sticking out their points. Bark may be smooth and grey or brown-grey and flaking – the last I have not seen. The nicest fir, I think.

Different varieties can be seen at different arboreta. Var. *georgei* is also named after George Forrest and was introduced by him as *A. Forrestii*, separated in 1930 and collected again in 1931, the year of his death. Forrest's record as a collector (of rhododendrons) is second to none, in spite of his predecessors. He wrote little, but if one of his journeys, in 1910, is typical, his career was hair raising. He escaped after being hunted for eight days by 'bloodthirsty bands of lamas', who caught his two companions and 'mutilated, disembowelled and beheaded them'. He was born at Falkirk and died in China at the end of his seventh expedition.

Abies delavayi, most silvery of silver firs

Eucryphia usually takes the form of **Nyman's hybrid eucryphia**, from the two Chilean species which suffer from the cold here – both had been resident for half a century before hybridizing. It is a dense, columnar tree, looking quite black, with beautiful off-white flowers in September. Evergreen, and can be 50 feet in the west. There is a fine specimen at Benmore, and others presumably at Nymans. It will grow in limey soil, if wet.

P. candicans, the Balm of Gilead poplar or Ontario poplar used to be common but is now rare, a victim of bacterial canker. It was introduced in 1773. A very attractive variegated form, of 1925, is '**Aurora**': cream, pale green, dark green and pink. Heavy pruning in spring encourages the strong shoots which bear the piebald, sometimes albino leaves, but it increases the risk of canker. The leaves of *P. candicans* are scented when young.

the variegated poplar 'Aurora'

The mark of the up-to-date garden is the **corkscrew willow**, *Salix matsudana* 'Tortuosa', from Pekin. Matsudo, Japanese, produced a flora of China. It is usually a narrow tree at least when young. At Oxford B.G., with water and high walls to help, it is well over 50 feet after only 10 years.

Sunrise horsechestnut. Another obscure species which provides a gardeners' wonder tree is *Aesculus neglecta*, neglected until it burst into 'Erythroblastos'.

contorted willow, *Salix matsudana* 'Tortuosa'

Ulmus villosa

[1910]

a white-berried *sorbus*, in Wigmore Bottom, Westonbirt

Older trees are salmon red rather than salmon pink, and all revert to green in summer. Of course it is a delicate, lovely thing, but for some reason I find the opening buds of the Japanese horsechestnut, *Ae. turbinata*, or even of the common horsechestnut, more exciting.

Ulmus villosa. This **west Himalayan elm** was known for 100 years before it was introduced to Kew, and grew there for some years before anyone realized how attractive it was. It has silver bark like a birch but with vigorously marked black rings – the bole becomes vertically gashed. The leaves are rather ash-like in appearance and the copious fluffy flowers, in picturesque loops and chains, are followed by hairy, pointed fruit. Villous, of course, means covered with soft hair. The trees at Kew seemed to have resisted Dutch elm disease, but one is now dead. *U. villosa* is rare in the wild, having been too much lopped for cattle fodder. This suggests that it does not coppice freely and might disqualify it as a street tree. But I do hope that this beautiful elm will survive and become more widely known.

Rowans

Sorbus trees are a modern enthusiasm. As late as 1914 all were included under *Pyrus*, section *Aucuparia*, because those great splitters, Bentham and Hooker, had done a bit of lumping for a change. Besides several varieties of the native rowan developed in the 19th century, the early 20th century saw the addition of *Sorbus* 'Embley', 1908, a Chinese form of *S. commixta* of Japan, and Sargent's rowan, *S. sargentiana*, 1908: these have orange-red fruit and various subtle and attractive qualities not immediately noticeable to the non-enthusiast.

Hupeh rowan, *Sorbus hupehensis*, is popular, a perky small tree with cool grey bark, purplish branches, leafstalks deep red at the base and cream-pink at the leaf: leaflets 11–13 matt green, markedly divided and sharply serrated only on the outer half. Flowers yellow centred with light-purple anthers in May, fruit eventually white or pink. The Hupeh rowan is said to be drought resistant, but all the same it seems to do best in western gardens – very healthy at Benmore.

S. discolor has white fruit, *hupehensis* and *vilmorinii* pink to white, and 'Joseph Rock' has large, pure, pale, Indian yellow berries. A cultivar of the European rowan, 'Xanthocarpa' also has yellow fruit.

Joseph Rock, who sounds like a Scottish seedsman, was actually an extremely clever Viennese professor of botany and Chinese at Hawaii, daring explorer in China and Tibet, seeker of chaulmoogra trees (oil used to treat leprosy) and finder of 1700 birds and 500 rhododendrons. He died in Hawaii, taking to Heaven a very wide knowledge of useful and ornamental plants, fluency in six European languages, Greek, Latin and Arabic, Tibetan, and several Chinese dialects, particularly his speciality, the aboriginal Na-khi. He discovered the northern dragon spruce and, at a Kansu monastery, a rare cultivated tree peony. This suddenly became extinct after a large fire, but the monks were able to restock from Rock's introductions to the wider world. The rowan named after him originated as a chance hybrid from seeds he collected in China.

A reliable, massively-fruiting rowan is *Sorbus* x *kewensis*, a hybrid of the native rowan with *S. pohuashanensis* (accent on the *e*), from Po hua shan.

Amazing southern beeches

Roblé beech, *Nothofagus obliqua* (the leaves are oblique or unequal at the base – typical of elms but not beeches). This was brought from S. America by Elwes. Extensive forests in the central valley, he says, had been removed for farming, but some roblé forest remains in remote Andean valleys. *Roblé* means oak, and the bark of old trees becomes oak-like, after a cracking stage when the juvenile bark breaks up. Though apparently warmth-demanding, *N. obliqua* does well in Britain and there are many large specimens. It is quick-growing and often self-seeding. The leaves are blunt pointed with 7–11 pairs of veins. The plot at Bedgebury, on poor sandy soil, averaged 70 feet after 34 years and roblé is the best performer of all the deciduous trees in the trial plots. The record is 85 feet in 22 years, at Windsor. The timber is redder than northern beech and roblé is said to be more like oak. The bark is said to be disliked by the grey squirrel, an important factor in some areas. It will not grow on chalk.

Raoul, rauli. The last of our southern beeches, *Nothofagus procera*, promises to be the hardwood tree of the future in western parts of Britain. In Chile it grows at higher levels than *N. obliqua* and responds to wetter climates. Though it is perhaps not as tall as its name *procera* suggests it is mature as a timber tree at 70 years old. Phenomenal growth rates are reported. It is also an extremely decorative tree in summer with a heavy load of leaves seemingly lightly supported. Lower branches often sweep the ground. The leaf is large for a beech, blunt at the apex and broad at the base, conspicuously ribbed with parallel straight veins, up to 18 on each side. Young trees have smooth, horizontally marked bark – later vertical fissures strike through. This southern beech – and there are several I have not mentioned – was introduced by F. R. S. Balfour of Dawyck. There are specimens in all arboreta and the tallest, 85 feet is at East Bergholt Place, Suffolk.

Metasequoia, **dawn redwood**, was known accurately from Pliocene Japanese fossils when it was found alive and well in Hupeh – in 1941 by a Chinese forester. Not only alive, it was growing in thousands over 250 square miles and was fed to cattle as foliage fodder. Now there is one in every self-respecting tree collection, and that includes many public parks. It is a street tree in American cities. *Metasequoia glyptostroboides* is rather similar to the swamp cypress, *Taxodium*, but of regular conic form, open foliage on curving branches, and more or less opposite leaves and twigs. Into leaf long before *taxodium*, it colours similarly in autumn. Cones rare except in hot summers.

Roblé beech, young bark

leaves of raoul

dawn redwood

The oldest living thing

bristlecone pine, Bedgebury

It lives in California, in the Inyo National Forest Park of the White Mountains, and in Nevada and Utah, and it can be 5000 years old: the **bristlecone pine**. The oldest trees belong to a species, *P. longaeva*, recently separated from *P. aristata* ('bearded, awned') and introduced to Europe only recently. *P. aristata* has been grown here since 1863; not, I gather, with much success, but there are specimens at Kew, Bedgebury, Leighton Hall, Wisley and at Edinburgh.

The foliage is described as 'foxtail' in character (the foxtail pine, *P. balfouriana*, is closely related), leaves in bundles of five with white resin specks which are absent in *P. longaeva*. Cones are purplish with bristles and blobs of resin. Bark smooth and dark grey. Variations in the annual growth rings of these ancient trees have been used to find out what the weather was like in past ages, with valuable results. The trees themselves are hulks with much dead wood, but even at over 4000 years they still produce viable seed. When the rainfall on the arid mountain slopes is small, they grow very little and produce no cones. The soil, or dry rock, is often eroded away for several feet below the original base, but the trees are not tall – rather they are twisted and sinuous – and so long as some roots remain underground they live. Young trees in California put out a ring of dense shoots at ground level, presumably to shade the roots, while the main shoot, sparsely encircled with branchlets, may grow only 3 feet in a century. Old trees are very resinous in all parts.

As they are quite shapeless in timber terms the bristlecones have been ignored by generations of Indians and settlers. Their immense age was first appreciated by Edmund Schulman, dendrologist of the University of Arizona, in 1948. He found that in some of the oldest trees the original heart, 4000 years old, was exposed to the sand-laden winds, and growth had continued in one sector after another. Frequently only a narrow strip of bark remained, but bright green foliage above proclaimed that life continued. Borings were skilfully pieced together to provide a unique record of climatic change over nearly five millenia.

The tallest trees, the redwoods, grow in the mist and rain of the coast; the largest, the Big Trees, in the alternate snows and heat of the Sierra Nevada; and, these, the oldest, only 50 miles to the east in the arid White Mountains. Extreme, not benign, conditions have provided these refuges for the most remarkable trees of the world.

Perhaps we should note here the rarest American tree in Britain. It is another foxtail pine, *P. albicaulis*. There is only one tree, and that is at Kew, 18 foot high in 1970. Its American name is the white-bark pine.

Gum trees

Eucalyptus species are so numerous in their native Australia and Tasmania, and so variable and given to hybridizing that a person called a eucalyptologist is required to identify them. He or she will need adult foliage, juvenile foliage, flower and fruit, and description of bark. Gum trees are fast growing, adapted to many different climates and soils, and productive of very good timber – one of the hardest timbers, jarrah, is from *E. marginata*, and wood called

Tasmanian oak or Australian ash comes from several species. Spotted gum is a tough, heavy wood from *E. maculata*. Karri, from *E. diversicolor* is available in very large sizes, stronger than jarrah but not as durable. Besides gum trees proper, some are sallees, from sallow or sally, some are 'ash', some are ironbarks; and dwarfs are mallees.

The best known gum tree in Britain is the **Tasmanian blue gum**, *E. globulus*. It is not really hardy and will probably be less planted now than the cider gum, *E. gunnii* (page 154) or some of those mentioned below. The blue gum has an honourable history world-wide as the fever tree, thought to discourage the malarial mosquito by its scent. It is one of the producers of eucalyptus oil, but it will grow in swamps and allows them to dry out, since like most eucalypts it casts little shade, turning its leaves edge on to the sun. It has been used in Algiers and the Po Valley and in hundreds of other places.

| *Eucalyptus niphophila* | *E. urnigera* | *E. viminalis* | *E. perriniana* |

1840	*E. coccifera*	peppermint gum, Tasmanian snowgum, Mount Wellington peppermint
1860	*urnigera*	urn fruited gum (over 40 trees at Crarae)
before 1880	*pauciflora*	cabbage gum, white sallee (45 feet since 1939 at Edinburgh B.G.)
1885	*viminalis*	ribbon gum, manna gum (bark hangs off in long ribbons)
before 1907	*delegatensis*	syn. *gigantea*. Alpine ash (Tasmanian oak timber)
1930s	*niphophila*	snowgum (similar to cabbage gum but more hardy, much praised)
1956	*dalrympleana*	broad-leaved kindling bark (grows in chalk)
1957	*perriniana*	spinning gum, mallee (known before, but a hardier strain)
recent	*camphera*	broad leaved sally (grows in damp frost hollows in N.S.W.
	mitchelliana	weeping sally (white-barked rare tree from Mt Buffalo, Victoria
	parvifolia	small-leaved gum (grows in chalk)
	simmondsii	Smithton peppermint. 1949 to 55 feet in 1970, Edinburgh
	vernicosa	varnish-leaved gum (ssp. *columnaris* 70 feet since 1949 at Kilmun)

There are 27 species on trial at Kilmun. Eleven species were planted at the John F. Kennedy Memorial Park, Co. Wexford in 1972. Older-established trees are at Crarae, beyond Inverary.

Voices in the wilderness

Planting is one thing, and conservation of trees and woodland is quite another. Ever since Tansley published his *British Isles and their vegetation* in 1939 we have been trying to understand the true history of 'Britain's Green Mantle'. Natural history turns out to involve a lot of human history. There are voices crying in the wilderness – Oliver Rackham is one – trying to tell us that none of it *is* wilderness and none of it needs the attentions of well-meaning but insufficiently trained conservationists. But don't leave it to the 'experts' – find out what the experts are up to.

Personally I distrust everyone; ecologists, conservationists, and especially Government departments – currently examining their powers. Since one department seems doomed to work against another, cash very often gets the casting vote. And I always seem to be hearing about bands of husky conservationists removing unwanted 'scrub'. What is so offensive about scrub, the first stage in the natural succession to woodland?

The sort of conservation I want is imaginative: as suggested in this story of Richard Mabey's. Recently, on a common, twenty gypsies over a period of two years illegally cut 200 small trees, hawthorn and holly mostly, for firewood. The trees were mostly cut at waist height with a chain saw. The gypsies were evicted, partly because of their wood-cutting activities. 'The results two years later could, without exaggeration, be described as spectacular. All but 14 of the 200 stools had sprouted abundant new shoots and there had been a massive regeneration of beech and oak seedlings on the now well-lit ground. Even sensitive woodland flowers like sanicle, goldilocks and ramsons have reappeared on the site. It would be an interesting experiment to grant permissive estover rights for a limited period in selected common woods. . . .'

My vote is for this sort of conservationist. No doubt power would corrupt even Mabey's fresh ideas. But everyone ought to read his book *The Common Ground*, because what it says, in no simple way, is very important to us all. Also, it's interesting. Start with the index: Cairngorms, candytuft, Cape Wrath, Captain Swing, Cartmel Common, catmint, cattle, Central Electricity Generating Board, chalk downs, Chanin, Paul; charlock, Chequers, cherry, wild; chestnuts, chickweed. That's what it's all about! But the trees are the most important.

26 April 1981

A heavy snowfall provides my last paragraph. Here in the Cotswolds the trees are generally a fortnight later in leaf than in the lower ground. Of our small trees planted in the last four years, a rowan and a hazel are in small leaf: they support the snow in grotesque lumps. A weeping birch, nearly in full leaf, is flattened but springs up again when released. Apple blossoms are wrapped in white bundles, and look unhappy. The ginkgo is hardly showing green yet. A narrow *Juniperus virginiana* is prostrate, rather surprisingly. A self-sown sycamore is only in bud, puce lozenges shining against the white. William, now turned 6, remarks sagely that the willow by the kitchen door (a tall osier) now looks like a weeping willow. I didn't know he knew what a weeping willow was.

The damage country-wide must be enormous. It is impossible not to be a bit gloomy, all things considered. We talk of ice ages.

Index of trees and men (and four women)

Abies alba 77 143; *cephalonica* 136;
  concolor 138; *grandis* 138;
  mariesii 157; *nordmannia* 143;
  pindrow 135; *pinsapo* 140;
  spectabilis 135; *veitchii* 161
abele 69 71
Acacia dealbata etc 124
Acer campestre 48; *cappadocicum* 153
  davidii 159; *griseum* 168
  japonicum 156; *capillipes* 159
  monspessulanum 16; *negundo* 98
  palmatum 127; *pseudoplatanus* 73
  rubrum 98 132; *saccharinum* 98
  saccharum 98
Aesculus x *carnea* 127; *flava* 114
  hippocastanum 88; *indica* 155
  neglecta 171; *turbinata* 172
Ailanthus 110
alder buckthorn 37 80
alder 20 49; cut-leaved 103 156
  grey 117; Italian 126
Alnus glutinosa 20 156; *cordata* 126
  incana 117; *rugosa* 117
almond 79 118 128
Amherstia 128
Angiosperms 7 11 12–15
Anna Paulowna, Princess 153
apple 41 60 77 80 130 159 174
Arbutus 52
Aralia 105
Araucaria 11 13 119 134
ash 28–30 57 59 80
aspen 32
Athrotaxus 20
Aucuba japonica 118
Azalias 123

Bay 82; bull 107
Betula alba 21; *albo-sinensis* 167; *nana* 18;
  papyrifera 108; *pendula* 21; *pubescens* 21;
  verrucosa 21; *utilis* etc 167
beech 21 31 125; copper 105; fern-leaved
  124; southern 152 171; weeping 124–5
Big Tree 15 143–146
birch 19 22 31; dwarf 18; paper-bark 108;
  silver 21 167; weeping etc 167
bird cherry 33 80
blackberry 47 58 63
blackthorn 45
Blenheim Orange 130
box 36 55
box elder 97
Brown, Capability 103 112 121
buckeyes 114–5
buckthorn 38
butcher's broom 60 78
bullace 43
Buxus sempervirens 36

Calamites 10
Calocedrus 147
Camellia 129
Carpinus betulus 42
Carya orata 99–100
Catalpa bignonioides 106; *speciosa* 160
Catesby, Mark 106
Cedar 55 77 137 141; incense 147;
  japanese 142; red 147; wood 97
Cedrus atlantica 141; *deodarus* 137; *libani*
  77 90 141

Celtis 55 81
Cephalotaxus 142 143
Cercidiphyllum 15 156
Cercis siliquastrum 82
Chambers, Wm 111 112
Chamaecyparis lawsoniana
  147; *nootkatensis* 148 162; *obtusa*
  148; *pisifera* 148
Chamaerops 129
Charlotte, Queen
cherry 45 46 80 164; laurel 81; plum
  43; sargent's 164
chestnut, sweet 54; American 55 93
Cinnamomum 13 128
Cobbett, Wm 96 150
cockspur thorn 101
Cornus controversa 159; *kousa* 158; *mas*
  80 82; *nuttallii* 151; *sanguinea* 37
Colletia cruciata 154
Compton, Bishop 97–99 105
Corylus avellana 19 20; *colurna* 78 84
Cotinus coggygria 90
Cotoneaster frigidus 127 128; *microphylla*
  123; species 128
cottonwood 160
cowstail pine 142–3
crab 41 42 80 159
Crataegus crus-galli 101; *laciniata*
  127; *monogyna* 34; *oxyacantha* 34 156
Cryptomeria 141–2
cucumber tree 108
Culpeper 61
Cupressus macrocarpa 140
  162; *sempervirens* 77 140
Cupressocyparis leylandii 161
cypress 13 55 77; bald, deciduous 96
  103; Hinoki 148; Italian 77 140;
  Lawson's 147; Leyland 161; Monterey
  140; Nootka 147 162; Sawara 148
cycads 10 12 15
Cydonia 79 129
Cytisus 51

Dallimore, W 7 162
damson 53 54
Daphne mezereon 78 111
David, Père Armand 159
Davidia 159 168
Dawn redwood 15 171
Delavaye 159 169
Dioscorides 55
dogwood 37; Pacific 151
Domesday Book 65 66 68
Douglas, David 132 etc 152
dove tree 168
Drymis 125
Dunkeld larch 161

Ebony 28 55
elder 47 78
elm 16 20 23 29 51 60 71 80 162;
  Camperdown 154; common 162;
  Coritanian 35; Dutch 59 92 102
  114; Exeter 124; Huntingdon 114; Jersey
  153; weeping 124 154; Wheatley 133.
  Disease 162
Equisetum 10
Eucalyptus 154 172–3
Eucryphia 169
Euonymus europaeus 52
Evelyn, John 24 34 95 102

Fagus sylvatica 31 32 105 124
fig 58
fir 77; balsam 132; Caucasian 143;

Douglas 136; grand 138; Greek
  136; Himalayan 135; noble 137–
  8; Spanish 136 140; and see silver
Forrest, George 169
Fortune, Robert 118 143
Fraxinus excelsior 29–31; *ornus* 105
Frangula alnus 37 80

Gerard, John 26 39 43 46 73 75 76–82
Gilpin, Wm 125
Ginkgo 10 11 13 15; *biloba* 112–113 174
Gleditsia 98
golden larch 148
Goodyer 55 81
gorse 51 52
grape vine 58
Green Man 34
Griffith, Wm 128
Guelder rose 38 78
gum trees 154 172–3
Gymnosperms 7 10 12–16 25

Hawthorn 34; Paul's Scarlet 156
hazel 19 20 29 31 61 71; Turkish 78 84
Hedera helix 28
hemlock spruce 103
Hiba 148
hickory 24 93 99 103
holly 21 25 28 61; Hodgin's 123
honey locust 98
honeysuckle 39 60
Hooker, Joseph Dalton 151 157
hop-hornbeam 105
hornbeam 42 46 72; fastigiate 162
horsechestnut 88; Indian 155; red 127;
  sunrise 169

Ilex aquifolium 28
d'Incarville 110 116
incense cedar 147
Ingram, Collingwood 164
ivy 28

Jacquemont, Victor 167
Japanese cedar 15; cherries 164; larch 149;
  maples 127 165; umbrella pine 13 148
japonica (quince) 129
Jeffrey, John 135 147
Jekyll, Gertrude 166
Johnson, Thomas 76 79
Judas tree 78
Juglans regia 55
Juniperus chinensis 97; *communis* 16 17 19
  22; *virginiana* 97 174

Katsura 156
Kaempfer, Englebert 112 118
Kent, Wm 103
Knight, Thomas Andrew 128 130
Koelreuteria 116

Laburnum 78 81
Lambert of Boyton 131 133
larch: *Larix decidua* 87 103 131;
  x *eurolepis* 161; *kaempferi* 149
laurel, cherry 81; spotted 118; Portugal 90
Laurus nobilis 82
Laurustinus 78 123
Lepidodendron 9 10
Libocedrus 15 147
Ligustrum lucidum 118; *ovaliformum*
  77; *vulgare* 77
lime 16 23 59 81 102; common 121; silver
  116; silver pendant 154; small leaved 23
  29; large leaved 29

Liriodendron tulipifera 95
Liquidambar 98
Litchi 116
Lobb, Wm 120 134 143 146
Lonicera 39
London plane 91
Loudon, J. C. 103 123 150

Magnolia acuminata* 108; *campbellii* 2
157; *denudata* 157; *grandiflora*
107; *kobus, sieboldii,* x *soulangiana* 157
malus baccata 159; John Downie
159; *pumila* 42 130; *sylvestris* 42
maple 16 34; cappadocian 153; Japanese
127 156; field 34; Montpelier
16; Norway 91; red 98; paperbark
168; snakebark 159
Maries, Charles 157 161
Marton Oak 35
medlar 58 79
Metasequoia 171
Menzies, Archibald 120 132
Mespilus germanica 58 79
Michaux, elder 118
mistletoe 39 61
monkey puzzle 11 119
Morus nigra, alba 75
mulberry 58 75
Myrica gale 41 60 78
myrtle, *Myrtus* 52

Nettle tree 55 81
Norway maple 91; spruce 16
Nothofagus species 152 171
nutmeg, California 143
Nuttall, Thomas 152
Nypa species 14 15

Oak 20 21 28 29 60 71 77; chestnut
53; cork 116; durmast 24; black etc
100; English 34–5; holm 75; Lucombe
116; red, scarlet 100; in Pliny 56; Turkey
56 107 116. Galls 36 107
old man's beard 39
olive 53 55 60
osiers 26–7 174
Ostrya species 105 106

Palm 14 15 129; sago 128
Parrotia 154
Paulownia 153
Pavia 114
peaches 79
pear 60 79 130; perry 130; willow leaved
117
Persian ironwood 154
Phillyrea 77 84
Phoenix 14
plane: *Platanus,* 15; *orientalis* 76;
x *hispaniola* 91; *occidentalis* 91
Pliny 53 81
pine 57 72 103 131; Arolla 54; bristlecone
172; Bhutan 128 135; Chile 150;
Corsican 113; lacebark 142; lodgepole
149; Monterey 134 139; Pinaster 103;
sugar 133 145; yellow 145. Southeastern
species 93
Pinus 131; *aristata* 172; *bungeana*
142; *cembra* 54; *contorta* 149; *coulteri*
54 135; *lambertiana* 133; *longaeva*
172; *jeffreyi* 54 135; *nigra* 113; *radiata*
134 139; *sylvestris* 16 18 22; *strobus* 94
101; *wallichiana* 128 135
Pocahontas, Princess 94
Podocarpus species 148

Pomegranate 79
poplar 11 53; balm of Gilead 169
black 69 72; hybrids 110 160
grey 69 81; Lombardy 103; white 69 81
Populus alba 69 81; *candicans* 169;
canescens 69 81; x *euramericana* 110
160; *lasiocarpa* 167; *nigra* 69
72; *tremula* 32; *trichocarpa* 160
Portugal laurel 90
privet 77; Chinese 118
Prunus avium 45 128; *cerasifera*
43; *domestica* 43 154; *insititia*
43; *laurocerasus* 81; *lusitanica* 90;
sargentii 164; *serrula* 104;
serrulata 122 128 164; x *yedoensis* 165
Pyrus communis 130; *cordata*
130; *salicifolia* 117
Pseudolarix 148
Pseudotsuga menziesii 132 136
Ptelea 105
Pterocarya 16 118

Quassia 111
Quercus 28 29; *cerris* 56 107; *coccinea*
100; *ilex* 75; x *hispanica* 116; *petraea*
27; *robur* 24 34–5; *rubra* 100; *suber* 56
quince 79 129

Redwood 15 141
Repton, Humphrey 122 150
Rhamnus cathartica 38
Rhododendron 116 123 150
Rhus typhina 95; *verniciflua* 168
Robinia 75 94 95 98 103
Rock, Joseph 170
Rosa canina 47
roses 47 77 118 123
rowan 22 33 174; Hupeh 170
Rubus species 47 63 132

Sabal 15
Salix alba 68 117; *aurita* 27; *babylonica*
107; *caprea* 27; *cinerea* 27; *coerulea* 117
fragilis 68; *herbacea* 18 41; *lanata*
18; *lapponum* 18; *matsudana*
169; *myrsinites* 18; *phylicifolia*
41; *polaris* 41; *reticulata* 18; x *sepulcralis*
125; *viminalis* 26
sallow 25 27 28 31
Sambucus nigra 47
Sarothamnus 51
Sargent, Prof S. 152 159 164 171
Sassafras 81 93–5
Scots pine 16 21 57 72 131
Sciadopitys 13 148
sea buckthorn 18 63
Sequoia 141
Sequoiadendron 15 134 143
Siebold, von 129 142, 153, 158
silver fir 16 58 77 and see fir; Delavaye's
169; Veitch's 161
snowball tree 38 78
snowbell tree 136
snowberry 129
Sophora japonica 111
Sorbus aria etc 46 165; *aucuparia* 22 33
80; *intermedia* etc 165; *hupehensis* etc
170; *torminalis* 43 44
spruce 15 103; blue 161; Brewer's 123 138
161; Hondo 161; Morinda 123; Norway
85 86; oriental 139; Serbian 161; white
and others 101
spurge laurel 78
Staphylea 78
strawberry tree 52

Stuartia 106 168
Styrax japonica 136
swamp cypress 15 97 103
sweetgale 19 41 60 62 78
sweet gum 98
Swida 37
Swedish whitebeam 165
sycamore 73–4 174
syringa vulgaris 78 84 89
symphoricarpus 129

Tamarisk 77
Tansley, Prof 24
Taxodium 15 96; *ascendens* 96; *distichum*
96
Taxus baccata 16 24 25 117
tea 106 143
teak 128
Thelycrania 37
thorn 60; cockspur 101; oriental 127
Thuja occidentalis 77 93; *plicata* 77 90
132 135 147
Thujopsis 148
Tilia cordata 23 29; x *eurapoea*
121; *petiolaris, platyphyllos*
29; *tomentosa* 116
Toreya 143
totara 148
Tournefort, J. P. de 116
Trachycarpos 129
Tradescant 81 96 98
travellers joy 39
tree of heaven 110
tsuga canadensis 108; *hetenphylla* 108
Turner, Wm 73 76 85
Tulip tree 14 95 103
Tupelo 103

Ulex 51
Ulmus angustifolia 36; *carpinifolia* 36
114; *coritana* 36; *diversifolia* 36; *glabra*
25–6 59 81 114 124 154; x *hollandica*
92 114; *major* 92; *procera* 92 162–
3; *plotii* 36 114; x *vegeta* 114

Varnish tree 168
Viburnum opulus 38
Victoria plum 154
Viscum album 39
Veitch, J. G. 34 148 149 161
Venetian sumach 90

Wallich, Nat 128 135
walnut 55 78 131
Wellingtonia 143
Welwitschia 12 13
Washingtonia 143
Whitebeam 42 46 165
Williams' Bon Chrétien 130
Wilson, E. H. 128 164 168
Willow, native species 27; corkscrew
169; crack 68; goat 25 27; herbaceous
18 41; weeping 106 125; white 68
willow podocarp 148
Winter's bark 125
Wisteria sinensis 129
woodbine 60 62

Yew 16 24 25 55; Irish 117 123
Yggdrasil 29 63
Yucca 123
yulan 157

Zelkova 113 114